MW00809601

JAGUAR CENTURY

779 XKT
16
NDU 289

JAGUAR CENTURY

100 YEARS
OF AUTOMOTIVE EXCELLENCE

GILES CHAPMAN

CONTENTS

NDU 289
1 PKL
2

Chapter One

THANKS, BILL

You will find, throughout this book, the author's admiration for Sir William Lyons can barely be contained. He was Jaguar's founder, shaper, strategist, and leading light. In fact, he was physically present for the first sixty-three years of the company's century, and, as we shall see, his legacy remains, a tall, elegant shadow guiding Jaguar down to the present.

A galaxy of high-performance cars that have made Jaguar extra-special, clockwise from bottom left: C-type, E-type Lightweight, 3.4-liter "Mk 1," Mk 2, XK120, and D-type.

Lyons had immense drive, something that all players needed as the British motor industry grew Lyons had immense drive, something that all players needed as the British motor industry grew in the 1920s. Rather than waste his energy on overambitious engineering ventures or empire building where the aim was to eliminate rivals and beat his chest, however, Lyons spent his time astutely assessing what customers wanted and could afford. In order to provide that, he recruited excellent people who he knew—with an almost uncanny intuition—would help him deliver on his vision.

Once he'd bought out his founding partner, he independently turned a going concern into a thriving business, shepherding it to industrial scale at his own steady pace. There were many points along this path when he could have sold up, cashed in, and spent the rest of his life enjoying his booty on the golf links or a yacht deck.

But after Lyons picked the Jaguar name for his cars—desirable vehicles of whose super-stylish design he was the mastermind—he was also building a marque that represented so much more than mere factory output. From 1948, when Lyons's newly recruited engineers came up with an astonishing new power unit, Jaguars became the cars that people simply longed to own. Lyons's near obsession with value, and his keen grasp of the aspirations of the typical, reasonably ambitious person, made this the sort of reality that could never be contemplated by Aston Martin or Bentley.

Even Jaguar's motor-racing activities in the 1950s were seen by Lyons as a way to sprinkle stardust over the car you could order from a Jaguar showroom. Indeed, he insisted that the C- and D-types be developed by the same team working on future road cars. When the first mass-produced Jaguars arrived in 1955, almost every driver in Britain knew that the company also made Le Mans–winning 180-mile-per-hour supercars.

The 1960s represent the purple patch of Jaguar greatness, with the Mk 2, E-type, Mk X, and XJ6 all taking high-profile roles as some of the most coveted things you could buy on four wheels. In the 1980s and 1990s, these and earlier cars, including the SS Jaguar 100 and XK120, were among the main totems of the emerging classic car movement.

Through circumstances and economics, politics and paralysis, Jaguar's fortunes seemed for a time to get jammed into reverse gear. After Lyons retired, the company struggled through the 1970s under the leadership of a dwindling coterie of his former lieutenants. The 1980s saw a revival, but even after a decade of frenzied efforts—and newfound independence—things remained tough. When Ford bought the company in 1990, the desperately needed investment finally poured in, but inspiration for the future proved elusive until design boldness made a return. A change of ownership to India's Tata might have been another unsettling tweak of the big cat's tail had the new custodian not helped Jaguar expand and flourish so spectacularly.

In the final chapter we will examine the I-Pace, a fundamentally different Jaguar for an automotive landscape that is still coalescing. Rapid, stylish, luxurious, and packed with character, the I-Pace has amazing gasoline consumption—in fact, it doesn't use a single drop. It might have seemed positively space-age to Sir William, but he would no doubt agree it offers the best and only way for this company to head into the future.

As the author noted recently, writing about a marque like Porsche or Ferrari can be a wearying business because one is apt to run out of different ways of saying *brilliant*, *excellent*, *stunning*, *fantastic*, *towering*, ad nauseam. The Jaguar journey over one hundred years takes us through ups and downs, with periods of awe-inspiring achievements and low points that have been very low indeed. It's a fascinating company to research and write about, and its very British story often follows the sometimes troubled history of Britain itself. The consistency and continuity of progress at Ferrari or Porsche has often been Jaguar's to envy. Yet through thick and thin, Jaguar has survived, and its cars today largely offer experiences and trigger emotions that others just don't.

This book chronicles Jaguar's first century in a way that will make sense and allow the reader to see exactly how it has progressed from the first sidecar to the latest SUV. It ropes in all the key characters, along with many outside forces. In straightforward terms, this book explains the factors that made Jaguars great and what they went on to achieve. And it illustrates the undulating narrative with carefully chosen images that capture the speed, glamour, and sheer deliciousness of the marque's canon, as well as many key historic moments.

Some Jaguar diehards may not like this bit: the book accords as much explanation of Jaguar cars and activities over the final third of its saga as it does to the golden eras of the SS Jaguars, the XK engines and sports cars, Le Mans, the "compact" saloons, the E-type, the V-12 engine, and the original XJ6, XJ12, and XJS. If you own an XF, F-Type, F-Pace, or I-Pace, then the impact of, for example, the Mk VII will seem as distant as black-and-white television is to today's videogamers. But this book should help you familiarize yourself with Lyons's genius and understand how the Jaguar phenomenon came to be.

Special cats, pampered pooches: Sir William and Lady Greta Lyons at home in 1972 with their pet terriers. In the foreground is an SS 1, parked behind is the then brand-new XJ12.

AN UNLIKELY COMBINATION

Blackpool in the 1920s: The founding of Swallow Sidecars, the early Swallow-bodied Austins and other cars, and the gritty determination of the two founders.

William Walmsley, astride a Brough Superior, and William Lyons, tucked into the attached Swallow sidecar, in a picture of the partners taken in 1923 at King Edward Avenue, Blackpool.

For parents today fretting that their sons, in particular, lack focus, seem easily distracted, and take a grudging view of any sensible future plans suggested for their young adult lives, the teenage years of William Lyons will seem wearyingly familiar. He later admitted himself, although with no great regrets, that he wasn't much of a scholar.

A winning combination: A 1920s motorcycle was transformed into a stable platform for commuting, or courting, with one of Swallow's striking torpedo-shaped sidecars.

A callow William Lyons astride a Harley-Davidson, one of the many motorcycles he rode and traded as a young man.

Hard graft, though, meant his parents were some way above the breadline. His father, William Lyons Sr., was an Irish immigrant to Blackpool, Lancashire, in the northwest of England who turned a keenness for music into his livelihood, trading in and repairing pianos from his own shop. His mother, Minnie, meanwhile, was from the Barcroft family of local mill owners. Their son William was born on September 4, 1901. The Edwardian era had just begun and motorcars were slightly frightening playthings enjoyed by very wealthy people on Sunday afternoons while almost everyone else walked, cycled, or rode a horse. Mr. and Mrs. Lyons gazed at their newborn in his crib not for one minute imagining that, almost exactly sixty years hence, their son would create the two most exciting automobiles of the moment.

William was a bright youngster, winning a place at Poulton-le-Fylde grammar school and later attending the Arnold School in Blackpool, where fees were charged. Evidently his parents wanted him to have a solid start; he'd been enrolled on a course to help him pass the exam for an apprenticeship with the Vickers shipyard in nearby Barrow-in-Furness. It was well intentioned. Lyons started fixing his schoolmates' bicycles at Arnold (the masters apparently took a dim view of his enterprise) and then bought a worn-out 1911 Triumph motorcycle from one of their older brothers. Quite accustomed to seeing large, complex machines dismantled at home, he reconditioned the motorbike and, being too young to ride it, sold it for a profit.

In the same year Swallow sidecars appeared, the Austin Seven brought reliable, thrifty car ownership to the masses, although it put comfort above style as it ate into the motorcycle-sidecar combination market.

Swallow's distinctive display at the annual Motor Show at London's Olympia in 1929—the Blackpool company had already carved out a name for itself for value-conscious motoring trendiness.

The young Lyons dug his heels in over ships but was more open to a new idea from his exasperated father. William Sr. knew the managing director of Manchester's Crossley Motors and wangled an engineering apprenticeship there for the lad, with evening classes at Manchester Technical College to make sure the rigorous theory matched the everyday practice. Tall, quite dashing, yet softly spoken, Lyons took up the new position at the age of eighteen, while continuing to get his kicks on two wheels by buying, riding, and tinkering with an old Sunbeam.

Although Crossley did produce some cars, its core activity was making military trucks, which were of no interest to Lyons. He lasted a year before handing in his notice and returning to Blackpool, taking up a position as salesman with the town's Sunbeam car agency, Jackson Brothers (soon renamed Brown & Mallalieu). Working as a car salesman did not have the stigma it might have today for parents with ambitions for their children—at any rate, secondhand cars barely existed—but his parents must still have wondered what he was doing with his life. In his new post, though, William learned all about cars in the real world—not just how they were put together, functioned, and were maintained, but also what persuaded someone to part with a considerable sum of money to actually buy one. He quickly grasped how to clinch a sale and was dispatched to "that London" to man the Brown & Mallalieu stand at the 1919 Motor Show at Olympia—an eye-opening experience for an eighteen-year-old able to observe the wealthy at close quarters as they contemplated their next new car. He must have had a whale of a time and his enthusiasm was poured into a growing list of responsibilities.

But it was not to last. A new general manager clipped the upstart's wings and by 1920 he was unemployed and killing time by helping his father with those pianos.

Lyons later wrote that "making a success of a business venture—*that* was my original aim in life." It came from a surprisingly parochial direction. Lyons shared his enduring love of motorbikes with a near neighbor in Blackpool's King Edward Avenue, William Walmsley, and was intrigued by his friend's sideline taking place in his home garage: sprucing up old military motorcycles from World War I and reselling them in the civilian market to discharged young soldiers keen to get their own set of powered wheels for the very first time. Part of this scheme involved building sidecars and selling the "combinations" at a decent profit. The elegant, torpedo-shaped form of Walmsley's "Swallow" sidecar, with its octagonal facets in polished aluminum and full-width wheel disc, added uncommon style to motorcycling; if you were taking a young lady out along the blustery Lancashire coast of the early 1920s, one of these sidecars for her to travel snugly inside, instead of riding pillion, would be an inducement. Indeed, young Bill Lyons bought one to attach to his very latest steed: an American Harley-Davidson.

Like Walmsley he'd been horse trading secondhand two-wheelers himself. But Lyons saw so much untapped potential in these natty sidecars that he proposed the two go into business together to make and sell them. The older man (Walmsley was thirty-one) was reluctant at first; he liked an easy life and he'd been doing okay on his own selling the Swallow at £28 a time, with wife, Ethel, lending a hand with her sewing machine to fashion the upholstery.

Workers at Swallow's Coventry factory in Foleshill busy themselves with various coachwork tasks, as ever larger numbers of Austin- and Morris-based cars take shape.

In fact, it was his father, Thomas Walmsley, who persuaded him to go for the partnership, after listening to Bill Lyons's plans. Thomas Walmsley and William Lyons Sr. each put up a £500 bank guarantee in August 1922, and soon after his twenty-first birthday Lyons was in business with the Swallow Sidecar Company in its very modest premises at 5 Bloomfield Road. It was the perfect partnership: the two Williams had complementary strengths and so rarely clashed. Walmsley ran the production line, initially turning out one sidecar a week, while Lyons looked after the administration and the marketing. In a matter of weeks, they had a small workforce of six.

It was obvious from the start that Lyons had the personal drive to take their business forward. For example, he sensed there was an eager market for Swallow's sidecars beyond the northwest of England, and so badgered organizers of the fully booked 1923 Motor Cycle Show in London until they let him have a stand after a last-minute cancellation. On top of that, he persuaded four motorcycle makers to each have a Swallow sidecar on their stands too. Show goers loved its sleek, avant-garde lines, and orders started to build. They worked extremely hard, but the two kindred biker partners were on a roll.

Somehow Lyons found time for romance, too, and in September 1924 he married Greta Brown. Perhaps not wanting to put his elegant new bride through the cramped ordeal of traveling in a sidecar, Lyons bought himself an Austin Seven, the "real car in miniature" that had been launched in the year of Swallow's foundation. At £122, a Seven was more than four times the cost of a Swallow sidecar. Lyons immediately liked its excellent, uncomplicated design, and like all early buyers he absolutely loved driving it. He found it patently obvious that the Seven's launch represented the biggest possible threat to his own products. It had four wheels, four cylinders, and four seats, and while wealthy and aristocratic motorists could chortle that it was so small you'd need to buy two—"one for each foot"—it possessed the comfort, weather protection, and safety that no motorcycle-sidecar combination could possibly offer.

By 1926, the Swallow Sidecar business had flourished to such an extent that a spacious new factory in Blackpool's Cocker Street was acquired, bought by Thomas Walmsley and rented to the two go-getting entrepreneurs. The company's thirty staff organized the move themselves over just forty-eight hours using a single truck; already people who worked for Lyons, such as Harry Teather—who would become a key member of the company in the years ahead—were displaying extraordinary loyalty to this dynamic young fellow.

In some of this extra space the company started to take in car bodywork and upholstery repairs, which sensibly kept skilled staff occupied during any production lulls. Up went a new sign: "The Swallow Sidecar & Coachbuilding Co." The expansive premises gave light to Lyons's next idea: a custom-built "sports car" version of the Austin Seven. Like all cars of the era, the little Austin had a separate chassis, and this versatility meant the manufacturer could offer several body styles (although none of them exuded any stylistic panache). Lyons may have been inspired by a Seven built by racing driver Gordon England, who gave it a rounded, lightweight body of treated fabric stretched over a wooden frame, although what Lyons envisaged was something more sporty *looking* than an out-and-out competition machine. And it had to be profitable.

While Lyons and Walmsley could easily collaborate on any new sidecar design, they adroitly recognized they needed someone with proper motor-industry experience to oversee a four-wheeler project. They found him in Cyril Holland, a former Lanchester Motor Company apprentice adept at making jigs and panels. He was given a wrecked racing car body to rebuild first and, having done a fine job on it, sat down with Lyons and Walmsley to plan the company's own first car.

This was the start of Lyons's extraordinary ability, despite having no design training whatsoever, to convey what he envisaged to a trusted circle of key people and to make sure the result fully matched his expectations down to the last detail. He may have done lots of sketching, but principally he was brilliant at finding the right colleagues and, through the medium of their craft, producing superb outcomes.

Lyons and Walmsley wanted a two-seater roadster body for the Austin Seven frame, made from lightweight aluminum panels, with a cowled radiator shell, gracefully tapered tail, flowing mudguards with running boards, and a raked-back, V-shaped windscreen. A chassis was bought from a dealer in Bolton for £114 and the promise that he could become the north of England distributor, and Holland and Lyons then got down to work.

They soon had a prototype running, with a set of light alloy panels supplied by a contractor in

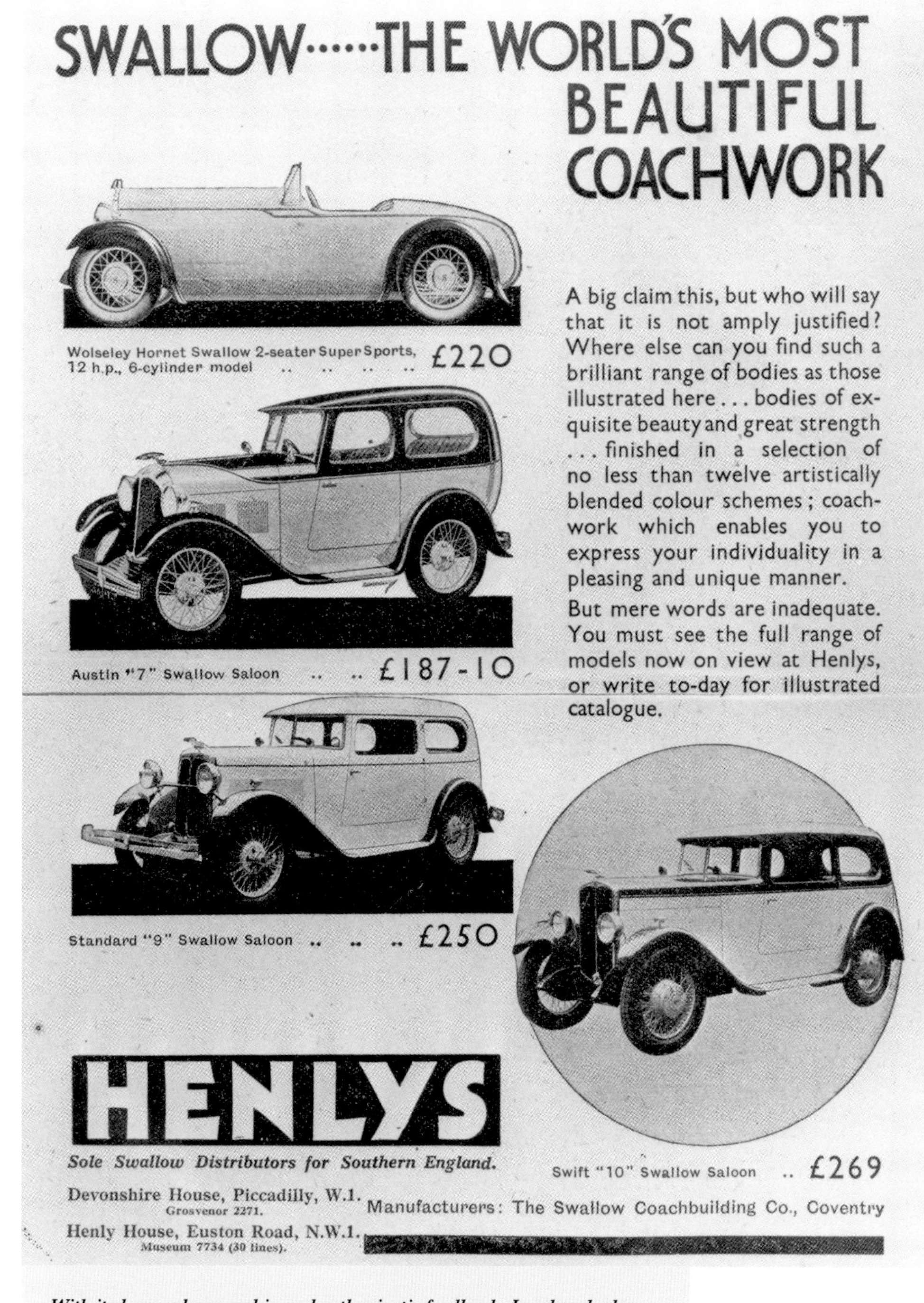

With its keen salesmanship and enthusiastic feedback, London dealer chain Henlys was key to Swallow's expansion, as Swift-, Standard-, and Wolseley-based models joined the tempting lineup.

Birmingham. While there were plenty of teething problems and misgivings about certain aspects of the car, with its flowing lines it looked positively sensational alongside a standard Austin. As well as a fabric roof, Swallow designed an optional metal hardtop for winter motoring. The intimate bench seat was leather upholstered, and the driver and passenger faced a polished wood dashboard.

A two-tone paint job was standard and the headlamps were mounted either side of the cowled radiator grille so that everything looked stylish and expensive, but the mechanical elements were completely unaltered. Hence, the car's only performance advantage, if any, was from its lighter bodywork and slightly more wind-cheating profile.

The public unveiling was on May 20, 1927, when the Austin-Swallow was announced at £175 plus an additional £10 for the detachable hardtop. Drab colors were the norm on cheaper cars but the little two-seater from Blackpool came in cream and red or light grey and green. The car predated the similarly conceived MG Midget, but both tapped into motorists' desire to stand out from the crowd without spending a fortune, and lent male drivers a certain raffishness that went down a storm at the height of the flapper era. Lyons, in charge of sales, found no shortage of dealers eager to stock his new cars, and many of them would go on to become major Jaguar distributors for fifty years or more. But nothing came close to the partnership offered by London's Henlys Garages. In exchange for exclusive sales rights to cover the entire south of England, it offered to guarantee the purchase of five hundred Austin Seven chassis and then market the cars with a proper advertising campaign, such was their confidence of being able to shift twenty a week through their own showrooms and appointed dealers. It was the most momentous thing that had happened to Lyons so far, and he drove the long route back from the meeting in London to Blackpool, silently wondering how he could jump from making just five cars a week to something that was not far off mass production.

However, by the time the deal had been formalized in January 1928, the Swallow operation had shifted up several gears. With a factory reorganization, more staff rapidly engaged, and bare Austin chassis often lined up outside the building in the rain waiting to be transformed, they were soon building twelve cars weekly, which was in addition to the twenty sidecars pouring out of the works every day. Henlys took its first delivery on January 21. Although Lyons's dream of running a successful business was now a reality, the next challenge he faced was coping with the expansion that this forced on him. The Cocker Street building was bursting at its seams, and now Henlys's relentless salesmen were urging him to design and build the Swallow four-seater saloon that some customers were requesting.

There was no question that new premises were required. The need to move, however, had another imperative. The company could easily find another base in Lancashire, but whichever it picked would still be a very long way from the bedrock of the British car industry in the West Midlands. That was where it acquired car chassis, raw materials, and the few skilled staff who would contemplate moving up to Blackpool for work. Swallow was a long way from the hub of this bustling industry from which it needed to draw so much lifeblood. The answer was to move the enterprise down south. It was not a decision made lightly, but once the proposal had been put to the fifty-strong workforce, an astonishing thirty-two of them agreed to pull up stakes and travel

This lineup of completed Austins outside Swallow's Cocker Street, Blackpool, factory in 1927 hints at the thriving operation within. The company would soon outgrow these premises and, indeed, the remote Lancashire town.

on the increasingly prosperous Swallow bandwagon.

As ever, it was Lyons taking the lead, and once the plan was hatched it had a momentum that was hard to resist. After all, just three months after the Austin Swallow was launched, the company unveiled a snappy, aluminum-bodied, two-seater conversion of the usually staid Morris Cowley. In the company's signature crimson-over-cream livery, it made an attractive alternative to the similarly conceived MG 14/40, although the Morris Swallow had no performance modifications to its engine. Then, in 1928, came the Austin Swallow two-seater saloon. Its shapely contours, low-set roofline, and unusual contrasting paint on the roof and some of the hood made it, if anything, the most distinctive car yet from the company—and the most rakish car of its size you could buy.

The Austin saloon signaled two interesting new imperatives for Swallow. The first was that it introduced the complex facets of a consumer product. No longer would the driver and passenger simply revel in the rush of fresh air on their faces; ventilating the slightly claustrophobic cabin had to be tackled comprehensively, with little funnels on the scuttle top channeling air in, a roof flap taking it away, and an optional opening section in the windscreen preventing the interior from developing condensation. The second issue, though, was one Lyons understood well, and it remains universal. A man might have chosen the car, but the approval of a woman would seal the final purchase. Both sexes loved the snappy image of these fancy Austins, but wives and girlfriends adored the option, frequently added to the purchase price, of a French-made Houbigant Ladies' Companion vanity set installed in the glovebox in front of the leather-covered passenger seat.

This study of the Austin Swallow saloon shows all its pintsize design flourishes, including the peaked roof over the windscreen, flowing mudguards, running boards, and, of course, snappy two-tone paintwork.

Chapter Three

SOMETHING A BIT SPECIAL

Coventry & SS: The growing company relocates to the Midlands to join the industry mainstream—and makes the audacious move to launch its first independent car: the SS I.

The inviting interior of the SS 1 was where hundreds of potential buyers pictured themselves, enjoying the ambience provided by fashionable art deco sunrise motifs on the door panels thanks to expert craft from cabinetmakers and upholsterers.

Moving a bustling manufacturing business to another street while continuing to meet a full order book is quite a task—lifting and shifting it two counties away is a mammoth undertaking, especially when the staff all need to find new homes while keeping the production line running. Not everyone could afford the comforts of Coventry's Queen's Hotel, where Messrs. Lyons and Walmsley were temporarily quartered as they settled their coachbuilding business in what had become the Detroit of Britain.

Walmsley had already done several recces of the city before Lyons, and in the bar of this very hostelry was introduced to Charles Odell, a real estate agent with lots of invaluable local knowledge. Odell was familiar with plenty of buildings. One in particular seemed right, a shell-filling factory built originally by the British government during World War I in Holbrook Lane, Foleshill, in the north of the city. It was pretty scruffy, having been idle since 1919, but there was 5,000 square feet of space—vastly larger than Blackpool—arranged over eight shops, and although the owner wanted a straight sale, negotiations led to a lease at £1,200 a year with an option to buy the freehold later. It must have seemed like a very major step, yet the place felt right; there were three similar adjacent buildings and two of them housed Holbrook Bodies, which built bodywork for Hillman cars.

In September and October, after the place had been renovated and spruced up, the big move began, and within a couple of weeks sidecars were crowding the newly acquired dispatch department, ready for delivery. The bedding-down process certainly had its problems. Lyons finally managed to persuade Cyril Holland, who had chosen to remain in Blackpool, to rejoin the firm with a big pay raise and a mandate to iron out production problems. It wasn't long before the factory was producing forty Austin Swallows a week. It ticked up steadily to fifty, and the combination of reduced costs on what today we'd call logistics, allied to brisk demand, meant that by September 1929 Swallow was able to buy its premises and the remaining vacant unit for £18,000.

The company had little difficulty surviving the 1929 Wall Street crash and resulting Depression because it was already selling style on a budget. In contrast, big names like Bentley and Sunbeam, with their expensively engineered sports cars, faced bankruptcy. In a 1977 TV interview, William Lyons graciously accorded his company's early success to his workforce. "I became impatient and felt it wasn't sufficient to build up a business on sidecars alone," he recalled. "The Austin Seven established the company on its feet. We had goodwill and enthusiasm from the workers. If we said we wanted to produce ten cars in a day, then they would work until late at night until they were done. We had the right spirit. It was very good."

The range of cars soon expanded. Although the Morris Cowley was dropped, Swallow's existing coachwork was ingeniously adapted for various other manufacturers' chassis, including the imported Fiat 509A and the Coventry-built Swift 10 horsepower. The latter was unveiled at the 1929 London Motor Show in an attempt to give the

slow-selling Swift a boost, and it exhibited all the winning motifs now typical of a Swallow car: natty two-tone paint job, V-formation windscreen with a peaked roof, and a stylish interior with bucket seats that tipped forward to allow access to the two behind. Some 150 were sold before Swift itself went out of business in 1931, but by then Swallow had allied itself to another Coventry-based marque, Standard. Its Big 9 and 16 horsepower models received the full, dramatic Swallow makeover, extending this time to a new radiator grille design that fully transformed these fairly humdrum British cars. (The figures in the cars' names, incidentally, referred to horsepower as calculated in a formula devised by the Royal Automobile Club for taxation purposes; actual engine output horsepower was much higher at 25.5 bhp and 45 bhp, respectively.) The managing director of Standard, John Black, sought to capitalize on

The original SS 1, unveiled in 1931, had the rakish long-hood look that was so desirable at the time, although Lyons—recovering after surgery at the time—was exasperated at the "conning tower" look of the cabin.

the symbiosis, and promised that Swallow could have all the chassis they needed as long as they continued to do their high-profile work on his products. The halo effect did them no end of good in the competitive and growing mainstream car market. In 1930 Swallow also offered a sporty two-seater body for the Wolseley Hornet.

Swallow was reaching the limits of what it could achieve by enhancing the products of others. While business was booming, Lyons could see that his mainstay, the little Austin, would soon lose its novelty. The time had probably come to ratchet up yet another gear and join the ranks of proper car manufacturers. Although the firm had no engineering department or drawing office of its own to make this happen, John Black at Standard was willing to help, and in 1931 the two parties had come to a deal. As

For the 1933 season there was a second-generation SS 1 alongside its SS 2 stablemate, with improvements to its looks and accommodations.

Advertising created by SS's dealer Henlys began to exude loftier ideals, stressing the car's performance, although in truth it was heavy and somewhat underpowered.

A specially designed underslung chassis, now supplied by Rubery Owen and powered by Standard engines, enabled Lyons to achieve the ground-hugging appearance he craved for the revised SS 1.

long as Lyons would contribute £500 toward development costs and agree to take a minimum order of five hundred units, Standard would make a chassis exclusively for Swallow, a rolling frame preloaded with Standard's mechanical components, including its six-cylinder 16 horsepower engine. The agreement was signed in spring 1931 to Swallow's specification for a lowered Standard 16 chassis with a 9-foot-4-inch wheelbase featuring semi-elliptic leaf springs outside the frame members, a down-swept center section, lowered radiator, an engine mounted 7 inches farther back than normal, and a wheelbase extended 3 inches. Power units would be Standard's side-valve six cylinders, in 2,054cc or 2,552cc sizes.

This emphasis on a ground-hugging frame was driven by the demands of how the finished car would look. While this was always the core concern for Lyons and his right-hand design assistant, Cyril Holland, there was also a lot of enthusiastic input from Henlys in London, who were itching for something new and irresistible to market.

The powerful, impressive Cord L-29 had been launched in the US in 1929 and it continued to set the pace for Hollywood glamour in *The Great Gatsby* mold. Henlys wanted something similarly low slung and speedy looking, albeit scaled down to the proportions of the typical British car. Lyons knew that if he could give them what they desired, then prosperity most likely lay ahead.

Working with Cyril Holland on a full-size, three-dimensional mockup, Lyons emphasized the powerful, long-hood look he wanted with tight-fitting cycle-type mudguards hugging the wheels, doing away with running boards. A low roofline with shallow windscreen and side windows was also part of the look, while a pair of large Lucas P100 headlamps gave a predatory feel to the car's nose. The pressure to get it right was intense, because an unveiling at the 1931 London Motor Show in October was needed to stoke sales for 1932.

A sudden setback changed their plans: the normally energetic Lyons was rushed to the hospital, where his appendix was removed. While recuperating, he discovered Walmsley, who had stepped in to finish the job, had tried to marry the new car's ultra-rakish look with a practical driving position and outward visibility by raising the roofline. Lyons was aghast. The cabin stuck up "like a conning tower," he fumed. Walmsley's defense was that he had no choice, because otherwise no one of average height could have sat comfortably inside it. It was too late to change the design—the show opening was just four weeks away—and Lyons did later concede that the compromise was inevitable.

On a more positive note, the company was quickly renamed the Swallow Coachbuilding Company (sidecars continued to be produced), and the decision was taken to christen its new car marque SS. Graphic artist Donald Reesby, who had helped with early sketches of the car itself, swiftly devised an art deco–style hexagonal emblem embracing the two letters. Lyons was sanguine about any assumption among his helpful suppliers that this stood for "Standard Special." But they were wrong. "We called it the Swallow Special, the basis on which we decided to promote our own individuality," Lyons later chuckled.

The snug four-seater SS 1, at only £310 and painted a striking red and black, was the undisputed star of the motor show, even though the

Built on the humble Standard 9-hp chassis, the SS 2 was a smaller car, but uniting the SS 1 cabin with a hood of normal proportions gave a more balanced design to this often overlooked but nonetheless important element of the SS success story.

company's stand was tucked away among the other coachbuilders rather than with the genuine carmakers. The interior oozed attainable luxury with its Vaumol leather upholstery and polished sycamore for the dashboard and door cappings. With its imposing headlamps, fabric-covered roof, and a capacious leather luggage trunk at the back, the dashing car looked perfect for an exciting trip to the French Riviera, and a rush of orders meant the first year's production was a sellout. Swallow gave an exclusive preview of the car to *The Daily Express* newspaper and may have been a bit disconcerted at the splash it received on October 9, 1931. "'Dream' Car Unveiled, Designed by 22 Salesmen," the headline read. The article went on to state, "The salesmen were unanimous on one thing: appearance is the best selling point in these days. 'Give us a motor-car with a £1,000 look, but which costs £300, and life will be easy!'"

The five hundred style-conscious individuals who ordered one were content to own a spritely 55-mph cruiser rather than a super-fast sports car. Top speed was no more than 75 mph and the car was in no hurry to reach 60 mph (97 km/h) in 23 seconds even with the larger of the two engines available (offered for a £10 surcharge over the smaller one). Headroom was cramped, as was the rear bench seat that could barely accommodate one doubled-up unfortunate. (Henlys devised a wacky solution to this: a fake luggage trunk with a pop-out dickey seat.) As SS had no engineering department, there were some niggling production faults, too, such as leaky seals to the windscreen and sunroof, and a cockpit apt to fill with exhaust fumes all too easily.

But none of this mattered. Owners had a car that looked like it cost two or three times the price. Its low roofline and long hood recalled the excitement of Woolf Barnato's Bentley Speed Six coupe from Cricklewood, built to commemorate a famous race with a train across France. Upper-class sports car drivers, nonetheless, were apt to be picky about the arriviste SS 1 with its lowly underpinnings. It was often dismissed as a "spiv's Bentley" or a "Wardour Street Bentley," suggesting it appealed to louche characters—and hopeful actresses—in the movie business who inhabited the Soho, London, thoroughfare. "Promenade sports car" was a dig at the SS 1's relative gutlessness in rallying, yet its likelihood of scooping up awards at Concours d'Elegance afterward.

There was a lingering resentment at the plurality of motoring in the late 1920s and early 1930s from people accustomed to car ownership as the preserve of the elite. The chairman could afford an expensive chassis and bespoke coachwork, yet he somehow found it an affront that a chief clerk desired the same thing on more modest means. There was nothing the snipers could do, though, to alter the clamor for this flashy new arrival.

Much less well known is that Swallow managed to get another brand new model into its 1931 motor show lineup: the SS 2. An extension of the working partnership

The 1932 SS 1 gave the car-buying public a rakish coupe with a long, long hood at a bargain price. Wire wheels and a leather luggage trunk suggested speedy journeys to exotic places.

with Standard this was, in effect, a relatively straightforward rebodying of the Standard 9 horsepower "Little Nine," more usually a small, four-cylinder family car. Swallow bought the chassis for these at £82 each (the custom-built SS 1 chassis cost the firm £130 a go), and only the steering column was modified to fit the lower lines of the SS 1 –derived body, while the hood length was similar to any other small Standard of this type. It made a very attractive small sports saloon and was a tremendous value at £210 complete with separate luggage trunk. The SS 2 gave the company something to offer its existing customer base of cost-conscious drivers as the Austin Swallow was phased out.

It's incredible to consider the work rate at what was still a fairly small company. No sooner were the SS 1 cars departing the Foleshill factory than Lyons dived straight into redesigning the car to get it dead right. The 1933 model, announced in October 1932, received a complete makeover with lowered window and door lines to integrate with the hood contours, and mudguards flowed elegantly through on to running boards. With all the initial batch of frames used up, the chassis was redesigned and custom manufactured by contractor Rubery Owen. It was now genuinely underslung at the back with members passing under the rear axle so the cabin roofline could be lowered to Lyons's satisfaction. Together with a 7-inch wheelbase stretch, this meant two people could now sit in the back in reasonable comfort (but still suffer claustrophobia—the pretend folding-roof irons on the outside looked impressive but in 1934 an optional rear side window was offered). The £325 cost does seem astonishing in retrospect for a handmade two-plus-two, although the cars may not have been very profitable compared to the sidecars.

A more intrusive prop shaft on this lowered version moved Henlys's silver-tongued salesmen to boast that the two entirely separate bucket seats were copied from armchairs in the company's boardroom (abject hype, of course), but they were still beautifully leather upholstered, while the inner door panels displayed that popular art deco motif of a rising sun, with a walnut center and stitched leather "rays." There were dinky little picnic tables in the back too.

This was a heavy car, with feeble Bendix cable-operated brakes. A new, aluminum head on the '33 engine gave slightly better breathing, but 75 miles per hour (versus the earlier 70) was the maximum speed. Customers, including comedy film star George Formby, loved it, perhaps fed by glowing press reviews such as this from *The Motor*: "The SS 1 is a new type of automobile in the sense that it is a car built for the connoisseur but is relatively low priced. All the attributes of sports models are incorporated in a refined manner."

The SS 2 remained unchanged in the 1933 catalog, but for the 1934 season announced in October 1933, the smaller model was brought into line with its bigger brother, with mudguards flowing elegantly into running boards, and a similar chrome-plated radiator cowl and instrument panel. Under the surface, the chassis was upgraded to that of the Standard 10 horsepower (the slightly more peppy Standard 12 horsepower engine could be had for an extra £5), the 13-inch-longer wheelbase and 8-inch-wider track allowing a much less cramped interior for both the £265 saloon (with a rear side window) and the £260 coupe (with fake folding-roof irons).

Sharing more parts between the two cars brought useful economies of scale, but Lyons widened the appeal of his range with a super-handsome SS 1 Tourer for 1934, an open four-seater with cutaway sections in the doors to accommodate the elbows of driver and passenger as they sped through the countryside in the sunshine (when it rained, the top could be erected and side screens from the small luggage compartment slotted into place). This car, with its dual cowls shaped into the top of the scuttle to suggest racing aspirations, didn't look out of place beside an Alvis or Lagonda and showed that Lyons, with help from Cyril Holland, was starting to build cars that were desirable on their own merits. Tapping into the growing 1930s vogue for streamlining, a four-seater SS 1 Airline saloon was added in 1934, its tapering tail suggesting aerodynamics at work; in reality, there was precious little science to its shape. It arrived at the same time as a very smart SS 2 Tourer.

Swallow was burgeoning, yet a difference in philosophy gradually opened between the partners. Walmsley lacked drive and was content to sit back and watch the money roll in. He wanted a comfortable life and the time to indulge his passion for model railways. The restless Lyons, however, sought to expand the company through ever-bolder moves. Their differing outlooks ultimately proved irreconcilable.

They had established SS Cars Ltd. in 1933 to start the separation of automobile and sidecar activities, and Lyons had bold plans for where he wanted to take the business as sales continued to snowball. After Holbrook Bodies had folded, he was able to snap up the other two buildings at the Foleshill site, and one of them came with a working sawmill that helped enormously in making the frames for car bodies.

When it came to taking the company public, which happened on January 11, 1934, Walmsley had decided he wanted to retire and devote his time to his multiple interests outside work. He shunned the idea of retaining a stake in the company and so his partner had to buy him out, although there is no account of any bust-up over the issue. The upside for Lyons was that he was now in total control as chairman and managing director and could reap the benefits of the vast efforts he poured into the business. And in 1935, all would be spectacularly revealed.

The SS 1 Tourer of 1934 was perhaps the most accomplished of all the company's early cars, with its dual cowls over the dashboard and delightful lines; breaking down on an open-air blast in the countryside was, hopefully, a rarity.

Chapter Four

CAT'S OUT OF THE BAG

Here comes Jaguar: William Lyons takes total control and launches his brand-new range, complete with a stunning sports car that begins to win races.

Lyons and his team were aiming to capture the expensive aura of a coachbuilt Bentley for their new sports saloon, and the prominent headlights and overall elegance achieved that. This is Jaguar's own preserved 1937 2½-liter.

Lunch at the May Fair Hotel in London in September 1935. Invited Jaguar dealers were asked to guess the asking price of SS's new Jaguar 2½-liter saloon. The average estimate was £632, but the actual price was to be £395.

With many years of hard graft under his belt, and now the sole proprietor of a marque that he had built from scratch, by the mid-1930s William Lyons wanted to build cars that need not apologize for either their style or their performance. Throughout 1934 and 1935 he was fully occupied with his plans for an all-new range of authentic SS cars to propel this step change, while the growing workforce was ramping up annual production at Foleshill to 1,800 units.

Before they were revealed, though, the company also signaled its intention to join the elite club of pure sports car makers. On March 15, 1935, the SS 90 two-seater was announced, a gem of a roadster with semi-elliptical springs all round and an SS 1 chassis truncated by 15 inches and underslung at the back so the car really hugged the ground. Behind the big Lucas headlamps and under the long hood was Standard's 2,663cc six-cylinder engine, given a mechanical overhaul to coax the power up to 68 bhp. The tuning package included aluminum con rods, an aluminum cylinder head, and twin RAG carburetors. The 100-mile-per-hour speedometer was there to flatter the owner, but all indications were that this lightweight machine might attain the 90 miles per hour of its title (although none was ever independently tested). Shock absorbers adjustable from the driving seat could sharpen the handling for swifter cornering. The image of a sports racer intended for Brooklands or Le Mans was amplified by the short, graceful tail treatment with the spare wheel embedded in it, and the snug cockpit of the prototype had cutaway doors and no top at all; even that on the production model was little more than a canvas headscarf.

At £395 it was another SS bargain, and the Honorable Brian Lewis spent 1935 campaigning one in various events including the RAC Rally and the Shelsley Walsh Hill Climb, where it came in a surprise third. The motorsports fraternity correctly surmised, however, that it just wasn't powerful enough to be competitive. The first production example was presented to Standard's John Black in June (possibly as a gift) but only twenty-two more were made, and

This Jaguar 1½-liter saloon was the lowliest model in the SS lineup, but its mix of winning style and economical running costs—and modest performance notwithstanding—made it the bestseller and an important car that underpinned Jaguar's early success.

the SS 90 was sidelined. This meant it was, in effect, a series of prototypes. But it was the first of its type from the company, and from this slightly shaky start all of Jaguar's sports car heritage has sprung.

For the car to be taken seriously by the automotive world's opinion formers, the issue of insufficient engine power needed urgent attention. Lyons sought out the young but renowned consultant engineer Harry Weslake. Within the car industry he was already famous for his work with Bentley, from whose racing engines he had coaxed a 50 percent increase in power. Weslake quickly identified the issue: with a side-valve engine like Standard's, the side positioning of the valves and the shape of the cylinders interfered with the inlet and exhaust flows. Potential for any improvement in efficiency was limited. Weslake instead devised a conversion to an overhead-valve system and designed a new cylinder head that let the engine breathe much more freely by taking in more air. A happy byproduct of this increased efficiency was better mechanical refinement levels—it ran more smoothly and quietly and used less fuel. The engine would be a little taller and more expensive to manufacture, but in the 2.6-liter version, brake horsepower took a quantum leap from 68 to 104.

It was a measure of the good relations between the two companies that Standard readily agreed to supply the new design to Weslake's careful specification. A handful were fitted to the last of the original SS 1–based lineup but, toward the end of 1935, production of all these older models was gradually wound down in preparation for the all-new range.

SS Jaguar saloons ready for export at the company's factory in Holbrook Lane, Foleshill, Coventry; by 1938, 50 cars were being made every week, which almost doubled the following year.

On the corporate front, and now as a company in which the general public could buy shares, SS Cars Ltd. was having a busy time. Sidecars were sidelined. In fact, a new company called Swallow Coachbuilding Company (1935) Ltd. was formed to concentrate on those. SS also considered buying the assets of the Sunbeam Motor Car Company from the receivers; the Wolverhampton firm had gone bankrupt after losses stemming from the Great Depression and its costly adventures in racing and speed record breaking, but its name and reputation were well respected. And, of course, Lyons had once sold the cars himself in his youth. Sunbeam might have proved ideal for marketing the new range, but ultimately Lyons decided as ever to go his own way. A list was drawn up of names that suggested athletic performance, and the team kept returning to words like puma, tiger, and jaguar. The last one resonated best and, once the company had checked that the Armstrong Siddeley aircraft engine of the same name was no longer being made, Jaguar it was.

Despite all this activity, Lyons's key focus remained on the new cars. He'd decided on a radical shift in ethos, and now wanted to create a cut-price Bentley in an audacious attempt to reel in more customers. He was after a sophisticated and expensive look with proportions and detailing just like a sports saloon from the most expensive of London coachbuilders such as Park Ward.

To achieve this, Lyons stuck to his idiosyncratic modus operandi of working with coachbuilding manager Cyril Holland; head of the wood shop Fred Gardner was also closely involved. On a full-size wooden buck, the metal panels were shaped purely from the boss's careful instructions and the odd basic sketch or note, then improved and altered as he saw fit until he deemed it just right. Lyons could not draw that well, but he was the only car company head in Britain who worked in this real-time three-dimensional way, with such extraordinary intuition about the appeal of the finished result. At the same time they were finessing the car's smart, sporty lines, the tight-knit team created a brand-new and very Bentley-esque grille design and worked on the details of the luxurious interior with its finely worked leather and polished wood trim.

Up to this point, Jaguar still did not have proper technical facilities, relying on Standard and Weslake for advice, but that was to change with the appointment of highly experienced ex-Humber engineer William Heynes on April 1, 1935. He immediately halted improvement work on the SS 90 and plunged headfirst into the intense development urgently required for the new SS Jaguar, much of which involved working with a wide range of suppliers around Coventry and beyond to define specifications, test components, and place orders. Heynes had to establish a drawing office from scratch and instigate disciplines that other manufacturers had spent three decades building up. He was thirty-two and thus very much a contemporary of the thirty-three-year old Lyons. They were the nimble young "disruptors"

The 3½-liter SS Jaguar 100 was the high-performance star of the range, able to top 100 mph and with 0–60 mph acceleration in an electrifying, for the time, 10.4 seconds.

In 1938 the SS appeal was further boosted with the arrival of the four-seater drophead coupe, seen here at a modern concours event and carrying SS's approved jaguar mascot.

chipping away at the middle-aged complacency that tended to prevail in the British motor industry at the time.

At a reception on September 21, 1935, at London's May Fair Hotel, the cars were unveiled to astonished reporters, dealers, and agents. Over a lavish lunch, Lyons urged his guests to estimate the new SS Jaguar 2½-liter saloon's price. When everyone's stabs at the figure were collated, the average guess was £632, and so there were gasps of amazement when Lyons revealed the list price as a paltry £395. As the average weekly wage was about £6, the car wasn't for drivers on a tight budget, but with a Bentley 3½-liter costing at least £1,500 at the time, the elegant new Jaguar represented astounding value. Indeed, to cater for those slightly less well off—and by way of replacing the smaller cars in the SS range—there was also a 1½-liter model at £295.

With plenty of minor details still to be finalized, the first cars weren't ready for delivery until January 1936. The SS Jaguar 1½-liter saloon featured a side-valve 1,608cc four-cylinder engine (making it a 1.6 rather than a 1.5) taken pretty much unmodified from the Standard 12 horsepower, along with that car's four-speed manual transmission. As might have been expected, performance was fairly modest, with leisurely acceleration and a comfortable cruising speed of about 60 miles per hour (97 kilometers per hour), but the super-stylish lines, natty wire wheels, and luxurious interior made this an impressive car that was neatly packaged. And, with just under 11,000 examples of this basic type built until 1949, it was the car that paid everyone's wages at Jaguar—a fact for which it has rarely received much credit in history books.

The 2½-liter saloon was a considerable step up, its 2,663cc six-cylinder Standard-based engine with Jaguar's overhead-valve conversion calling for a 6.5-inch (16.5-centimeter) extension of the 1½-liter's 112.5-inch (285.8-centimeter) wheelbase. The urbane styling could easily accommodate a longer hood, of course, but with 105 bhp at the driver's disposal (the 1½ had just 52), it could dash from standstill to 60 mph in about 17 seconds, and the 87 mph (140 km/h) top speed was more than adequate for Britain's road network.

It is now amazing to consider this, but the launch of the SS Jaguar saloons overshadowed the arrival of the SS Jaguar 100, the new two-seater sports car from the Lyons-and-Heynes team. It appeared alongside the mainstream model at the London Motor Show at Olympia in 1935, and

An SS 100 tackles a maneuver at a Junior Car Club meeting at Brooklands track, Surrey, in March 1939. The car's power and agility made it a favorite for both amateur and professional drivers, although SS largely left it to customers to enter their own races and rallies.

there was even a third debutante present alongside them: a so-called SS Jaguar tourer, which was an open four-seater "run-out" model based on the four-year-old SS 1.

Derived from the canceled SS 90, the new SS 100, with its fold-flat windscreen, shapely mudguards, stubby tail, and cutaway doors, was the very essence of the 1930s roadster. The SS 100's chassis had a short 8-foot-8-inch wheelbase, beam axles front and back with half-elliptic springs, and underslung rear suspension. The power unit, of course, was the overhead-valve six-cylinder, which made it a 95-mile-per-hour car for a mere £395, with steering, brakes, and gearbox all well up to the job.

SS 100 deliveries started rather late in 1936, and several owners were keen to enter it into competitive events with cautious approval, although limited official support, from the Coventry factory. In July 1936 motoring journalist Tommy Wisdom, driving with his wife Elsie "Bill" Wisdom, took an SS 100 to a storming victory in the International Alpine Trial, one of the first events that could be called an international rally as we know them today, while Sammy Newsome's car roared up the Shelsley Walsh Hill Climb in September in 51.62 seconds to come first in the up-to-3,000cc unsupercharged class. J. Harrop's car won the RAC Rally in March 1937, and in September that year Wisdom was the 3.0-liter class victor again in the Paris–Nice Trial. Such results had a high profile at the time and started to bring decent kudos as the SS 100 was seen to wallop cars from other, long-established and world-renowned sports car marques.

This famous car also acted as a mobile plinth for another distinctive element of the Jaguar story: the leaping Jaguar radiator mascot. Mascots ("hood ornaments" in the US) had for years been popular additions to radiator caps at the prows of cars. In 1935, accessory firm Desmo introduced one specifically for owners of SS's new Jaguar cars, but it was a poor match for the elegance of the cars themselves. Bill Rankin, recruited to handle public relations for SS, is said to have described it as resembling "a cat shot off a fence" and, as Lyons took a particular dislike to it, came up with a plan for the firm's own mascot. An enthusiastic amateur artist himself, Rankin made some renderings of what he considered an anatomically correct depiction of the powerful South American mammal, and then asked motoring artist (and SS owner) Frederick Gordon Crosby to turn it into a stylistic sculpture, the creature crouching on its rear legs, ready to launch itself at its prey. The "Leaper" chrome masterpiece measuring 7.75 inches from fang to tail tip was the result, and was introduced in 1938 as an official accessory, priced at an additional two guineas on any new car order, or ordered for fitment to an existing one. The bronze original was for years fitted to Crosby's own cars and remained in his family's ownership until 1996.

After a couple of years of production, during which SS gradually got into its stride as a full-fledged volume motor manufacturer, its cars for the 1938 season, previewed in autumn 1937, showed worthwhile evolution. The star technical upgrade was a new 1,776cc four-cylinder engine in the 1½-liter (still called a 1.5 but almost a 1.8-liter car now) with an overhead-valve conversion to the Standard unit, which made the car considerably livelier. There was also a very elegant new drop-head coupe on both the 1½- and 2½-liter chassis. A third line of 3½-liter cars, however, featured a new 3.5-liter OHV engine, almost bang on at 3,485cc, and with 125 bhp at 4,500 rpm, this one put some real fire in the Jaguar belly. The 3½-liter saloon was now a 92 mile-per-hour car, but it was in the SS 100 that the engine perhaps occasioned the most spectacular transformation, taking top speed to just over 100 miles per hour for the first time—as high as 105 miles per hour in the right conditions—and giving this lightweight slingshot, costing just £445, 0–60 acceleration in an electrifying 10.4 seconds. Heynes's careful specification of

With the SS 90, Jaguar finally had a sports car that appealed to true enthusiasts. Here, one is seen taking part in a 1935 trials event. With some modifications, and a lot more power, the car was turned into the SS 100.

robust components to cope with this added urge, such as its ENV rear differential, made sure the car was well up to the job when it came to hard driving.

Just how much more powerful this bigger-engined SS 100 was became obvious when Sammy Newsome tackled Shelsley Walsh and got to the top of the hill in 45.94 seconds, six seconds quicker than his previous effort in September 1936. J. Harrop's 3½-liter took tenth overall in the 1938 Monte Carlo Rally, and another won the 1939 Welsh Rally outright. Even after World War II, the cars continued to perform very strongly in competitive motorsports.

In 1938 SS was making fifty cars every week, and a year later that had nearly doubled, with the construction of new purpose-designed assembly buildings at Foleshill that catered for such rapid expansion. This was partly down to another efficiency Lyons had identified and put into practice, replacing the ash wood frames of the cars' bodies with all-steel structures. This reduced vehicle weight and slashed manufacturing costs. Lyons always maintained his low prices were possible because SS was such a lean organization.

In 1938 came another unveiling, this time a beautiful coupe version of the SS 100 that was a star turn at the 1938 London Motor Show. The sleek looks of the faired-in rear mudguards, and the curved shapes of the side windows and roof pointed directly to future Jaguar designs, but as war clouds gathered, this highly desirable car (it would have sold at £595) remained a tantalizing one-off. Indeed, SS car manufacture was immediately wound down after war was declared in September 1939. By 1940 it had been halted altogether, and SS Cars' facilities were turned over wholesale to military contract work. This naturally included making large numbers of sidecars for army dispatch motorcycles, but also work repairing Whitley bomber aircraft for Armstrong Whitworth. Among the very last brand-new SS cars delivered was the final SS 100 in early 1941, the last of 314 of these classics that would strongly influence Jaguar's future direction.

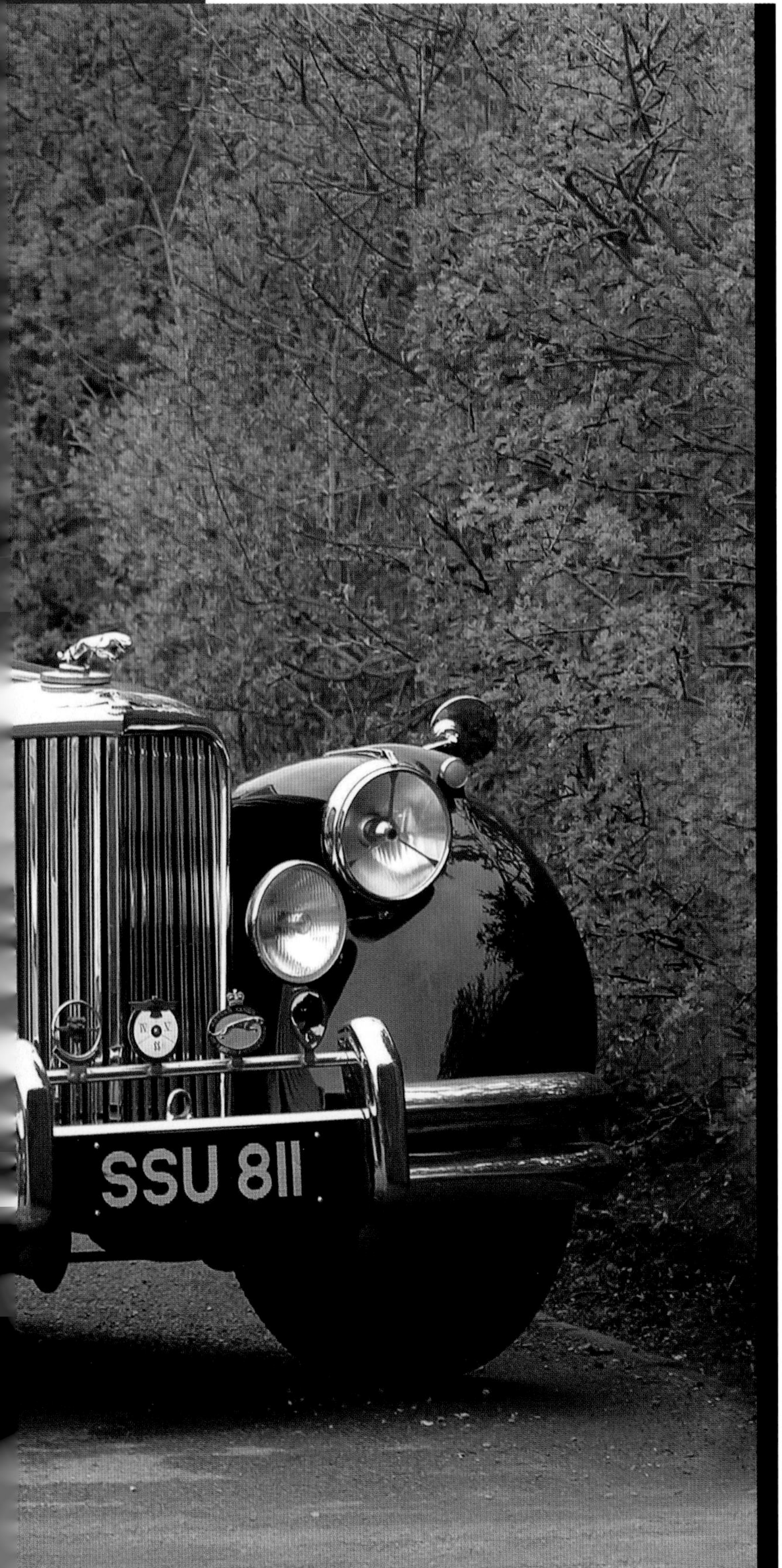

Chapter Five

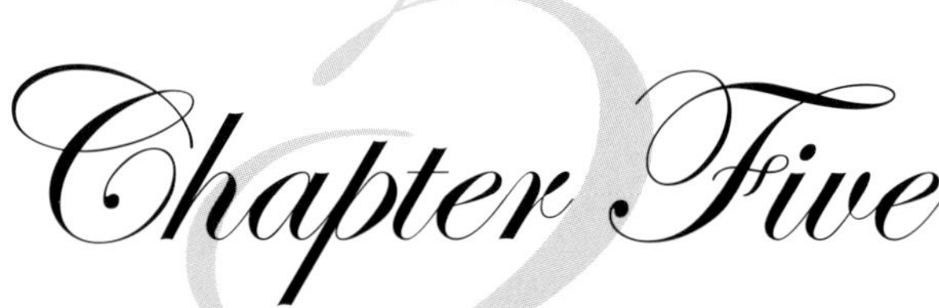

HOW THEY WON THE WAR

World War II and the XK engine: Helped by war contracts, SS swells in importance in the industry, and in the darkest days of the conflict its engineers create the company's first engine—a stunning achievement. Jaguar Cars Ltd. is formed in 1945.

The two-door, four-seat convertible version of the Mk V exuded 1940s glamour and, in export markets, began to lay the groundwork for the overseas demand that would fuel Jaguar's later growth.

The government-backed investment that poured into SS Cars during World War II, enabling it to play its part in the national effort to defeat Germany, changed the company fundamentally. Any last shreds of the keen amateurishness from which it had originally sprung were banished. This was now a business with engineering at its core, allied to seasoned manufacturing and assembly techniques and accomplished salesmanship. It was a deeply transformative time.

Acting as a subcontractor to defense firm Armstrong Siddeley led to installing lots of new equipment, in turn increasing the young company's ability to meet exacting manufacturing standards. With aircraft to both repair and make parts for, a substantial new factory building was erected just up the road; at an overspill former shoe factory in Leicester, an intake of new engineers started to machine a large number of vital components.

It might state "MG" on the front of the EX135's streamlined contours, but "Goldie" Gardner's speed-record machine, in its later guise, ran the experimental 2-liter four-cylinder rendition of the Jaguar XK engine that, ultimately, never went into production.

More than 9,300 sidecars of different military types were produced. While these stand as the most recognizable of Swallow products, the vast quantities of other items built in the same period give an idea of the extraordinary range of the company's output. As cataloged by Jaguar historian Andrew Whyte, these run from wingtips for Spitfires to dinghy storage covers for the Shorts Stirling, from fuel tanks for the de Havilland Mosquito combat aircraft to landing gear doors for the Whitley bomber, and from large numbers of ammunition body frames to aircraft deicing tanks and oxygen bottle cradles.

The largest number of any one item was a 10 hundredweight amphibious trailer, of which the company made more than 30,000 examples in three sizes. Work in this area led to SS building two prototypes for lightweight vehicles intended to be parachuted into enemy territory and be usable the moment they hit the ground. Completed in 1944, they never went into production because of rapid advances in transport aircraft design. But this exacting project became an extremely useful training ground for a newly recruited engine designer named Claude Baily, working with Walter Hassan, SS's chief experimental engineer, who'd joined the company in 1938 after years working on exciting ventures like the supercharger developed for Bentley Motors by Sir Henry "Tim" Birkin.

If SS didn't exactly boom during the darkest days of the war—when Coventry in particular was targeted for German bombing raids—then it at least thrived. Lyons had voiced his yearning to his closest colleagues in the late 1930s to build a 100-mile-per-hour sports saloon to outshine every possible rival, and in the 1939–1945 period plans were carefully and discreetly formulated for ways to achieve that ambitious goal. In 1939, for example, the company had bought near-neighbors Motor Panels from its receivers as a source for in-house car bodies, but for some reason, possibly its old-fashioned methods, Lyons changed his mind and sold the business three years later. Chief engineer William Heynes, however, made more progress on the power-unit front. He could frequently be found on fire-watch duty, sitting on the factory roof and scanning the night sky as other areas of Coventry took major hits from enemy aircraft. On Sunday nights in 1942 he did his shift with Hassan and Baily, and the three of them kicked around ideas for the sort of engine they'd love to make. Lyons, apparently, joined these meetings occasionally, or if he didn't then he conveyed his input, which had to be taken into account. He foresaw a time after the fighting ended when consumers' money would be tight, and smaller-engined cars, such as the SS Jaguar 1½-liter, would need to be the priority. But he had another imperative. Customers had to admire what they saw when they lifted their cars' hoods. A new engine would have to be as much of a source of pride—equally handsome in its own way—as the car's exterior lines.

As early as 1943, and in utmost secrecy, a couple of working four-cylinder prototypes had been built and tested. One, code-named XG, was a pushrod development of the old Standard 1,776cc motor, but the other, the XF, was a twin-overhead-camshaft 1,732cc unit. It was markedly more responsive and offered increased mechanical refinement. An engine like this would be more expensive to manufacture, but such an advanced specification, previously the preserve of the most expensive and exotic European sports cars, could help "future-proof" it as rivals scrambled to catch up.

By the time peace was declared in Europe, a much-developed four-cylinder engine was undergoing continuous, rigorous testing. Its key specification highlights were its dual overhead cams, two valves per cylinder, hemispherical combustion chambers, polished cam covers, and two SU carburetors. With a three-bearing crankshaft, it had a cylinder bore and stroke of 76x98mm to give a capacity of 1,790cc.

The first year of peacetime was a momentous one in several ways. In March 1945 the name of the company was changed to Jaguar Cars Ltd., turning the model title into a marque and consigning SS to history. It was a timely move. The public was well aware of the notorious *Schutzstaffel*, or SS, the

Where once luxury cars were crafted for the moderately affluent, during World War II, the SS factory in Coventry was turned over to armaments. The wingspans of these Whitley bombers being rejuvenated fills all available space.

A cross-section of the "XK100" four-cylinder version of Jaguar's all-new engine from 1948, at which time the smaller unit was still being seriously considered for production.

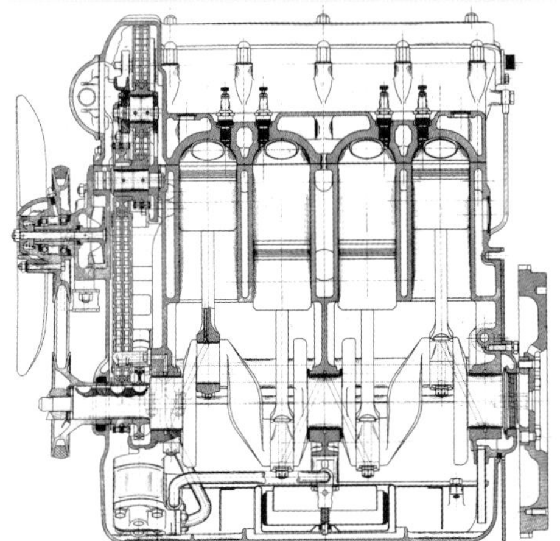

Some of the SS workforce pose with a Gloster Meteor under construction; this pioneering jet fighter was introduced toward the end of the war. Experience working as a subcontractor on such projects hugely helped SS, and then Jaguar, shift from craft- to technology-based manufacturing.

The XK engine in all its straight-six, twin-overhead-camshaft glory. The demands of flexible high performance and mechanical robustness informed the unit's design, although making it a joy to behold was a factor too.

Dozens of newly manufactured XK engines undergo bench-testing at the Foleshill factory prior to installation in completed XK120s.

Nazis' paramilitary "Protection Squadron" whose vicious rule had terrified all right-minded German citizens. The name had to go.

The company's sidecar-making business, Swallow Coachbuilding Company (1935) Ltd., was also moved on, sold in January 1946 to a firm that maintained aircraft at Walsall Airport. It continued making the sidecars there for ten more years, and the Swallow name was part of the deal.

The range of Jaguar saloons and drop-head coupes was put back into production pretty much as it had been in 1940, with the notable exception of the SS 100 two-seater. Not that the SS 100 didn't play its part in Jaguar's 1940s reestablishment. A single example carefully stored away for the five long years of war was recommissioned and put at the disposal of a young driver named Ian Appleyard whose family company, Appleyard of Leeds, was Jaguar's Yorkshire distributor. He achieved the distinction of winning Best Overall Performance in the 1948 Alpine Rally as well as second place overall, and garnered a class win in the Tulip Rally the following year. It was impressive stuff for a car whose design was more than ten years old. More than just a friend to the company, Appleyard literally became one of the family when he married Lyons's daughter Patricia.

William Heynes had proved himself so capable at moving Jaguar forward that in May 1946 he was appointed to the board as technical director. Four months later the company made a key appointment when it took on as service manager Frank England, a friend of Walter Hassan with an enormous amount of experience as a mechanic, team manager, and Alvis service chief, and a first-class organizer and coordinator. On account of his towering height, everyone called him Lofty.

XK engine assembly is in full swing at Foleshill in 1950 as Jaguar gears up for the launch of its crucial Mk VII sports saloon. The company was leaving nothing to chance as it prepared to take on the global automotive establishment.

The XK engine mounted in an XK120 chassis at the factory in 1951. It is extraordinary to contemplate how far Jaguar had come at this point, its first basic in-house car launched just twenty years before (including five years of war footing).

Lyons was one of the very first car-industry leaders to promote women on their merits to senior positions. Alice Fenton had been an assistant in Lyons's father's Blackpool music shop before she joined Swallow. As Lyons was working around the clock to grow the firm, she helped him appoint and liaise with the company's very first dealers as his secretary and assistant, and she was one of the intrepid crew who moved the business down to Coventry. By 1956 she was appointed home sales director, overseeing the launch of Jaguar's new compact 2.4-liter saloon, and would no doubt have become a very well-known figure if she hadn't died of a cerebral hemorrhage at the tragically young age of fifty in March 1960.

The 1940s were important for Jaguar's people, but the decade really belonged to an engine. The company's engineering team had extended its twin-overhead-camshaft concept to include a six-cylinder version with a bore and stroke of 83 × 98mm to give a cubic capacity of 3,181cc. By mid-September 1947 this prototype in bench tests started showing a very promising power output of 142 bhp at 5,000 rpm. Moreover, it made a quantum leap in mechanical smoothness—the sort of refinement that it really had to offer in a pace-setting luxury saloon. Once this was firmly established, the four-cylinder engine was abandoned and never offered in any production model, despite a few preliminary announcements. However, it would still enjoy a burst of glory and a place in the record books. Captain Alfred "Goldie" Gardner set more than one hundred speed records between 1936 and 1950, and one of these used experimental Jaguar four-cylinder engines; fitted to his streamlined MG EX 135, a 1,970cc version became the first 2.0-liter car to cover a mile at 173 miles per hour, achieved on a Belgian motorway in 1948.

The final specification for Jaguar's first complete engine was decided. In order that it would be even more athletic than the old modified Standard unit, the stroke was lengthened to 106mm to give a final capacity of 3,442cc. It produced a beefy 160 bhp. The XK, as it was christened, was based on a cast-iron block with a seven-bearing crankshaft featuring steel con rods and without cylinder liners. On top was the all-aluminum hemispherical head including the twin camshafts. There were two timing chains to reduce noise and the engine sucked in fuel through two 1.75-inch SU carburetors. The engineering department's concept of a large capacity and those "hemi" combustion chambers gave the motor astonishing torque and made it happy and robust enough to be revved hard. Yet it also possessed the showroom appeal Lyons knew was crucial. With its magnificent polished alloy cam covers and exhaust manifold in gleaming stove enamel, it would be the apple of every owner's eye.

The XK proved itself a truly amazing engine. Over nearly forty-five years some 700,000 examples were produced, powering race winners as potently as it did tanks. It was the absolute bedrock of Jaguar's widely acclaimed high-performance reputation.

The mid- to late 1940s were severe times in Britain's motor industry. Raw materials were in short supply and to qualify for bigger allocations carmakers had to argue their case that these would be used to create products with good export potential, as the earning of foreign currency was an essential part of the British Treasury's plan to tackle the vast deficit built up during the war. No credible action plan meant no cold, hard steel. At the same time, the "captive" market once provided by the British Empire was crumbling as countries gained their independence from London, most notably India in 1948.

While many British cars were either too feeble or too old-fashioned to have much competitive appeal internationally, Lyons applied his energies to selling abroad. Ever since the 1930s a trickle of SS cars had left UK shores each year, but the first proper export consignment of Jaguar 3½-liter saloons set sail in January 1947 for the US, where they were marketed by New York entrepreneur Max Hoffmann from his Park Avenue showrooms. Just over a year later Lyons set sail on the liner *Queen Elizabeth* for a five-week sales drive on the West Coast, adding no fewer than three California distributors to his network, including Kjell Qvale's International Motors, which had opened up the US market to the delights of Britain's MG sports cars. European inroads were made with the appointment of Emil Frey as a Swiss concessionaire, and even limited local assembly of cars in Belgium.

Whether Lyons told these important appointments, whose sales skills he immediately recognized, of Jaguar's exciting upcoming plans isn't clear. That they wanted a piece of the action was certain, though, and there was a brand-new model in September for them to begin promoting immediately: the Jaguar Mk V. Tellingly, it was the first car from the company designed from the get-go to be built in both right- and left-hand drive configurations.

This car is often adjudged an "interim" model and yet, engines apart, it was almost all new. It should perhaps be seen as a crucial bridge between the SS days and the stylish and accomplished Jaguar saloons that would become world famous in the 1950s.

After hours inside the Foleshill factory in the early 1940s gives a chance to see some of SS's vital work in progress for the British war effort, in this case fuselages for the RAF's Whitley bomber planes undergoing repairs.

The Mk V's most important feature was its all-new chassis frame with deep box sections and crossbracing to vastly improve its stiffness. At the front was a new independent suspension system using double wishbones and torsion bars—conceived by William Heynes—that made the car much safer and more predictable in its handling than previous Jaguars. Hydraulic brakes were another major step forward, while the way the car rode was further improved by losing the underslung element of the chassis at the back that could give a bumpy ride, the frame now sweeping over the rear axle.

Those engines were the familiar 102-bhp 2.7-liter and the 125-bhp 3.5-liter Standard units from the obsolete 2½- and 3½-liter cars, respectively, with four-speed manual transmissions; the XK had yet to make its debut. The car's styling, though, was a masterful modernization of the sleek SS-era trademark look. Overseen as ever by Lyons's expert eye, the theme was one of fairing-in, as the headlamps were now incorporated into the pressed-steel bodywork either side of the Bentley-like front grille, following the style of contemporary American car design, rather than freestanding. Another clue to the future importance of the North American market was a system of flashing indicator lights for US models, incorporated into the sidelights and taillights. Lyons used some genius design ploys to update the old shape and compensate for losing the lower underslung chassis. He enclosed the rear wheels behind metal "spats" (as seen on the one-off SS 100 coupe in 1938) to elongate the side profile, and introduced the ovular "tuck-in" curve to the rear quarterlight as a sleek sign-off to the window line; this last detail would become an instantly recognizable Jaguar motif throughout the 1950s and 1960s, copied as late as 1969 by stylists of the Ford Capri to impart a harmonious look to that car's side profile. Finally, on the Mk V, lower-profile tires on 16-inch disc wheels (down from 18 inches) lowered its height. As either a four-door saloon or a two-door drop-head coupe, it was a super-stylish machine with a chassis that made it markedly more drivable. An overlooked Jaguar, yet an important one, contemporary testers found the £1263 3½-liter

The Jaguar Mk V, launched in 1948, is a stylistic bridge between the 1930s and 1950s, with headlights now carefully integrated rather than free standing, but its independent front suspension was its key technical advance.

An important car in Jaguar's design evolution, the Mk V introduced features such as the arc and curve of the window line and enclosed rear wheels that became signatures of more famous models to follow.

model stable, supple, and easy to steer at high speeds, if not perhaps when straining at its 90 mile-per-hour maximum.

But what, you may well ask, of Jaguar's savvy dependence on a range that included smaller, more affordable cars? For sure, the market at home was characterized by postwar austerity. But Lyons's sights were now trained on the international arena where he could see huge demand for the brand of power and style he had in mind. There was, though, another factor. The Standard Car Company's boss, Sir John Black, having partnered with SS and now Jaguar in engines, cast envious eyes at what was being achieved at Foleshill. He dearly wanted to buy Jaguar, and made many overtures to do so, but even though the shares were publicly traded, Lyons had the controlling interest, and he politely but firmly rebuffed any takeover approaches. The spiteful, bombastic Black found this very hard to take and plotted revenge. Standard bought the remaining assets of the Triumph car company (a close SS rival in the 1930s, its Coventry factory had been destroyed by German bombs in the war) and launched the 1800 Roadster and Saloon in 1946. They were powered by the 1,776cc four-cylinder engine with Weslake-style overhead-valve conversion once made exclusively for the SS 1½-liter cars. The Triumphs were distinctive alternatives to the Jaguar 1½-liter for a couple of years until, with the Mk V, Jaguar departed the four-cylinder market for a full fifty years. For Jaguar was poised to make its first great leap forward.

Chapter Six

SPORTS CAR GENIUS

XK120 to XK150: The XK120 is built as a limited-edition showcase for the XK engine but demand is so massive Jaguar has to radically change its game, squaring up to everyone from Chevrolet to Ferrari in the world sports car arena.

The pure, beautiful lines of the XK120 were created over three days early in 1948 by Lyons, who was eager to build a showcase for the XK engine in double-quick time.

These details of the XK120 highlight the roadster's purposefulness: the hood was basic, there were sidescreens instead of windows, a no-nonsense cockpit, and reasonable luggage accommodation.

With Jaguar's future prospects pinned firmly to its all-new saloon car, naturally there was consternation that this crucial new project (covered fully in chapter 7) took rather longer to complete than anticipated. The Mk V would be unveiled in the autumn of 1948 to a broadly positive reception, and the exciting XK engine was now all ready to go but was, for the moment, without a berth. The situation had set the Jaguar team thinking, and it was decided to build a limited-production sports car that could act as a rolling showcase for the engine and also prove its stamina in a few races and demonstrations; with the remarkable continued competition success of the old SS 100, there remained a valuable reputation to capitalize on.

This was barely six months before the first postwar London Motor Show would open at Earl's Court in October 1948, but the tight time scale didn't faze Lyons. While chief engineer Heynes shortened and modified a Mk V chassis frame to accept the XK engine, Lyons set to with his trusted craftsman Fred Gardner to design the car itself. He later said that the design took three days. As the shape was beaten out in aluminum in a few weeks it became obvious early on that here was something extra-special: a low-slung two-seater roadster with pure, fluid lines where separate mudguards were replaced with fully enveloping wings and the tail came to a beautifully tapered finish. Three months later they had a running prototype.

In truth, the car wasn't particularly original. A harsh critic might point to the 1940 BMW 328 Mille Miglia Roadster and claim the new Jaguar was a very close copy. Experts in the exquisite prewar Italian coachwork for Alfa Romeos and Lancia, or some of the 1947 output from French coachbuilders for one-off Talbots and Delahayes, can easily find design parallels. Whatever the external influences, Lyons melded them with his own ideas for a car of stunning beauty and purity of line, incorporating the metal spats from his 1938 SS 100 coupe to fully enclose the rear wheels and making every aspect—such as the raked V-shaped windscreen and the lack of external door handles—adapt to the wonderful form. In overall proportion, up-close detail, and, of course, visual impact, it was the highest accomplishment in double-quick time.

The 1948 Motor Show in London was packed with new cars as the British motor industry finally presented its future postwar face to the public. But no car—not even the innovative and affordable Morris Minor, nor the highly advanced Bristol 401—made such an impression as the new Jaguar, presented under the name of XK120 Super Sports to signify a projected top speed that would make it the fastest production car on the planet. It was the glittering star of the event.

Unlike for showpieces unveiled at shows today, Jaguar boldly stated an astoundingly low asking price of £998. It was deliberately priced a whisker below a grand because all new cars costing over £1,000 incurred a purchase tax rate of 66 percent; below that it was a "mere" 30 percent, meaning a new XK120 on the road in Britain would cost £1,298. The limited edition would be capped at 240 cars, which was just enough to recoup the cost of making this mobile velvet cushion on which to display the gem of a brand-new engine.

Jaguar took a stand at the New York Auto Show in February 1949, the earliest such event there that could be called international in flavor because a huge contingent of foreign marques took part for the first time. The month after it was at the Geneva Salon. Each time the XK120 created a furor, especially in the US, where there was a clamor to get one. New York City importer Max Hoffmann claimed he had sold ninety of the cars, at $4,000 apiece, on the basis of the brochure illustrations alone.

The initial scope of the XK120 project didn't merit "tooling up." For such a small production run, Jaguar had intended to return to the artisan method (still used by Morgan today!) of a seasoned ash wood body frame clothed with aluminum panels. Now a new reality dawned on the company.

It had hit upon something with enormous sales potential in the US and, rather than turn away thousands of potential orders, the firm could use them to lobby for a far bigger allocation of steel if it could put the XK120 into something like mass production. As the car would almost certainly be capable of bringing in valuable dollars for the UK's shell-shocked economy,

The XK120 at Jabbeke, Belgium, in May 1949, with Jaguar test driver "Soapy" Sutton at the wheel, where the thrilling new Jaguar achieved 132 mph to cement its status as the world's fastest production car. "Lofty" England holds the flag.

Once on the racetrack, the XK120 begged to be driven hard and fast, and here Leslie Johnson is in the battle-scarred HKV 500 (the Jabbeke car, converted to right-hand drive) at Silverstone in 1949, heading for the 120's first race victory.

Whitehall's Ministry of Supply readily agreed. Hoffmann immediately booked the entire production run for the next six months, which meant, at a stroke, eighty percent of XK120 output was earmarked for North America. Little wonder that Lyons was elected president of Britain's Society of Motor Manufacturers & Traders shortly after. A new plan was formulated just as swiftly as the first one had been. After the initial batch (there were in fact 242 of them in the end) of XK120s was hand built, the car would move to a production line with an identical looking, steel-framed and paneled body, while retaining aluminum for the doors, hood, and trunk. It took a year to do this, but the hiatus actually came in quite handy.

Naturally, there was broad skepticism that this new pretender to the crown of king of the sports car was indeed faster than anything else. The 1946 Healey 2.4 had been trumpeted as the first 100-mile-per-hour production car and was officially timed at 111 miles per hour, and finished thirteenth in the tricky Mille Miglia road race. Ferrari, meanwhile, was another newcomer, and in 1949 it more than earned its laurels when its V-12 166 won the 24 Hours of Le Mans (Italian-American Luigi Chinetti shared the driving with English aristocrat Lord Selsdon). It was all about the crucial difference between claiming and proving. Jaguar had to stand up and be counted.

In May 1949 the company issued invitations to journalists to join it at the Jabbeke Highway in Belgium to see what the XK120 could really do. The two-lane A10 motorway from Ostend to Brussels (today part of the E40 pan-European route) had a section near Jabbeke that was dead straight and flat for 8 miles and had a notably smooth concrete surface. It was a precious gift to the high-performance motoring world, the likes of which simply could not

With its well-known NUB 120 registration number, this is probably the most famous XK120 of all—the car in which Ian Appleyard and his wife, Pat (Lyons's daughter) achieved so much rallying success, notably winning the Alpine Rally in 1951 and 1952.

be found in Britain at the time, and the Royal Automobile Club Belgium was in those days able to close sections for high-speed runs, and act as official timekeeper.

Walter Hassan was going to drive the car but fell ill, so his place was taken by chief test driver Ron "Soapy" Sutton. The left-hand-drive car was only the second XK120 built, and it was adjusted with a tiny wind deflector in place of its windscreen, modified top-gear ratio, metal tonneau cover over the passenger seat, and a streamlined undertray. The engine, though, was completely standard. The car was timed completing the flying mile at 132.596 miles per hour, more than qualifying it as the world's fastest production car. In fact, at one point on the two-way average, Sutton kissed 135 miles per hour; even with the windscreen and top in place the XK120 could reach 126 miles per hour. Soapy's final party trick was to trickle past the invited media at 10 miles per hour in top gear.

This was a fantastic endorsement of the XK120's performance, but it was proven in a more real-world situation in August 1949 when the car made its competition debut in a production sports car race at Silverstone. The ever-capable Lofty England was on hand as team manager. Two of the cars loaned by the factory to drivers Leslie Johnson and Peter Walker finished first (that hard-working Jabbeke car again, now converted to right-hand drive) and second, respectively. Johnson (this time in Walker's car from Silverstone) bagged Jaguar its first US racing result by coming fourth in a sports car race at Palm Beach, Florida, in January 1950; four months later came the first US win, in the Palm Beach Cup with Phil Hill and Don Parkinson driving. Indeed, throughout 1950 XK120s proliferated in events large and small, campaigned by amateurs and professionals alike. There were some very impressive results, such as Leslie Johnson's fifth place on the Mille Miglia; a one-two-three finish in the Tourist Trophy in Dundrod, Northern Ireland, with a very young Stirling Moss taking the laurels (Lyons instantly signed him up as a works driver); and Peter Walker's victory in the Silverstone production sports car race again, in which Jaguar also scooped the team prize.

Showing what a versatile contender the XK120 was, it also excelled in rallying. Lyons's son-in-law Ian Appleyard, with intrepid wife Patricia navigating, famously brought two straight wins on the demanding Alpine Rally in 1950 and '51, also coming first in the 1951 Tulip Rally, where another XK120 came second. Mr. and Mrs. Appleyard didn't win the 1952 Alpine but they completed it so faultlessly, with not one penalty point incurred, they won a special gold cup that tasted almost as good as the winner's champagne. This was all in the same white car with its distinctive NUB 120 number plates.

Back in 1950, Jaguar made its cautious debut in the 24 Hours of Le Mans, the most punishing endurance race of all. Three XK120s were entered and although one was out early with clutch trouble, the others finished twelfth and fifteenth. That was very credible, indeed, albeit not good enough to garner much acclaim; the cars had too much weight and not enough power to lead the pack there. Lyons and Heynes realized, though, that a Le Mans victory could do their company an enormous amount of good, so another audacious scheme was hatched, this time to build an XK120 model specifically for top level motor racing (more in chapter 8).

The regular production XK120 open two-seater, steel-bodied that is, was a car for pure enjoyment in good weather, and it was no surprise that the US West Coast accounted for the bulk of sales, which was excellent news for Jaguar and for Britain. The company made sure that, among customers eager to get their cars, screen idol Clark Gable was the first. The high-quality, tight-fitting cockpit was purposeful rather than opulent, and weather protection consisted of a workaday canvas top and detachable side screens. Lighter wire-spoke wheels to improve handling meant part of the car's signature style was lost because the sleek rear spats no longer fit over the wheel hubs and had to be left off. The old "race on Sunday, sell on Monday" mantra was part of what made the XK120 successful but in everyday life people who could afford an exciting car like this—especially those beyond the warm-weather states—really needed a few more creature comforts.

Jaguar responded in 1951 with an XK120 fixed head coupe whose supremely elegant styling was only slightly compromised by a rather claustrophobic cabin. The emphasis was on luxury and the car had a lustrous wood veneer dashboard and door cappings (the roadster just had leather-covered door tops), wind-up windows, and a proper heating and ventilation system. To counter any accusations of having gone soft, though, there was an optional SE pack with an added 20 bhp and wire wheels. A car very similar to this—in fact, William Heynes's very own road car—was the next XK120 to achieve legendary status. A team of drivers headed by Stirling Moss took it to the Autodrome de Montlhéry race circuit near Paris in 1952 and drove the car nonstop for seven days and nights at an average of over 100 mph. It went like a train and provided more proof that modern Jaguars were not just glamorous but robust under sustained pressure. For one whole hour it belted around the banked oval at 130 mph.

The third and final variation of the XK120 arrived in April 1953, a drop-head coupe derivative. Here was an open car intended for high-speed touring and everyday comfort, and to that end it was equipped with a much more substantial mohair top with a zippered rear window and the fixed head's wind-up windows.

Any XK120, though, was a joy to drive. *The Autocar* captured its character succinctly in its April 1950 road test write-up: "Nothing like the XK120, and at its price, has been previously achieved—a car of tremendous performance and yet displaying the flexibility and even the silkiness and smoothness of a mild-mannered saloon. Press the right foot down and a snarl comes into the exhaust... and on a familiar road the bends and even the landmarks seem to have been redesigned overnight and placed much closer together!"

If there was one area letting down the car it was in its brakes: large 12-inch drums with Lockheed hydraulics all round, the best that contemporary technology could furnish but not really adequate for a car with such acceleration.

In its home country, the XK120 was always a rare sight. Only 1,660 of the 12,045 cars built had right-hand drive. The US took most of the 7,606 roadsters, 2,672 fixed heads, and 1,767 drop-heads.

If the XK120 roadster had triggered sighs of longing, then the fixed head coupe put potential buyers into rapture with its sleek and harmonious contours. The only drawback was that the cabin was apt to feel rather cramped.

The impact of the XK120 on Jaguar cannot be emphasized enough. The most exotic car then produced in Britain catapulted the firm on to the world map as one of the truly great car marques and added stardust to Jaguar's mainstream luxury saloons. However, its status as the fastest production car on earth was envied by rivals, and in September 1953 it was finally snatched away—by the Spanish. A Pegaso Z102, a supercharged former Le Mans car, went to Jabbeke, where Celso Fernández pushed it to a record-busting average of 151.032 miles per hour. Almost immediately, Lyons phoned his new chief test engineer, Norman Dewis, to ask what he was going to do about this affront. Dewis was skeptical the XK120 had enough potential to beat the Pegaso, especially without a supercharger. Nonetheless Jaguar was back in Belgium in October. It was taking its chances against blustery autumn weather with an ingeniously modified car. Apart from a higher compression ratio,

From the back, the XK120 fixed head coupe was just as visually satisfying as from the front, although the prominent overrider "bumpers" were necessary to ward off light knocks.

Fearless company test driver Norman Dewis became a legend in his own long lifetime. Here he is in characteristically cheerful form at Jaguar's favorite demonstration arena, the Jabbeke Highway in Belgium, in 1952.

A padded leather roll on the door top and the ability for the windscreen to be removed and replaced by aero screens were attributes harking back to sports cars of the 1930s.

a beefier prop shaft, and a close-ratio gearbox, it was mechanically unaltered, but had been made more wind-cheating by removing sidelights, streamlining the headlights, and adding a Perspex bubble canopy that cut height so radically that Dewis had to sit on a chunk of foam instead of a driving seat—once the top had been battened down on top of him. Even the tread on the tires was reduced to cut drag. To everyone's incredulity, Dewis crushed the Pegaso's feat after hitting an officially timed top speed of 172.412 miles per hour. The fastest-car crown was convincingly grabbed back.

Norman Dewis with the carefully modified XK120, featuring a wind-cheating Perspex bubble roof, in which he reached an amazing 172 mph in 1953 to grab back the fastest-production-car laurels from Spain's upstart Pegaso.

Jaguar continued to update its cars with the same restless frequency of the prewar SS operation, and in 1954 the XK140 series arrived to replace the XK120. The most immediately obvious alteration was the heftier bumpers, which took away a little visual finesse but were deemed necessary to ward off careless urban car-parkers in the key North American market! To drive the new range was to discover an even more sparkling response than before, as the SE engine was now standard and given an extra 10 bhp for a 190-bhp output at 5,500 rpm. To continue to offer an upgrade above even that, a new SE model had 210 bhp on tap thanks to the special cylinder head from the C-type racing car (see chapter 8). This meant that in fully equipped, road-legal guise the XK140 SE (or XK140 MC as it was marketed in the US) was potentially a 125-mile-per-hour road rocket.

Jaguar's attention had shifted to the C- and D-type by the time the XK140 was launched, but that didn't put off privateers. This XK140 fixed head coupe is the only one ever to enter Le Mans, in 1956 with Roger Walshaw and Peter Bolton, where it was disqualified in error while running in eleventh place after 206 laps. It's been restored recently.

By shifting the engine forward 3 inches, all XK140s were less constricted inside for driver and passenger, and the drop-head featured an even more fully insulated top to banish the winter chills, plus a tiny rear seat for toddlers, smallish dogs, or (more likely) a briefcase or picnic basket. The fixed head coupe featured the most radical of external alterations,

Hollywood idol Clark Gable was photographed in September 1952 with his new XK120 as it was loaded at Kent, England, for shipping to France on a Bristol freight aircraft.

The Jaguar XK150 roadster introduced in 1958 came with disc brakes and, eventually, a 265 bhp 3.8-liter engine as it faced ever-sterner competition from the Chevrolet Corvette.

Interior of the XK150, now with wind-up windows across the range and a one-piece, curved windscreen through which to admire that long, shapely hood.

with a much-extended cabin over that small rear seat to make it roomier and airier inside.

Telescopic shock absorbers better cushioned road imperfections and a new rack-and-pinion steering system, taken directly from Jaguar's racing cars, was state-of-the-art and felt very precise. With motor racing now focused on more specialist cars, though, the emphasis edged toward sporting luxury for the XK. Driving fast—and in style—all day long with agility and control in the corners and comfort on the straights was what customers wanted. So first came an overdrive for calmer top-gear cruising, and in 1956 the rather surprising option of automatic transmission arrived to make the driving experience as undemanding as possible.

After just under 9,000 of these cars had been sold, the XK sports car lineup was overhauled one more time in May 1957. Jaguar and Dunlop had been collaborating on the development of disc brakes for years and now they came to a Jaguar road car, following their British debut the year before on the Triumph TR3. They were race-proven on the Jaguar D-type and, because they could be relied on time after time to stop the car assuredly from very high speeds, the 12-inch Dunlop disc brakes on all four wheels remedied the chief failing of the XK line: drum brakes that were, after repeated heavy use, prone to fading.

The XK120 styling was now almost a decade old and feeling a little dated no matter how elegant and harmonious it remained. Rivals such as the Mercedes-Benz 300SL, BMW 507, and Lancia Aurelia Spyder were upping the ante, so the XK150 adopted a more straight-through wingline, less undulating, that made it look a little bit fatter. Moreover, the stringback-glove brigade was dismayed that there was now a choice of a drop-head and fixed head coupe only. The one-piece windscreen and widened hood were all modernizing touches, but what had happened to the sports car character?

The XK150 roadster was actually known as the "Open" in factory parlance, and almost all of these glamorous, powerful machines were made in left-hand drive, mainly for US export.

It was back with a growl in 1958 and the launch of the strictly two-seater XK150 roadster, with the new styling theme plus a better top and wind-up windows. With engines in the latest 1957 Chevrolet Corvette lineup offering power options from 220 to 283 bhp, Jaguar was duty bound to respond, and the new S option for the XK150 had a "straight port" cylinder created by veteran Jaguar consultant Harry Weslake, which, along with a battalion of three SU carburetors, gave a storming 250 bhp—enough to make an XK150 a 130-mile-per-hour beast. And there was even more to come when the XK engine was enlarged to 3.8-liter capacity in 1960. The standard version offered 220 bhp while the 3.8 S, the acme of XK sports car development, boasted 265. These cars were available for but a short time. Production wrapped in October 1960. Jaguar was now one of the world's greatest sports car marques.

Undoubtedly more practical for day-to-day driving than an "Open," the drop-head coupe version of the XK150 was almost as scintillating to drive; the stacked-up hood when folded and the dash-top rear-view mirror were in conflict, though.

464 HYV

Chapter Seven

GRACE ... SPACE ... PACE ...

Ambition fulfilled: The Mk VII sets new standards in every direction, making Jaguars the preeminent sports saloons and cementing connections with royalty. The series takes a dramatic new turn with the technologically adroit Mk X, but has the marque reached its limits?

This is the Jaguar Mk VII M personally owned and loved by the Queen Mother for eighteen years. It often returned to the Jaguar factory for maintenance and updates, including fitting the one-piece windscreen from the car's successor, the Mk VIII.

It is little exaggeration to state that the Mk VII saloon, at its debut under the bright lights of the London Motor Show at Earl's Court in October 1950, was the culmination of all the company had worked toward for the fifteen years since the Jaguar name first appeared.

It was the most mouth-watering sports saloon on Earth, and fully lived up to William Lyons's decree that it must be "the match of any similar car, built anywhere in the world, at any price."

The pattern that emerges with SS and then Jaguar in their earliest years is one of major impacts underpinned by well-proven building blocks that could ensure success. The Mk VII is a prime example.

The twin-cam, 3.4-liter XK straight six engine, for instance, while intended primarily for this very car, had been in painstaking development for many years, proving itself in the XK120 for months on both road and track. It was more than ready for its role and came partnered with a four-speed manual gearbox, made by Moss, that was sturdy and well tried. And then there was the strong box-section chassis frame with its independent torsion bar front suspension that was first seen on the Mk V in 1948 and carried over with careful upgrades.

The modern and elegant full-width four-door bodywork, though, was completely new, and with its extended rear overhang to give a graceful tail treatment, along with

A Jaguar Mk VII performs ribbon-cutting duty at the official opening ceremony of the Motor Industry Research Association's proving grounds at Nuneaton, Warwickshire, on May 21, 1954.

a much larger trunk, you would never have guessed the car used the identical 12-foot wheelbase of the Mk V. It looked as good as any bespoke Bentley. Lyons had labored in his idiosyncratic manner on the styling, with craftsmen fitting a full-size wooden mockup with a series of panels continually modified until the boss was satisfied. He was particularly obsessed with the way light played on the curves, and he apparently used a self-assembled combination of string, metal rods, and bits of wood in his experiments to fine-tune his thinking and get the optimum look. But he also had opinions from American car buyers ringing in his ears from his regular trips to the US. The headlamps were now fully embedded in the car's frontage on either side of a tall and simplified radiator shell, while the rear wheels were faired in behind Jaguar's trademark metal half-covers. The two-piece windscreen reflected the limitation of curved safety glass technology in those times, but the sweep of the side-window shapes was in harmony with the wings that were blended so smoothly into the car's flanks.

The US influence was obvious not so much in the design forms of the Mk VII but in its scale. A full six-seater, at 16 feet long this was a very big car in a British context, yet beside contemporary Lincolns, Cadillacs, Packards, and Hudsons, it would have seemed shorn of excess. The interior craftsmanship, too, would have exuded a sporting luxury rather different than the Detroit norm, with rich leather upholstery, deep Dunlopillo cushioning, burr walnut cabinetwork, and cozy West of England cloth headlining. At night the cabin was illuminated by a wonderful violet glow from the dashboard dials.

The dreamily Twilight Blue car unveiled in London carried a £988

In the "bigger picture" that Lyons had inside his head, this was what motor racing was all about—using success on the track, as here with the D-type, to bolster the allure of the Mk VII sports saloon

The inviting rear seat of the Mk VII ushered passengers into a world of hand-finished opulence, with fold-out walnut picnic tables, built-in clock, and even a magazine rack.

price tag, a steal for what was offered, and as Britain was just emerging from grim, postwar austerity—with all gasoline rationing restrictions lifted that year—the omens looked great for the Mk VII (it should have been a Mk VI, of course, but Bentley was already using that title, so Jaguar had to skip a "mark"). It was for this car that Jaguar, possibly guided by its advertising agency but certainly by Alice Fenton's instinct for what summed up the car, introduced its brilliant slogan, "Grace ... Space ... Pace ..." The stickiest issue was supply; the Mk VII was principally for export only and the home market allocation was almost a token gesture. The same blue car a month later found itself in the splendor of New York's Waldorf Astoria hotel for a preview reception. After just three days on display Jaguar had five hundred orders; a few months later and it could boast of having secured $30 million in US sales.

Despite hitting the scales at almost 2 tons, the Mk VII was fast—very fast. Nothing comparable could beat it for acceleration as it sprinted from standstill to 60 miles per hour (97 kilometers per hour) in just over 13 seconds. In independent tests top speed was proven to be 101 miles per hour, yet it was also the handling of the car that set it apart from most other large saloons of the period. It was sensational. America's *Road & Track* noted that the Mk VII could be "power-slid around a slippery corner just for the fun of the thing," while Gordon Wilkins of Britain's *The Autocar* found the car "handled magnificently in the worst possible conditions, sliding continuously on snow and ice for hours on end." It should, perhaps, be added that only experienced drivers would have felt confident throwing this large car around so casually! Directly below the driver's feet, crammed between the chassis members, was the car's anchor in the form of a large Clayton Dewandre brake servo cylinder—a unit of sometimes dubious reliability but one that helped coax exceptional stopping power from the Jaguar's large drum brakes, and a point in its favor for rallying and racing.

Yes, that's right. Jaguar was determined to prove that its luxury saloon could earn its competitive spurs. In the *Daily Express* International Trophy Production Touring Car race at Silverstone, Mk VIIs won five years in succession: the victorious drivers were Stirling Moss in 1952 and 1953, Ian Appleyard in 1954, Mike Hawthorn in 1955, and Ivor Bueb in 1956. In two of those years, Mk VIIs filled the top three places. There was no other British car quite like it; potential rivals from Armstrong Siddeley, Daimler, Humber, Riley, Rover, and Wolseley could offer comparable comfort, but their roadholding and responsiveness were abysmal by comparison. Internationally, perhaps only the Lancia Aurelia with its complex, all-aluminum V-6 engine came close, but at £2,863 was frighteningly expensive.

Jaguar had planned very carefully for the start of Mk VII manufacture and the high volume anticipated. Instead of making the bodywork in-house, the shells were manufactured by the Pressed Steel Company in Oxford and delivered to Jaguar in Coventry on transporters. That freed up some space at the Foleshill factory but nowhere near enough to cope with demand. By 1952 Jaguar had taken over a huge new plant at Browns Lane, Allesley, Coventry, in which to set up production lines for both the XK120 and the Mk VII.

Critics regarded the Mk VII as pretty much automotive perfection. In 1952, *The Motor* declared it "one of the best cars submitted for road test in the post-war years."

Both this and the American magazine *Auto Age* raved about

Elegance and cohesion were the hallmarks of the Mk VII, whose tapered forms and well-balanced proportions were a reflection of the clarity of thought that went into Jaguar's 1950 sports saloon watershed.

The accomplished lines of the Mk VII were testimony to Lyons's good taste and intuitive eye. This large and impressive saloon was every inch the world-class product that he aimed for.

Ian Appleyard on course to take a fine second overall place in the 1953 Monte Carlo Rally in a Mk VII; in 1956 Ronnie Adams would take his example to a rousing overall victory.

In 1954 the Mk VII became the Mk VII M with a slew of small improvements, chief among them a 30 percent hike in engine power, but externally it looked as good as ever.

the car's braking. A Borg Warner automatic transmission system became an option for export cars from 1952 (the first auto fitted to a Jaguar) and overdrive was added as an option, but these were pretty much the only changes to the car until 1954 and the introduction of the Mk VII M, which offered a 30 bhp power increase and a few other detail improvements. Jaguar built a top-secret lightweight Mk VII intended for racing, with a D-type racing engine and magnesium body panels, but it never saw an actual race; instead, a fairly standard Mk VII M pulled off the considerable feat of winning the 1956 Monte Carlo Rally, driven by the team of Adams, Biggar, and Johnston. Just as exciting in the boardroom meetings at Browns Lane in 1956 was the news that Queen Elizabeth, the Queen Mother, had picked a Mk VII M as her personal car, and in doing so bestowed the first Royal Warrant on Jaguar. She must have loved it dearly because the metallic claret car was in her regular use for the next eighteen years.

With some 21,000 Mk VIIs sold, the big Jaguar was renamed the Mk VIII in 1956. The key outward improvements were a curved, one-piece windscreen (the Queen Mum's car came back to the factory to have that upgrade too), a range of two-tone paint schemes, and more exposure for the rear wheels as the spats started to look a mite old-fashioned. The standard engine now offered 190 bhp (210 from one running the C-type-style cylinder head). The least you could expect was around 105 miles per hour at top speed.

Two years later, the basic car was overhauled further and renamed Mk IX. The two major new features were roughly in parallel with the XK140's transformation into the XK150, namely a 220-bhp, larger-capacity 3.8-liter XK engine and four-wheel servo-assisted Dunlop disc brakes. But there was also a Jaguar first: power-assisted steering. Plus, for cars sold in the UK, a sliding steel sunroof was now included as part of the standard package at the still extremely reasonable price of £1,995.

In the end, more than 46,500 of the Mk VII-IX series were built. In autumn 1961, though, the Mk X replacement had some major and startling surprises in store. It was bold, broad, and bristling with technical excellence; a lavish new Jaguar saloon for the 1960s.

The forward-leaning grille and four headlights fronted a long, low torpedo-shaped saloon that gave the appearance of straining at the leash and being eager to rocket forward. It was a huge car in every respect, and not least in its width that, at a bollard-scraping 6 feet 4 inches, remains among the widest ever for a British road car. It was 5.5 inches longer than the Mk IX and 8.5 inches lower. Below the surface, the 1940s-era separate-chassis construction had been ditched in favor of a full monocoque, with body and chassis combined in one unit. That in itself would have eradicated a lot of noise, vibration, and harshness, but there was also an all-new, fully independent rear suspension system based on that in the E-type launched the same month in 1961 (see chapter 10). Designed by Heynes and his colleague Bob Knight, this brilliant system used wishbones and four coil spring/damper units mounted on a metal crossbeam that was insulated from the car's body by rubber bushes. The amazing compromise it gave between soothing ride comfort and tenacious roadholding was an absolute revelation, and the disc brakes, mounted inboard at the

Duotone paintwork, cutaways in the rear wheel covers, and a one-piece curved windscreen distinguished the Mk VIII, while the 210 bhp engine with C-type head ensured this large car could reach 105 mph.

Four-wheel, servo-assisted disc brakes were standard equipment on the Mk IX introduced in 1960, and under the hood was a 3.8-liter, 220 bhp edition of the XK engine, which it shared with the XK150.

back were exceptionally effective too. *The Autocar* was astonished: "The inherent impression of security in this car is such that passengers are usually unaware they are travelling as fast as the speedometer indicates." It might have been the biggest Jaguar, but on the move it quickly shrank around the driver to feel like anything but hard work on the road, and in a hurry. For the time the sensation of being in control of a Mk X, even in the city center, was one of total confidence from a commanding driving position. It was arguably the best riding steel-sprung car in the world until 1968, when that mantle passed to ... the Jaguar XJ6!

Under the hood was a 265-bhp-at-3,000-rpm, triple-carburetor 3.8-liter version of the XK engine, also shared with the E-type. The peak 260 lb-ft of torque at 4,000 rpm provided plenty of overtaking energy, while the abundant power made this a 120-mile-per-hour car. A four-speed manual gearbox was available, with optional overdrive, but most buyers (four in five) naturally chose the automatic option; it accelerated faster anyway, achieving 0–60 in just under 10 seconds.

The interior was once memorably likened to an Edwardian library, with polished walnut cappings to doors and rear seat backs, dashboard, dash rail, inner windscreen pillars, and door frames, and fold-out picnic tables for the front-seat passenger and two rear-seat occupants. A limousine option isolated the rear seat for privacy with a fixed bench seat up front for the chauffeur topped with a glass division. Electric windows were always standard but air-conditioning was available as a later option.

In 1964 came a new 4.2-liter engine with an identical power output but additional flexible torque at

283 lb-ft at 4,000 rpm to make the Mk X even more responsive on fast journeys. And then in 1966 came a name change to 420G, to align it to the smaller Jaguar 420 model and a G for "Grand." Accompanying detail changes were minimal: more supportive front seats, a transistor clock, and a padded leather roll across the dash top rather than the wonderful but potentially dangerous wooden rail.

The Mk X/420G sold to business tycoons, showbiz stars, wealthy villains, and consulates around the world. And yet, in its key US market as much as elsewhere, it rather failed to catch on, despite Jaguar boasting of early sales to the US and Canada worth several million dollars. With some 18,500 examples sold until it was quietly dropped in 1970, average annual sales were less than half of the series it superseded. There were a few reliability issues on early examples, for sure, but it was the vast size of this car, very much the equivalent of larger US models, that deterred most. Lyons later admitted it was too big, and all subsequent Jaguar saloons were considerably more compact.

As a small tangent to the Mk X/420G saga, the car's floorpan, suspension, engine, and drivetrain lived on for another twenty-two years after the car departed the Jaguar range. Following the convoluted series of mergers that resulted in the formation of British Leyland Motor Corporation in 1968, in which Jaguar was a key element, it fell to the company to provide a replacement for both the Daimler Majestic Major and Austin Princess limousines, relics from the 1950s that were in continual demand from undertakers, embassies, and town halls around Britain, guaranteeing a steady, profitable demand. Jaguar took the 420G platform and stretched the wheelbase by 21 inches to accommodate a limousine able to carry eight people. The traditionally styled coachwork of the resulting Daimler DS420 was a formal and seemly evolution of the razor-edged "Empress" style created on Daimler chassis by London's coachbuilder to the Royal Family, Hooper & Co. With assembly taken care of by Vanden Plas in North London, this regal Daimler remained available until 1992, completed by craftsmen but relying on the excellence of the Jaguar Mk X to make it function. But if a sudden burst of speed or a defensive, urgent driving maneuver was called for, the Jaguar within was always ready to spring into action.

The torpedo-shaped lines of the Mk X were just one aspect of this futuristic new super-saloon introduced in 1961; the independent rear suspension system in the monocoque-construction body structure put it streets ahead of rivals.

The stately Daimler DS420 Limousine of 1968 was built on an extended Mk X/420G floorpan, a modified form that meant the big Jag was destined to survive until 1992 and become a fixture of ceremonial British life.

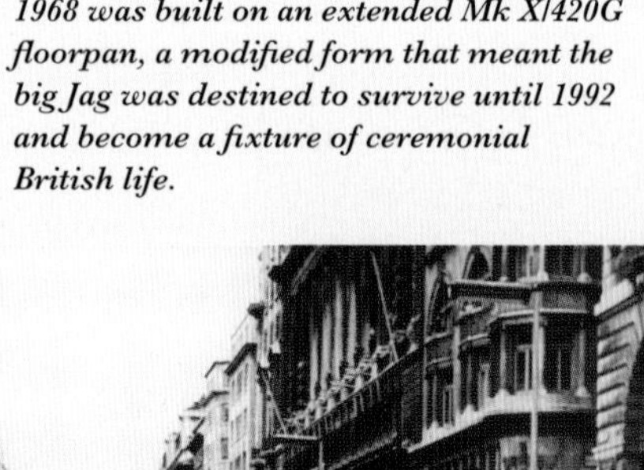

For the Mk X's rear-seat passengers, the ride comfort was so cosseting that they'd be tempted to take a nap on the dreamy bench seat. Or, of course, catch up on paperwork with the lovely folding writing tables.

Jaguar's craftspeople excelled in cabinet-making and upholstery, found inside the Mk X's spacious passenger compartment, with the walnut veneer even extending up the internal window surrounds for a uniquely indulgent ambience.

Chapter Eight

MASTERS OF ENDURANCE

Racing: Jaguar began by supporting amateurs in races and rallies, then hit the big time with its scientifically schemed C- and D-type racers, which triumphed at Le Mans on five thrilling occasions.

Once Jaguar had decided to build a pure racing car, a new burst of design ingenuity was released as the wonderful XK120C, or C-type, sought to overcome the standard car's bugbear of excess weight.

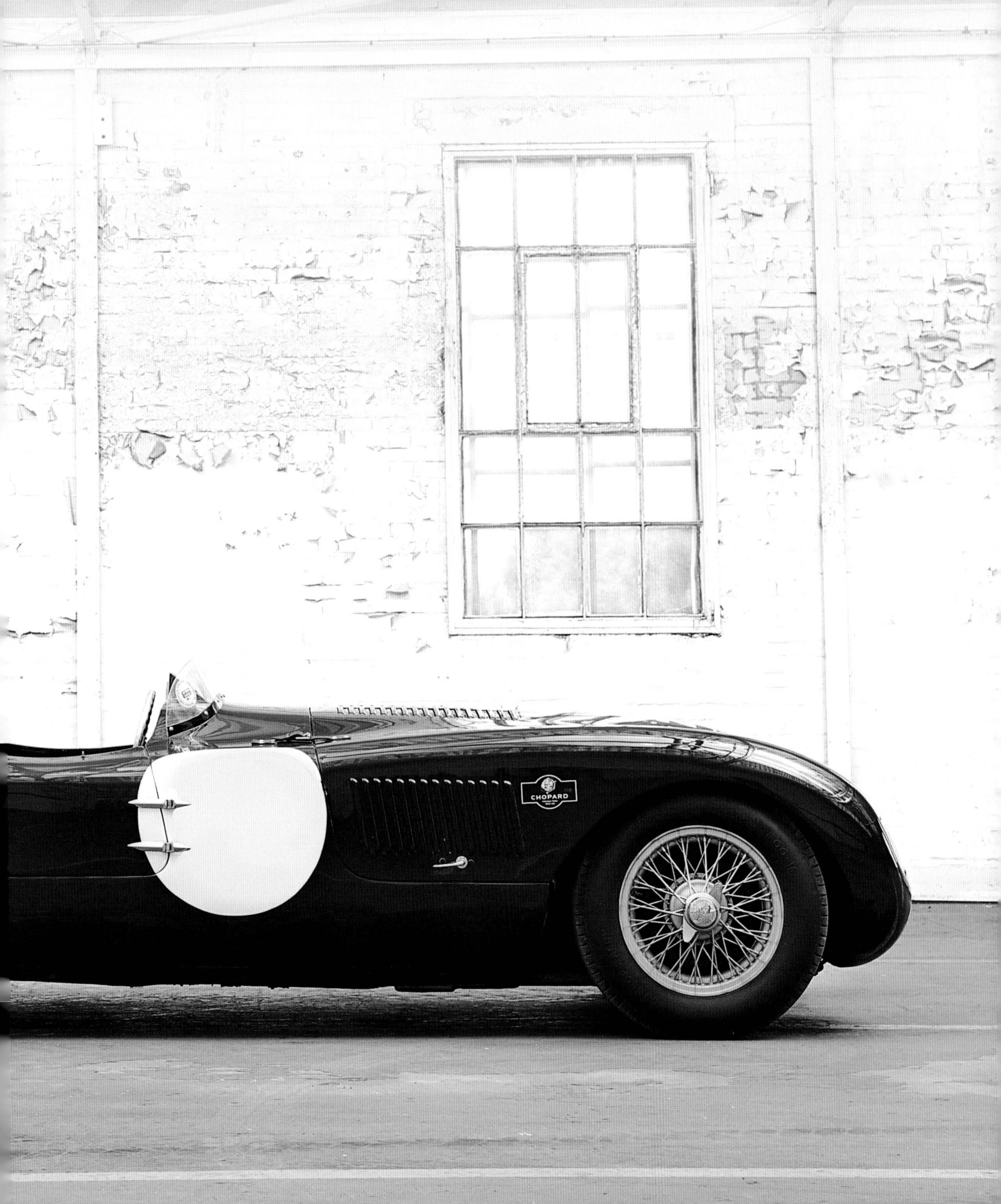
CHOPARD

A young Stirling Moss at the wheel of his C-type in the 24 Hours of Le Mans in 1951, where he set the course lap speed record at a storming 105.24 mph, although it was teammates Peter Walker and Peter Whitehead who drove the C-type to its first win.

Stirling Moss and Norman Dewis together tackled the 1952 Mille Miglia around Italy, their C-type experimentally equipped with Jaguar's new Dunlop disc brakes, which proved hugely effective.

Jaguar's XK120, as explained in chapter 6, was irresistible to racing drivers. Its abundant power and eagerness and, for its era, excellent roadholding made it eminently suitable for timed road and rally events and competitive track racing. Between 1949 and 1951 came more than one hundred competition victories in Britain and Europe, among which a win in the Tourist Trophy made a name for a talented young fellow named Stirling Moss.

Yet many competitors driving an XK120 did so for the sheer fun of it, and the Jaguar factory was happy to let owners race the cars, sometimes helping out with prerace preparation and occasionally lending cars to drivers who showed talent. The attention gathered from these mostly amateur, minimally financed efforts was extraordinary. Former Jaguar executive Bob Berry, a sometime racing driver himself, said, "The publicity was enormous and, in the space of only three years, the once insignificant company became a household word across the world. No promotional campaign, no matter how large or how lavish, could have achieved even a fraction of the impact of three short years of motor racing and virtually all of this was undertaken by private owners. The situation was almost unreal."

The one area where the XK120 had not particularly excelled was in France's 24 Hours of Le Mans, the grueling annual endurance event where motoring legends were made—such as Bentley's five historic victories there between 1924 and 1930. It remained the ultimate prize in motor racing. In 1950, two of the three Jaguars entered did well, taking twelfth and fifteenth overall places, but it was obvious their weight and insufficient power had stopped them from finishing any higher. In October of that year, Lyons, Heynes, and England made the bold decision to open a racing shop within the company's experimental department; more specifically, they would build a car with the goal of dominating Le Mans, with England managing the racing team.

It is easy to spend—and squander—a king's ransom going motor racing. The costly lure of the starting grid had bankrupted several carmakers in the past. Yet the Jaguar approach, as ever, was lean and resourceful. There was no separate racing department. As Berry remembered, "The engineers, draughtsmen, testers, and mechanics were all drawn from our existing resource and handled racing car projects as the need arose. On most occasions, work had to be fitted into the production car workload, often in the evenings and always at weekends. Our racing mechanics and fitters were drawn from among the experimental and service division staffs and competition for racing assignments was fierce."

Not only that but standard Jaguar parts had to be used wherever possible, and that applied as much to engine components as it did to small items like ignition leads or even lamps. The thinking was supremely sound on two fronts. First, huge cost savings would

Duncan Hamilton on his high-speed way to victory at the 1953 24 Hours of Le Mans, where the disc brake-equipped C-type surpassed all challengers.

Scenery on the Italian route of the 1952 Mille Miglia (1,000 Miles) was breathtaking but diminished stopping power on the thousands of corners—that was no longer an issue with disc brakes. Here Moss and Dewis explore the course, the car bearing Jaguar's factory "trade" number plates.

be made (essential for Lyons's approval, as the company's money was also, really, his money), and the test programs of well-proven parts already in production could be much tougher under race conditions, with replacements being manufactured close by in Jaguar's machine shops. And second, all the valuable results of race simulation testing could be fed straight back into production cars as refinements. The benefits of problem-solving and decision-making in the sort of limited timescale motor racing demanded would have an immediate, albeit indirect, benefit to the Jaguars sold to customers worldwide. Consequently, in Jaguar's racing adventures ahead, engines almost never failed, and the cars always started any race they were entered in.

Work quickly progressed on the race-focused XK120C (for "competition"), which would soon be far better known simply as the C-type. It was built around a triangulated "spaceframe" tubular steel chassis designed by Heynes with leading Jaguar engineer Bob Knight. The independent front suspension, as on the standard XK120, was by torsion bar and wishbones, while at the back the trailing-link suspension setup included a novel torque reaction link to improve traction.

Working with Heynes and Knight, aerodynamicist Malcolm Sayer, a new recruit from aircraft company Bristol Siddeley, applied his scientific knowledge of wind cheating to the lightweight aluminum two-seater bodywork. Meanwhile, a standard-production XK engine was tuned fairly modestly to produce 204 bhp, with larger exhaust valves, higher-lift camshafts, and larger SU carburetors.

A team of three cars was built in just over five months, and they were ready in good time for the 1951 Le Mans race in June. The driving pairings were Stirling Moss and Jack Fairman, Peter Walker and Peter Whitehead, and Leslie Johnson and the Italian Clemente Biondetti.

The meticulous preparation paid off in a spectacular way after the two Peters won the race on the C-type's very first outing. The car ran faultlessly and relentlessly, and in racking up 2,243 miles it covered more distance than any car at Le Mans before it. The other two cars dropped out of the race due to failure of the oil delivery pipe, but Moss's fearless driving did bring the Le Mans course lap record to Jaguar, too, at 105.24 miles per hour. Later in the year, the C-type proved it was no flash in the pan by finishing first, second, and fourth on the Tourist Trophy in Dundrod, Northern Ireland.

Naturally, there was jubilation within Jaguar at this stunning achievement, and the whole tight-knit team felt emboldened. In May 1952, a single C-type was entered in the Mille Miglia, the famous 1,000-mile race (against the clock) around the twisty roads of Italy, with Moss at the wheel and Jaguar chief test driver Norman Dewis codriving and navigating. Ostensibly, they entered because they thought the car had a realistic chance of winning, but in reality their goal was to test—under cover—the experimental disc brakes Jaguar had codeveloped with Dunlop. Originally used on aircraft, the brakes were first planned for use on cars for the 1948 Tucker Torpedo, though they never made it to the few examples actually built. Discs quickly dissipated heat, unlike the universally used drums, and so gave the same, reliably predictable performance time after time; Jaguar had lent Dunlop an old XK120 to refine disc brakes for motor vehicles, and a close working partnership followed in 1951–1952. At one point, Moss's car was running in third place, although ultimately a damaged steering rack ended its day. The brakes, which never ran hot or faded at crucial moments, showed huge promise, but Moss was tantalized by the new Mercedes-Benz 300SL that was enjoying its maiden race outing; it seemed to possess a turn of speed that made it impossible for any C-type to catch it.

Quite a number of professional racing drivers, including here former Formula 1 World Champion Giuseppe Farina, drove C-types on the road.

Jaguar's exceptional in-house talent clustered around the first of their new D-type sports-racing cars; left to right: Malcolm Sayer, William Heynes, Bob Knight, Ron "Soapy" Sutton, Jaguar staffers Arthur Ramsey and Keith Cambage, and, at the wheel, Norman Dewis.

Prerace test sessions at Le Mans in 1954 with Tony Rolt at the wheel of the first iteration of the D-type, chassis number XKD 401.

Scottish Ecurie Ecosse drivers Ron Flockhart and Ninian Sanderson brought Jaguar its fourth Le Mans victory in 1956 with their D-type.

The 300SL came in second behind the winning Ferrari.

This concern spooked the normally methodical Jaguar team, and for Le Mans a month later the C-type received untried last-minute modifications in the form of lower and elongated front and rear ends to make it more aerodynamic and, therefore, quicker. With little time for testing at realistic race speeds of 150 miles per hour (241 kilometers per hour), the unforeseen consequence of compromised airflow for cooling arose only once the race was underway and all three were forced to drop out because of overheating issues.

To add to the chagrin, some cold analysis of the Mercedes 300SL that won revealed it was actually up to 15 miles per hour (24 kilometers per hour) slower overall than the C-type with its original body. "We were determined never again to depart from the precept of careful thought and maximum testing," wrote Bob Berry later. "High maximum power looked impressive on paper but in a race what really mattered was a wide spread of power and torque in the middle speed ranges."

Later in 1952, a C-type proved the disc brake's supremacy when Stirling Moss and Peter Whitehead won a three-hour sports car race at Reims in France, and in 1953 the factory team was back at Le Mans with three C-types returned to their original shape but boasting disc brakes, maximum power teased up to 220 bhp with Weber carburetors, and numerous other small evolutionary changes, including rubber fuel tanks suspended in aluminum shells to trim unnecessary weight. Plus, of course, an extensive testing regime had been undertaken.

Jaguar achieved another sensational result: C-types finished first, second, and fourth. The winning drivers were two larger-than-life characters, gentleman racers with plenty of experience, Major Tony Rolt and Duncan Hamilton, and they set a new distance record of 2,539.7 miles (4,087.3 kilometers) and became the first Le Mans competitors ever to drive the twice-round-the-clock punisher at an average speed of over 100 miles per hour (161 kilometers per hour). Stirling Moss and Peter Walker were second, Peter Whitehead and Ian Stewart fourth. Meticulous planning and the car's reliability played their key parts, of course, but disc brakes, with pads made especially thick to last 24 hours, were the trump card. No other cars had them then, not even Ferraris. They allowed the C-type to attain 150 miles per hour (241 kilometers per hour) on the 3.7-mile (6.0-kilometer) Mulsanne Straight on the circuit with the drivers able to decelerate for the corner far later than their competitors with complete confidence that the braking capability wouldn't vanish.

Taken together with a C-type win (for Moss/Whitehead) in a new 12-hour endurance race at Reims and a class win on the Nürburgring 1000 km, plus fine showings for XK120s and Mk VIIs in many other races and rallies, 1952 was a golden year for Jaguars in competition. The C-type itself went into limited production, costing at least twice the price of a standard XK120; forty-three of the fifty-three built were sold to private individuals. It is telling that the first three Formula 1 world champions—Giuseppe Farina, Alberto Ascari, and Juan Manuel Fangio—all owned one ... and drove them as road cars!

Jaguar truly had the racing bug, and for 1954 the company intended to stay ahead of the game. With no possibility of developing a different power unit, William Heynes had led investigations into weight-saving materials and construction techniques. A new "D-type" Jaguar was created with a magnesium alloy monocoque tub for the center section/cockpit attached to a square-section tubular structure at the front, which cradled the engine, gearbox, suspension, and precise new rack-and-pinion steering arrangement. Aerodynamicist Malcolm Sayer had spent countless hours at his drawing board and in

Much excitement at the 1956 Le Mans finishing line as the D-type takes the checkered flag.

the wind tunnel to perfect the all-new shape. His principles were based on inverting an aircraft wing for downforce rather than lift; the form was so wind cheating that even an apparently insignificant item like a rearview mirror could make a substantial impact on its airflow management. To keep the car stable on long, fast straights, Sayer specified that a fairing be fitted, flowing back from the driver's headrest. The cockpit was an uncannily calm, draft-free environment in which to concentrate on driving, even at 170 miles per hour (274 kilometers per hour).

In tests at Le Mans in May 1954, the prototype proved so effective that Tony Rolt immediately shattered the circuit lap record by a full 5 seconds, and preparation continued apace to ready the three team cars for the race a month later.

This 1954 Le Mans proved a battle royale. Ferrari and Jaguar fought closely throughout the race, but constant heavy rain reduced the edge that Coventry's disc brakes, now with hydraulic power assistance, gave to the British car. Then contaminated fuel and clogged filters plagued the Jags, leading to two of the D-types (piloted by Moss/Walker and Whitehead/Ken Wharton) dropping out. But Rolt and Hamilton overcame the problems, bringing the D-type home second, a mere 1 minute and 45 seconds behind the victorious Ferrari. There was a little consolation for the factory when Whitehead and Wharton paired up to take top honors in the 12 Hours of Reims a few weeks later, confirming the D-type's brilliance in the absence of bad luck.

Only with this D-type did the mechanical elements depart substantially from Jaguar's regular production parts. "Dry sump" lubrication maintained far more consistent oil pressure, better cooling, and the chance to mount the engine lower in the chassis. For 1955, engine capacity was boosted to 3.8 liters, and there were new camshafts and a new cylinder head with bigger valves and revised valve angles. Power was up as high as 275 bhp, while the bodywork was immediately identifiable by a longer nose cone, a new windscreen and headrest, and a tailfin raised and tapered for a shark-like profile. This D-type could accelerate from standstill to 60 miles per hour (97 kilometers per hour) in 4.7 seconds.

Mike Hawthorn and Ivor Bueb won the 1955 Le Mans. Hawthorn took part in a tremendous tussle for the whole of the first hour with Fangio's Mercedes-Benz and Castelotti's Ferrari, during which he established an astounding new lap record speed of 122 miles per hour (196 kilometers per hour). However, just over two hours into the event, excitement turned to tragedy. A minor collision caused the Mercedes-Benz 300SLR driven by Pierre Levegh to barrel roll, and when it hit an embankment most of its heavy components were catapulted into crowds of helpless spectators. More than eighty people lost their lives in the worst motor-racing accident of all time. Le Mans organizers let the race continue to

avoid a mass exit by the crowds that would have jammed roads needed for rushing emergency vehicles. Mercedes-Benz immediately withdrew its other cars, and Jaguar's victory was noted but, naturally, there could be little joy in it. The 12 Hours of Reims, where Jaguar usually excelled, was canceled as the racing community reeled.

The D-types were back at Le Mans in 1956, largely unaltered from the year before apart from a full-width windscreen to meet a new rule aiming to rein in the very high speeds now attained. There were also now limits on fuel consumption, and one of the cars was equipped with an experimental fuel-injection system to make it more efficient.

It was heart-rending for the team when two of the cars collided on only the second lap, and the event was all over for the duos of Paul Frère/Desmond Titterington and Jack Fairman/Ken Wharton. Hawthorn and Bueb in the fuel-injected D-type gave a stuttering performance until a cracked fuel line was fixed, and then they fought their way from twenty-second place to finish sixth—excellent, all things considered. Jaguar's wisdom at offering D-types to outsiders paid off handsomely when Ninian Sanderson and Ron Flockhart of Scotland's Ecurie Ecosse won the race in a car painted in their team's dark blue rather than the British racing green of the factory entries. Jaguar's image was bolstered even more by the Belgian-entered D-type that finished fourth overall. The D-types went on to fill the top four places at the 12 Hours of Reims.

At the end of 1956, and after five years, Jaguar decided to end its factory racing program. There was little more left to prove with four Le Mans wins in the bag, and in 1956 Jaguar became the first and only marque to finish first in both the 24 Hours of Le Mans and the Monte Carlo Rally in the same year. It was a sad day for everyone who'd been on that incredible journey to success, much as it was entirely logical. The baton was passed to private entrants, and they certainly did not disappoint. In 1957, an Ecurie Ecosse D-type again trounced all comers at Le Mans, driven by Flockhart and Bueb, with the same team's Sanderson/Jock Lawrence car finishing second, and an amazing three more of the invincible Jaguars in the top six.

Jaguar management had been quite taken aback by the reaction to its racing program. Not just externally, where the results and acclaim added incalculable luster to the image of the road cars, whose sales worldwide continued to balloon, but among the company's own workforce. Bulletins giving updates were broadcast over the public-address system in the Browns Lane factory, and there was clamor for printed newsletters handed out to staff giving reports of race triumphs. The morale boost was completely unexpected; a happy

With plenty of D-type parts left over from its racing days, Jaguar created the XKSS as a road-going version of it, but only 16 examples were made before a fire at the factory killed off the nascent project.

May 1963 and Hollywood legend Steve McQueen, howling along Sunset Boulevard, pops out for a pint of milk in his beloved XKSS. The car's ferocious speed was apt to land him in frequent trouble with the law.

byproduct was that job vacancies were swamped with the best applicants from around Coventry's "motor city," eager to join the most dynamic company in the business. Jaguar loyalty started to become an increasingly valuable company asset.

However, the company had, perhaps, overestimated the number of potential customers for a D-type of their own and, once the racing program ended at the end of 1956, thoughts turned to what to do with the surplus sets of components lying around. In a very short time, the basic D-type was lightly transformed into a road-going two-seater named the XKSS with two full-size seats, a passenger-side door, and a proper windscreen, side screens, and roof. Chrome bumpers were fitted and, as there was no trunk space whatsoever, a luggage rack perched on the back to carry a suitcase or two, taking the place of the deleted tailfin. The plan was to build a limited edition of 150 examples.

With a 250-bhp edition of the dry-sump 3.4-liter XK engine, the car was something of a hot rod, with thrilling responses to suit only the most skilled of sports car drivers. Most of them went to the US, where they were sold for $5,850 apiece; little surprise that speed-loving Hollywood actor Steve McQueen ordered one immediately. He kept it for ten years, and its brutal high performance brought him two driving bans.

Jaguar had barely decided where to go with the XKSS when fire ripped through the factory in February 1957 and incinerated nine of the twenty-five examples built so far. Most of the jigs and tools used to build this and the D-type also went up in flames. The venture ended there and then. But as one exciting era at Jaguar came to a sudden end, it was but a short and spirited drive to the next.

JAGUAR
3·8 LITRE

Chapter Nine

SPORTS SALOONS FOR EVERYONE

Mk I to S-type: The 2.4-liter establishes a new market for Jaguar—the compact sports saloon. And the older the series gets, the better it is to drive, producing super-quick cars vital to racing and getaway drivers alike.

Often the only way to tell which XK was lurking within the Mk 2 was via the discreet hood badge; the cars needed careful maintenance, and neglect in secondhand ownership wrecked thousands of them.

Jaguar cars of the early 1950s were mainstream cars. They had wide and obvious appeal, and any averagely competent driver could find ready enjoyment behind the wheel—experiencing their superior precision and responsiveness compared to rivals—while passengers relaxed in the comfort and enticing ambience of their interiors. They were not mass-produced vehicles, still sticking to the time-honored construction method of separate chassis and body. Unitary construction, popularized by the Citroën Traction Avant in 1934 and introduced to the British car industry four years later by Vauxhall, meant an all-steel, welded structure where the frame and body formed a single entity. Apart from eliminating noise and vibration, this one-piece monocoque skeleton was stronger and safer because all the elements of the architecture supported each other and were completely integral. Unit-construction cars were also lighter and thus more efficient.

Project Utah finally came to fruition in 1955 with the launch of the new compact 2.4-liter saloon, on which Jaguar had worked hard and spent £1 million, to join the monocoque-construction movement.

It was the way of the future, no doubt about that, and Jaguar realized it would be essential to expansion. Once fully established in its new home at Browns Lane, the company quickly laid plans for a new, smaller unit-body Jaguar. The company had adroitly spotted a gaping hole in the market for just such a compact, modern sports saloon; there was little to indicate such progressive thinking was stirring among rivals. Cars like the Daimler Conquest Century, Riley RM 2.5-liter, Sunbeam-Talbot 90, and Wolseley Six-Eighty were all aging rapidly as Jaguar's "Project Utah" swung into action in 1952.

It was a culture shock to depart the coachbuilt era and create a monocoque structure. The technology was still relatively new and Jaguar worked closely with its supplier, Pressed Steel, on the new shell. Key tenets of the design were that it should be both sporty to drive and comfortable to travel in. To that end, William Heynes and his engineering team created a new suspension system with coil springs at the front in a separate subframe and semi-elliptic leaf springs at the back, cantilevered and assisted by a Panhard rod to help accurately locate the rear axle and transfer suspension loads to the strong center part of the monocoque. It was an unusual arrangement that, despite the absence of a fully independent rear suspension, helped endow the new car with excellent handling at high speed.

The long-toyed-with four-cylinder version of the XK engine remained a possibility at the inception of Project Utah, but Jaguar still couldn't achieve the level of refinement it desired. As it turned out, a Ford Zephyr won the 1953 Monte Carlo Rally with its standard 2.2-liter straight six engine; it was unthinkable that Jaguar could offer a lesser unit in a car that would rival the

Work had already begun on a smaller-capacity six-cylinder version of the XK. In July 1951 an engine with a bore and stroke of 88×66mm began testing, giving a capacity of 1,986cc, but this was deemed inadequate. Instead, the 86mm bore of the 3.4-liter engine was retained but the stroke reduced to 76mm. On the test bench, the resulting 2,443cc size was good for as much as 155 bhp at 6,000 rpm—that would really give the new car a steely edge, even when tuned down for production. Twin Solex carburetors were specified, and the final power output was an energetic 112 bhp.

While it could never be described as a pretty car, the William Lyons-approved lines of the new "2.4-Litre saloon" were a pleasing amalgam of Jaguar hallmarks (bulbous, rounded front wings and narrow grille redolent of the XK140, the faired-in rear wheels, and gracefully tapering hindquarters) massaged on to a "straight-through" wingline in keeping with contemporary style pacesetters in Italy and the US. As this streamlined (or at least, streamlined-looking) bodywork called for the wheels to be tucked inside, a rear track measuring 4.5 inches (11.4 centimeters) narrower than the front was necessary.

Everything about the car's size and specification was just right for the UK market, and little wonder it was one of the most keenly examined new cars at the 1955 London Motor Show. Dealers were frantic with test drives and orders for the £1,532 newcomer, the world's first compact and sporty "executive" car. Jaguar must have been hugely relieved at the reception because developing the car and remodeling those newly acquired Browns Lane assembly halls around its high-volume needs represented an investment of £1 million, a colossal sum by the company's historically cautious standards.

All things are relative, and the abundantly powerful nature of the larger Jaguar Mk VII M perhaps made the 2.4-liter feel a little underwhelming. Body engineers had taken no chances with the strong new chassis-less structure; at 3,045 pounds (1,381 kilograms), however, it was more than 400 pounds (181 kilograms) heavier than the Ford Zephyr Six Mk I, and apt to feel a little underpowered. The car could only just crest 100 miles per hour (161 kilometers per hour), reaching 60 miles per hour in 14.4 seconds. Still, the well-resolved suspension front and back provided excellent roadholding by the roly-poly standards of the era. "Appreciation begins with the discovery that the driving position, and especially the seat, are exactly right," purred the *The Motor* in approval of a car fitted with the optional overdrive. "The delightfully smooth—and silent—performance of the engine is incidentally matched by its shining appearance, and there is evidence of mechanical attention to detail in half-concealed items like the polished dipstick."

Inside, the richly appointed leather-and-walnut cabin and full instrumentation were exactly what every aspirational new Jaguar convert wanted. But to keep the headline price tempting, quite a lot was missing. Only if you paid extra for the Special Equipment package did you get such things as a rev counter, foglights, a cigarette lighter, windscreen washers, and (would you believe) a heater!

This was entry-level Jag territory, but the factory was keen for customers to spend more if they wanted to. Three stages of tuning kits, for instance, were soon offered to raise power to 119, 131, or 150 bhp, while those who wanted more effortless ownership could opt for a Borg Warner automatic transmission starting in 1957. For export markets such as the US, the standard 2.4-liter simply did not live up to

Once given the 3.4-liter XK engine, the Mk 1 was utterly transformed into a high-performance machine that was soon tearing up the saloon car racing tracks . . . but was in dire need of better brakes.

The rear view of a 3.4-liter Mk 1 used in historic saloon car racing, which gives a good idea of the hefty roof pillars that were a sign of the strong structure within.

An artfully resolved facelift resulted in the Mk 2 in 1959; handling, looks, braking, and visibility were all much improved.

the storming, fire-breathing image Jaguar had cultivated. Fortunately, though, precious little work was needed to install the original 3.4-liter XK engine in the 2.4's place, nor did the company use the 190-bhp standard edition but the 210-bhp-tune unit that was not far off the engine that once powered the C-type racing car. Small semicircles were cut away from the rear spats so that appropriately racy wire wheels, with their protruding hubs, could be fitted, and a wider grille fronted a bigger radiator.

The performance transformation was absolutely electrifying, as the new 3.4-liter saloon launched in 1957 could rocket to 60 miles per hour in 9 seconds and reach speeds up to 120 miles per hour (193 kilometers per hour). Nothing about it felt ponderous or heavy, but something *did* feel distinctly edgy. It developed a rather hairy reputation that needed fixing. "The car seldom did anything frightening, but I often had the feeling it might," Lord Montagu of Beaulieu wrote about his, while the Honorable Alan Clark, a car-mad member of British Parliament, recorded, "The 3.4 Mk 1, that really was a car; it didn't have any brakes at all." It desperately needed disc brakes, which arrived as an option in 1958 and were fitted to practically every car sold. The beast was tamed, but its widowmaking reputation came back to haunt it in January 1959. Britain's first-ever Formula 1 World Champion, the charismatic Mike Hawthorn, died at the wheel of his. The reckless Hawthorn had been racing against his friend Rob Walker in a Mercedes-Benz 300SL when he clipped a bollard at a reported 80 miles per hour (129 kilometers per hour) on the A3 Guildford Bypass, lost control, and hit a tree. The precise cause of the crash will never be known, although the driver and not the Jaguar, much modified by Hawthorn, was most likely the culprit.

The compact Jaguars, together with their Mk VII–IX sisters, dealt a fatal blow to many once-admired British saloon cars. Buyers could get all the style and performance they wanted at an excellent price, and so handmade saloons from great names like Alvis and Bristol suddenly seemed absurdly expensive (while Aston Martin and Bentley remained a considerable cut above). Armstrong Siddeley cars were axed in 1960 almost entirely because Jaguar systematically took their market; it was a similar story for Lea Francis, while the British Motor Corporation's big Wolseleys and the Rootes Group's matching Humbers faded into the background as bulky, undynamic, and outmoded also-rans. For any traditional British driver who felt a Jaguar was too louche and flashy, a Rover P4 or P5 was the best alternative. The Vauxhall Cresta PA and Ford Zodiac MkII packed style and value, but the image was too blue-collar to match successful people's snowballing aspirations. The first compact generation proved very successful, and by 1959 some 20,000 2.4s and 17,500 3.4s (largely for US export) had considerably broadened Jaguar's appeal and accessibility. It was time to rethink them for the decade ahead.

In naming the fully revised version the Mk 2, the outgoing cars were forevermore known as the Mk 1. Aficionados generally disdain later-life "facelift" models as the ruination of a much-loved original; think of the early and subsequent Chevrolet

Wire wheels continued to be a highly desirable option on the Mk 2, and cutouts on the rear wheel covers could accommodate the knock-off spinners needed to secure them.

Camaro, Alfa Romeo Spider, or Porsche 911. The Jaguar Mk 2 is a rare reversal of that. It was a vastly better car than the Mk 1, and has always been much more coveted.

The remarkable revamp they received, overseen by Lyons, brought enlarged windows and slim, elegant screen pillars that lightened and lifted the whole look, ridding the small Jaguar of its rather slug-like original form. The windscreen was wider and the quarter windows of the rear doors had that stylish wraparound, ovular curve that characterized the firm's larger saloons and sports coupes.

Below these fine new clothes, the front and rear track were now identical at 55 inches (140 centimeters), with slim half-spats that also helped break up any remaining slab-sidedness, while the front-suspension geometry was adjusted to reduce body roll in cornering. Every model had four-wheel disc brakes as standard. Inside there was a fully revised dashboard layout. Lyons had always liked the instruments, the speedometer especially, to be in

Young executives were drawn to the sporty, compact Mk 2 like flies to jam, and with disc brakes on every model it now offered the ultimate package for anyone who was going places.

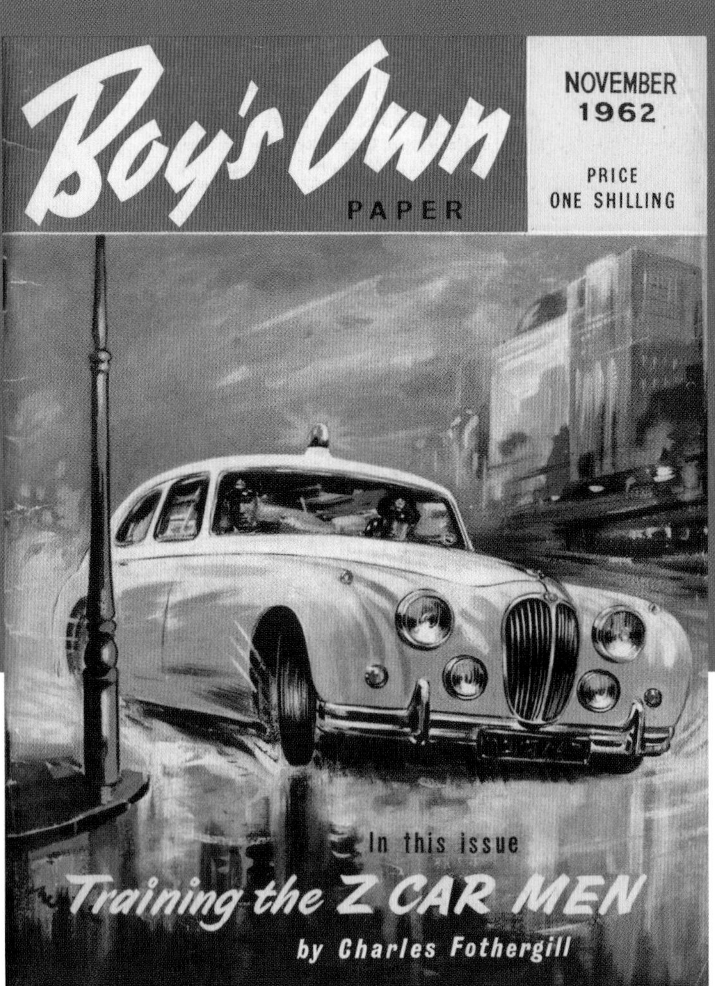

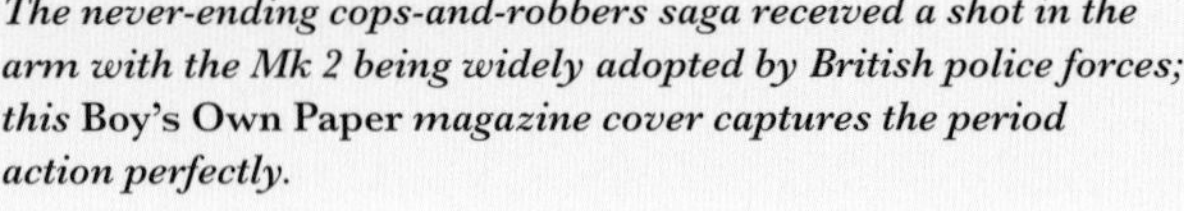
The never-ending cops-and-robbers saga received a shot in the arm with the Mk 2 being widely adopted by British police forces; this Boy's Own Paper *magazine cover captures the period action perfectly.*

For a few years, Mk 2s were pretty much unassailable on the racetracks in the British Touring Car Championship and many other events; their abundant power and controllable (in expert hands, that is) handling proved a winning combination.

the center of the dashboard so the front-seat passenger could feel more involved in the Jaguar experience, but now the main dials were directly in front of the driver, with a battery of switches in the center. It felt much more focused and remained the standard Jaguar dashboard layout into the 1970s.

There was also a third option on top of the 120-bhp 2.4-liter and 210-bhp 3.4-liter model: a 220-bhp 3.8-liter. A Mk 2 with this feature, as well as wire wheels and overdrive, was the best sports saloon in the world, and the thrilling acceleration allied to a 125 mile-per-hour (201 kilometer-per-hour) top speed created an instant saloon car-racing phenomenon. The Mk 1 3.4-liter had tackled plenty of rallies, with brothers Don and Erle Morley's outright win in the 1959 Tulip Rally a highlight, along with the team prize in the 1959 Monte Carlo going to three similar cars. This new, big-engined Mk 2, though, excelled in wheel-to-wheel touring car racing—track events for near-standard production saloons. Wherever the cars were entered by teams such as John Coombs Racing and Equipe Endeavour they tended to dominate. In the multi-heat Tour de France, for example, Bernard Carsten drove a 3.8-liter to victory four times from 1960 to 1963, covering a furious 3,600 miles (5,794 kilometers) in the last one. From Brands Hatch to the Nürburgring, Mk 2 3.8s were the cars to beat. They won five major endurance races at the latter, and were everywhere in the British Saloon Car Championship from 1958 to 1963. The super-demanding Brands Hatch Six Hours was won by Mike Parkes and Jimmy Blumer in 1962 and Roy Salvadori and Denis Hulme in 1963, both times in a Mk 2 3.8. On the other side of the world, similar cars snatched the Australian Touring Car Championship in both 1962 and 1963 for Bob Jane, and then in 1963 Peter Nöcker won the first-ever European Touring Car challenge in the Mk 2.

By then Fords in the form of the American Falcon V-8 and the British Lotus Cortina four-cylinder were beginning to squeeze the straight six Jags out of contention. Jaguar astutely realized that the Mk 2 3.8-liter's mercury had peaked, and so set out in March 1963 to gold-plate its star reputation. A team of drivers corralled by Lofty England—including motorbike Tourist Trophy champion Geoff Duke and car racers Peter Lindner,

The British School of Motoring could teach existing license holders how to control a car at high speeds on the racetrack, and naturally this Jaguar Mk 2 was part of its fleet based at the Brands Hatch circuit in 1963.

It was only the pincer grip between the powerful American Ford Galaxie and the nimble British Ford Lotus Cortina that finally weakened the Mk 2's saloon car racing prowess. This battle royale about to erupt is at Brands Hatch, Kent, in August 1963.

Jaguar took this near-standard Mk 2 3.8-liter to the Monza track in Italy in March 1963 with a team of drivers, where they proceeded to break four international speed records, which included covering 10,000 miles at an average of 106.58 mph.

John Thaw as TV's Inspector Morse is possibly the most famous of small-screen Mk 2 drivers; the 2.4-liter car used for filming had been found in a scrap yard, and was often so temperamental that it had to be pushed into the shot.

The S-type saloon of 1963 brought the sophistication of independent rear suspension to an updated and enlarged Mk 2; for several years it was Jaguar's best-selling model.

Peter Sargent, John Bekaert, and Andrew Hedges—departed for the Monza track in Italy with a near-standard car (but with its final drive ratio lengthened so it could cruise at 100 mph (161 km/h) at a relaxed 3,500 rpm). In relay they proceeded to smash four international Class C speed records for 3,000–5,000cc cars: four days spent at an average 106.62 mph (171.59 km/h), three days at 107.02 mph (172.23 km/h), 9,320 miles (15,000 kilometers) at 106.61 mph (171.58 km/h), and 10,000 miles (16,093 kilometers) at 106.58 mph (171.52 km/h). It was quite a haul, although they just missed out on establishing an international seven-day average beating 100 mph (161 km/h), breaking two axles in their attempt as the Jag thundered round Monza for a week.

But the fact that Jaguar Mk 2s symbolized high-speed driving became apparent to the ordinary British motorist. The country's first dedicated motorway, the M1, opened in 1959 and several police forces, through whose regions the three-lane asphalt ribbon stretched, ordered Jaguar Mk 2s as patrol cars. There were no speed limits before 1965, so the Jaguars in police service were regularly given vigorous exercise in pursuit of their duties—as well as miscreants. By 1969 the British motorway network had reached almost 1,000 miles (1,609 kilometers) in length, with prowling police Jaguars a common sight in rearview mirrors nationwide.

The criminal underworld, quite understandably, needed to fight fire with fire, and these Jaguars—the stiff structure, excellent suspension, and hair-trigger acceleration—were frequently stolen and used for speedy escapes. In the hands of a getaway driver used to handling it, a Jaguar could not be caught. A Mk 1, for instance, was part of the elaborate £2.6 million cash heist from a London–Glasgow mail train in the so-called Great Train Robbery in 1963. A fictionalized version of events in the 1966 Peter Yates film *Robbery* had Mk 2s really showing their backstreet fleetness to rude effect. The notoriety of the Mk 2 became firmly entrenched.

The Mk 2 that remains etched into most people's memories, however, is a lowly 1960 Mk 2 2.4-liter that accompanied actor John Thaw in his thirteen-year role on British TV as *Inspector Morse*, Colin Dexter's perceptive but morose, ale-savoring, opera-loving Oxford detective. The actual car used for filming was bought from a scrapyard at the start of filming in 1987—so mechanically decrepit it was often pushed in and out of scenes by the crew. But it became a small-screen icon admired by a peak TV audience of 18 million and, once fully restored in 2005, sold for more than £150,000 at auction.

With the disappointing reception given the formal Mk X and the rip-roaring success of the feisty Mk 2, chauffeur-driven comfort seemed to be losing out to driving a race-bred winner. In the early 1960s Jaguar started to ponder something in between, identifying yet another niche to spread into. The S-type made its first appearance in September 1963, which was great timing since the Rover 2000 and Triumph 2000 would impress the new breed of upwardly mobile, executive car buyers just one month later. The hushed serenity of the Mk X now came to a nimbler, Mk 2-based four-door sports saloon as the S-type adopted the brilliant independent rear-suspension setup from the bigger car and the E-type. As ever, the rear subframe, cradling its four coil springs and four shock absorbers, was carefully insulated from the body with plenty of rubber bushes, resulting in a much more cosseting ride quality. Around this system was a 7-inch-longer (17.8 centimeters) tail section with partly

As Britain's motorway network approached 1,000 miles at the end of the 1960s, the S-type was one of the most familiar police pursuit vehicles patrolling it.

The 1966 420 was the ultimate evolution of the Mk 2 family. The power unit was the 4.2-liter version of the familiar XK engine, the fully independent suspension came from the S-type, and the four-headlamp frontage matched that on the largest Jaguar, which was renamed 420G in concert with it.

A different grille and badges on the 420 turned the car into the otherwise identical Daimler Sovereign of 1966, making this the first instance of Jaguar indulging in the kind of "badge engineering" that was endemic to the British motor industry of the 1960s.

Sailing on: Jaguar kept the old Mk 2 going as the 240 and 340 (the 3.8-liter engine was dropped) from 1967 to 1969; the specification pared back with plastic seats and thin bumpers, but still offered great value for money.

The 3.8-liter Mk 2 of Roy Salvadori is hounded furiously by Stirling Moss in an identical car in the British Touring Car Championship race at Silverstone in May 1960. They finished in this order, first and second respectively.

shrouded wheels, which also included twin 7-gallon (26.5-liter) fuel tanks, one in each rear wing to free up trunk space where the single 11-gallon (41.6-liter) tank used to hog the floorspace. Meanwhile, the roof was slightly longer at the back to give some extra headroom. The car may have resembled a junior Mk X at the rear, but the frontage was still recognizably Mk 2-based, albeit with some artful Lyons resculpting around the front wings and in the little peaks over the headlights. Slimmer bumpers ousted the hefty chrome Mk 2 cowcatchers. The interior, with bigger seats and a slab of gleaming walnut across the front, brought Mk X levels of opulence to the cozier Mk 2, and with remarkably good ergonomics despite the gentlemen's club ambience.

All this effort took its toll on how the car tipped the scales, with a weight gain of 335 pounds (152 kilograms) over a Mk 2. For that reason, only the punchier 3.4- and 3.8-liter engines were offered, with a choice of automatic or manual transmission. *Autocar* loved it, stating in March 1965, "It seems tailor-made for the man who likes to drive himself, yet wants a car which will look right anywhere, be it in a farmyard or outside a luxury hotel. There can be few big saloons in which the ride is as good as in the Jaguar S-type."

In that year, and again in 1966, the S-type was Jaguar's bestseller, and by 1968 some 25,000 examples had found appreciative buyers with the 3.8-liter outselling the 3.4-liter by three to two.

With a new 4.2-liter XK engine, offering more torque for a more athletic feel in midrange acceleration, installed in the E-type and MkX, it would have been logical to offer it in the S-type too. Instead, in 1966, the company created another new model with it, the 420, which added a new, four-headlamp nose section to the S-type to complete the transition to a more acceptably sized Mk X–style offering. Indeed, the larger car was then renamed the 420G. The wider, shallower grille was in stark contrast to the chrome-plated "waterfall" of the other smaller Jaguars, but then this car also had to assume a separate identity. With a new fluted radiator grille and different insignia—but almost nothing else—it was marketed as a Daimler Sovereign, the first instance of a Jaguar being entirely "badge engineered" in the livery of its venerable sister marque (Daimler had been acquired by Jaguar in 1960—see chapter 11).

Notwithstanding all this activity with new saloons, the old Mk 2 continued in production as the entry-level model to a Jaguar lifestyle. Its value in this respect wasn't overlooked, either. In 1967 the 3.8-liter engine was dropped and the two remaining cars were rebranded as the 240 and 340. Prices starting at £1,364 were keener than ever, relatively speaking, although the upholstery was now in a plastic called Ambla (a PVC made by Imperial Chemical Industries) rather than leather, and slimmer, cheaper bumpers were fitted.

The wide and messy range of Jaguar saloons would all be replaced in one fell swoop by the XJ6 in 1968. By then cumulative output of the Mk 2–type cars (including the Daimler V8-250) was more than 120,000 over nine years. Jaguar had become a medium-sized car manufacturer. In fact, in pumping out so many, some of the exclusivity had been eroded. In the early 1970s, with secondhand Jags glutting the market, values fell away, essential maintenance was often skimped on by careless owners (servicing was needed at least every 3,000 miles (4,828 kilometers), often sooner, and even then worrying oil leaks were endemic), and rusty Mk 2s could be found in backstreets if they still barely functioned, or languishing in scrapyards if they'd been neglected. "Banger races" in the 1970s—demolition derbies on dusty tracks that usually hosted greyhound racing—were full of time-expired Jaguars; the irony was that the strength of their unitary-construction frames, and even the waning power of their XK engines, made them as accomplished at this form of destructive motorsports as they had been at many others.

For Mk 2s that somehow survived the 1960s, though, there was a new appreciation of their attributes in the early 1980s classic car boom. Before long cars that might otherwise have been crushed or wrecked were being rejuvenated as vital and totemic members of this preservation scene. City bankers, rather than purchasing brand-new BMWs, were sometimes spending tens of thousands of bonus pounds on specialists to have a Mk 2 restored and subtly improved (for example, to use lead-free gasoline) for use as captivating everyday cars.

Chapter Ten

THE MOST BEAUTIFUL CAR

E-type and V-12 engine: The most exciting sports car the world has ever seen arrives in 1961, marrying science, luxury, performance, and stunning looks. There are special lightweight racers and soon after the start of the 1970s an incredible new engine emerges: a V-12.

Malcolm Sayer's design was tamed with beautifully integrated bumpers, while a number plate rendered as a bonnet sticker helped to keep the contours pure.

YKE 374A

When a racing team has seen victory in endurance racing with such sweeping assurance over so many years, a point comes when there is little left to prove. In 1957, Jaguar's emperor, Sir William Lyons, recognized that now was the time to retire gracefully and decreed that the factory competition department would be disbanded. There was, naturally, glumness that the adventure was over. However, the company's deep wells of team spirit, loyalty, and high-performance expertise would be redeployed to add renewed luster to its range of road cars.

After all, what was the point of all the efforts to dominate at Le Mans if the company couldn't capitalize on the acclaim? The XK series would soon be ten years old, and bold thinking was called for again. Anyway, the company would enthusiastically foster the campaigning of Jaguars in the hands of private teams. With this new strategy in mind, former racing engineers began work on a brand-new design, codenamed E1A, that would in effect tame and transfer the D-type's winning ways on the racetrack to a sports car focused on road use. The sleek shape was an obvious evolution, but so was the monocoque construction, and the smallest engine, a 2.4-liter XK, was installed. The key difference was an experimental independent rear suspension system, for which the car was a rolling testbed for extensive development. Here was the true progenitor of what was destined to become the E-type.

This is E1A, the earliest E-type prototype built to test the extreme limits of Jaguar's new independent rear suspension.

Meanwhile, though, a second prototype, E2A, was intended to keep the motorsport spirit alive. With its prominent tailfin jutting out from behind the driver's seat, it seemed every inch the D-type successor, but it was built very differently in 1960. E2A used a steel chassis with lightweight aluminum body panels, while its unique engine was a 3.0-liter version of the XK equipped with a Lucas fuel-injection system—something to keep pace with the power unit in the Mercedes-Benz 300SL. The mystery Jaguar, entered by Briggs Cunningham's personal team, dropped out of the 1960 24 Hours of Le Mans, but the wealthy American took E2A to the US and slowly built up its stamina over several events, culminating in a victory at Bridgehampton for Walter Hansgen. After that it was returned to the Coventry factory, where Jaguar could assess how well the car had stood up to unforgiving race conditions. Such was the real-world experience needed in those days before computer analysis.

The shape was right, fully redolent of the heroic D-type; there were thousands of miles of road and race testing in the bag; and the new suspension system had been pressed to its limits. Lyons was confident Jaguar could head determinedly for an all-new sports car rebirth.

The day came rapidly, on March 15, 1961. Journalists were invited to lunch at Le Gastronomic de Parc des Eaux Vives on the southwestern shore of Lake Geneva. As they took their places, their eyes were drawn excitedly to a giant wooden packing case in the dining room. When the sides of the crate were pulled away, there must have been gasps of wonder as the E-type was revealed

Prototype E2A was an aluminium-bodied racing testbed; despite flaking out at Le Mans, it was taken to the US by Briggs Cunningham and turned into a winner.

It's March 15, 1961 on the shore of Lake Geneva, and Lyons presents his new E-type to a deeply admiring press corps.

The sleek and ritzy E-type coupe was widely known to be Lyons's favorite, and it remains one of the all-time greats among classic sports cars.

for the first time. Outside the restaurant was a similar car, registered 9600 HP and chassis number 885002, which was used to whisk off the postprandial reporters for demonstration runs and photography sessions. Meanwhile, the other car and the packing case were transported to the Geneva motor show, where the theatrical unveiling was repeated for the public the next morning.

It triggered a media storm, the likes of which has rarely attended the car world before or since. Five hundred cars were ordered at the Swiss show, and when the car made its US debut at the New York Auto Show a month later—unveiled as the XK-E by *Playboy* pinup Marilyn Hanold—orders were taken at the rate of one every five minutes. Approval came from characters as diverse as Enzo Ferrari and Frank Sinatra.

The aggressive, dart-like profile of this E-type roadster, with its lengthy, bulging hood and its tapering, pointed tail, cut a unique dash. But the coupe seen at Geneva was, if anything, even more beautiful. It was the version on which Lyons had had most input, shaping it in partnership with his expert sheet-metal fabricator, Bob Blake. It featured a clever hatchback third door, hinged at the side, and the fastback lines, Jaguar's first since the 1930s, were expertly accentuated by Lyons's use of glittering stainless-steel window frames and slim, wraparound bumpers. It was Lyons's personal favorite E-type and a stylistic masterpiece. Nevertheless, in-house aerodynamicist Malcolm Sayer made sure both E-types obeyed his science, spending long weeks in the wind tunnel with scale models to ensure excellent coefficients of drag.

The basic D-type construction method was retained—the E-type would be built around a monocoque center section with a bolt-on front

Jaguar's tireless test driver Norman Dewis holds a very early E-type steady on the high-speed banking at Britain's Motor Industry Research Association track in Nuneaton, Warwickshire.

Playboy model Marilyn Hanold presents the XK-E in roadster form at the 1961 New York Auto Show, with the backdrop perhaps overdoing the big cat theme a little.

subframe in tubular steel to carry the engine and front suspension, and a similar rear cradle, mounted to the body unit with rubber blocks, for the back axle and rear suspension. The suspension system itself, the painstaking work of Jaguar engineer Bob Knight, used coil springs/wishbones all around, with torsion bars front and rear. Dunlop disc brakes were naturally an important part of the package, only now power assisted on all four wheels and with the rear ones mounted inboard.

Both Lyons and Sayer were over 6 feet (1.8 meters) tall and, though the car measured over 14 feet (4.3 meters) long, the neat little cockpit was cramped—with its machine-turned dashboard and bucket seats clad in Connolly leather—and sweaty in hot weather. But they worked wonderfully together on the E-type's few compromises: a front number plate, for example, would have ruined both looks and aerodynamics, so owners were obliged to have a large sticker on the hood.

Decades later, Jaguar's director of design, Ian Callum, paid fulsome tribute to what Jaguar achieved:

"I know the E-type inside out and its design purity is amazing. In fact, I think Sayer actually pushed the E-type beyond William Lyons' natural "comfort zone." After all, he employed "wing aerodynamics," as you would on aircraft, which are actually designed to achieve lift, to give the E-type a pure bullet shape. If you can imagine the car without its wheels, it's very like an aircraft fuselage—the ultimate in pure forms. In fact, the wheel arches come right down below the line of the top of the wheels so the shape isn't spoilt."

In those days, car design was parochial, and the E-type was very much a Coventry sort of car like a Mercedes-Benz was a Stuttgart

At some 16 feet, the E-type was as long a car as its torpedo-like profile suggested, and the refined suspension also gave it limousine-like absorption of road surface imperfections.

The cockpit on the E-type roadster was snug-fitting and purposeful; note the triple wipers needed to keep the shallow windshield clear in a deluge.

Graham Hill practices for the Spring National race meeting at Oulton Park in April 1961—the E-type's very first competition outing, which it won.

You can almost feel the ground shake as two E-types roar away at the head of a sports car race at Aintree in 1961, with two Aston Martins in furious pursuit. The example registered BUY 1, driven by Jack Sears, came second and was later used as a race development car.

Rows of newly-built E-type roadsters await their eager owners outside Jaguar's Browns Lane, Coventry headquarters in 1961.

sort of car. The cultures didn't cross boundaries and so, of course, Jaguar didn't need to look elsewhere for its inspiration. That's another reason why the E-type—and, in my opinion, especially the coupé—is such a pure design. It's a benchmark for the "wow!" factor.

Under that elongated hood sat the 265-bhp, triple-carburetor edition of the 3.8-liter XK power unit carried over from the now-obsolete XK150. *Autocar* declared it, with a 0–60 time of 6.9 seconds, the fastest-accelerating car it had ever road tested. They also managed to push an E-type just beyond 150 miles per hour (241 kilometers per hour) in top speed testing. The figure was astonishing, shaming even Aston Martins and Ferraris, but it was also controversial. Owners found they couldn't coax their own E-type coupes much beyond 140 miles per hour (225 kilometers per hour) on the recently opened M1 motorway—which, until 1965, was free of speed limits. It seems likely those road-test demo cars had specially doctored engines so they could kiss the magic 150. *Autocar* also established that, considering its performance credentials, the E-type was pretty fuel-efficient, giving about 18 mpg (7.7 km/l) in everyday use. Handling and roadholding were deemed excellent, neutral, taut, and well damped in experienced hands, and the car's ride quality was an utter revelation. Bob Knight's painstaking fine tuning had produced a car whose absorption of bumps and coverage of ropey asphalt was more limo than hot rod.

When an average house in Britain cost £2,700, the £2,097 E-type roadster was certainly an indulgence for the well-off. On the other hand, the Aston Martin DB4 cost a hefty £4,084, and a Ferrari 250GT a monstrous £6,469. Jaguar simply could not build them quickly enough but, as ever, there was no

Wherever an E-type turned up in its early days, such as here in the paddock of a British race meeting, a crowd would gather to gawp and yearn.

hint of complacency. A 4.2-liter engine arrived in October 1964, offering near-identical power output but much more torque, allied to a vastly improved gearbox (Jaguar's own, no longer a unit brought in from Moss) now boasting synchromesh on first. The brakes were better and the seats more comfortable, although the shiny aluminum finish on the dash had proved too distracting, so the console was changed to plain black. Collectors today prize the purity of the early 3.8-liter cars, but this later 4.2 Series 1, nicknamed the "Series One-and-a-Half," was much better to own and drive. A two-plus-two "family" E-type was introduced in 1966 with a 9-inch-longer (23 centimeters) wheelbase to envelop two tiny rear seats for children. Automatic transmission (mostly to satisfy North American demand) was offered too, and the watering down of the E-type's character continued with the Series II in 1968. Most changes—bigger bumpers, plastic rocker switches instead of aircraft-style metal toggles, a collapsible steering column, and deleting the glass headlight fairings—were to abide by new safety legislations, while US antipollution laws meant a less powerful engine for that market, one that now featured twin Zenith-Stromberg carburetors. Optional power steering and twin electric cooling fans admittedly made the car less taxing.

Under Lyons's careful supervision, the E-type had been planned as an exemplary road-going machine. Racing, though, remained infectious, and Formula 1 hero Graham Hill took first place at the April 1961 Spring National meeting at Oulton Park—the E-type's first competition outing. One month later, Mike Parkes was second only to Willy Mairesse's Ferrari 250GT SWB at Spa, Belgium, in the E-type's international race debut. Taking their cue, scores of dashing owners would drive their girlfriends to Brands Hatch or Snetterton in their E-types on the weekend, whereupon they put up spirited amateur performances, and privateer wins were frequent. Jaguar itself tried to resuscitate the spirit of the D-type in 1963–1964 with a tiny run of highly specialized, aluminum-bodied E-type Lightweights. These have a lot of allure with collectors today, yet they didn't much dent Ferrari's supremacy among 1960s sports-racing machines. One of these exotic creations, using experimental fuel injection, produced 344 bhp, the most potency ever from a 3.8-liter aluminum-block XK racing engine. But even this, from Peter Lindner's exceptional car, wasn't enough to keep the E-type consistently at the head of the racing pack.

With Jaguar's rising global profile demanding ever more effort to sustain, the company decided on a return to top-level racing. Both a new car and a new engine would be required. For the latter, Jaguar pursued the V-12 avenue ruled by Ferrari.

It was the most ambitious strategy Lyons had ever planned; and as the company's largest shareholder, he put his own money behind it. He asked engineer Claude Baily to build a V-12 of 5.0 liters and with twin overhead camshafts per cylinder bank to outdo everyone else. The powerplant was installed in a brand-new, mid-engined two-seat sports racer with E-type overtones and, as ever, exceptional aerodynamics from Malcolm Sayer. The car, called XJ13, was the culmination of accumulated Jaguar thinking that had been around since the very late 1950s. But the V-12 didn't actually run until August 1964, and from that point on the march of change in areas like tire width created a constant struggle to make it competitive. One astonishing achievement the XJ13 did manage

Pale sunrise and purple evening . . . getaway hours! Sleek, beckoning roads and away-from-it places . . . getaway playgrounds! This is your moment. Relish the power of Super National. Getaway people get Super National.

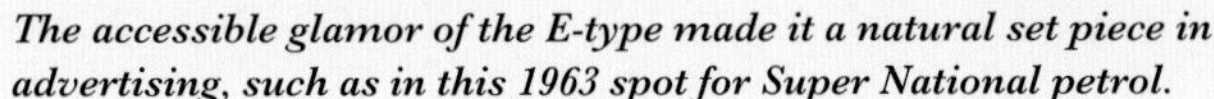

The accessible glamor of the E-type made it a natural set piece in advertising, such as in this 1963 spot for Super National petrol.

The E-type Lightweight put Jaguar briefly back into top-flight motor sport contention; this one is competing at Silverstone in 1963.

was to post the lap record of the Motor Industry Research Association (MIRA) high-speed bowl at 161 miles per hour (259 kilometers per hour) in 1967, driven by David Hobbs, which stood for years. But it was also at MIRA in 1971 that the XJ13 met its end, when fearless test driver Norman Dewis was lucky to dash unharmed from the blazing wreckage after a high-speed crash caused by a burst tire. Although the car would be rebuilt and displayed again in 1973, the venture was over. For Jaguar's dominance of the V-12 engine, though, things were just beginning. Lyons wanted such an engine that could be sold, he told *Autocar*, at a "Jaguar price." Jaguar engineers (Baily had retired, so Walter Hassan and Harry Mundy led the project) started a design program to simplify the pure racing engine in a manner that would make it the first of its type in the world to enter genuine mass production.

A Jaguar worker touches up the paintwork on an E-type roadster bodyshell as it moves slowly through the Browns Lane manufacturing process.

This meant swapping the hemispherical combustion chambers for cheaper heron-Type heads and moving to a single overhead-camshaft per bank of six cylinders. Despite the obvious complexity involved, the engine had to be robust enough for everyday use and able to be maintained at every dealer's service bay. In addition, improved low-speed torque and acceleration at higher engine speeds were better suited to a road car, and it was considerably more compact. Lyons wanted his new engine to power a luxury saloon that would outshine the Mercedes-Benz S-Class and even the Rolls-Royce Silver Shadow, but the XJ6 (see chapter 12) already embodied so much that was new that adding the V-12 was asking for trouble. Just as the XK120 had been the cradle in which to launch the XK motor, a new sports car was needed, and so an audaciously altered Series III version of the E-type would usher in the V-12 epoch in 1971.

When this car made its debut, its familiar profile softened and harmonized with the sweeping curves of the XJ13, one thing was clear: it was a guaranteed 150-mile-per-hour supercar. As a long-wheelbase two-seater roadster or two-plus-two fixed head, both with power steering as standard, the wondrous refinement of the 5.3-liter engine was astounding. The 272 bhp on tap completely recharged all the E-type vigor that had been lost to emissions-cutting detuning. It fully represented Jaguar's determination to restore the power to the E-type that tightening laws had squeezed out of the car. It now whispered its way from 0 to 60 in 7.2 seconds, with bottomless reserves of torque, meaning this big cat could keep sprinting and leap past every other car on the road, such was its midrange overtaking prowess.

Perhaps surprisingly, the V-12 did finally stamp the E-type's mark on the racing grid. The American Group 44 team, tightly run by Bob Tullius, won the 1975 Sports Car Club of America B-Production Championship trophy in 1975, campaigning a V-12 roadster. This truly fabulous motor car, though, suffered unfortunate timing. Even though the asking price was still a bargain at £3,343, the 1973 fuel crisis decimated demand. Unlike the first thrifty E-type, this was a 12-mpg gas-guzzler. Jaguar built a forty-nine-car runout edition in September 1974 in jet-black paint with a commemorative plaque on the dashboard. Some of them were still unsold in showrooms a year later.

Emblematic of Jaguar, and indeed Britain, the E-type was decadent and hedonistic, yet also a pinnacle of scientific engineering. The company built 72,520 examples; most went to the US and only 12,330 were sold in the UK.

The term *icon* is overused, but among cars it fits the E-type, most especially after New York's Museum of Modern Art added one to its permanent collection in 1996 as a brilliant example of "sculpture in movement." In 2004, London's Design Museum devoted an entire exhibition to the E-type, curated by design critic Helen Evenden who said, "I am captivated by the gorgeousness of the car, the glamor of it ... the unusual mixture of masculine and feminine qualities." In 2008, the E-type topped a reader poll in *The Daily Telegraph* as the most beautiful car of all time. Jaguar could not have hoped for better.

With extended wheelbase, two extra seats for children, and that side-opening tailgate, the E-type became a practical family car in 1966 with the launch of the 2+2 model.

Jaguar's astounding new V-12 engine found its first home under the long hood of the Series III E-type in 1971, putting impressive new lead into an old but serviceable pencil.

The curiously messy rear end of the Series III V-12 roadster; Lyons always felt the exhaust pipes were the one unresolved aspect of the car, and now there were four of them, plus bumpers raised awkwardly to meet US impact laws.

The new engine put some muscle back into the E-type's limbs, particularly as there was no question it was now firmly in the 150-mile-per-hour supercar league.

The hand-welding gives an idea of how much manual labor still went into producing cars, such as this Series III coupe, at Jaguar in 1971—robots were strictly sci-fi stuff.

Quality is vital to
SMOKING
STRICTLY
PROHIBITED
IN THE BODIES
OR IMMEDIATELY
OUTSIDE CAR BODIES
WHERE SOLUTION
IS BEING USED
stops tracks working
FIRE PREVENTION
THE LION

Chapter Eleven

BOLDER WITH EVERY MOVE

Expansion: With steady precision, William Lyons built Jaguar into an important and diversified British industrial group, taking on Daimler, Guy, and Coventry Climax before finally cutting a deal intended to safeguard his unique company's future.

The final assembly hall at Browns Lane around 1962, humming with activity as Jaguar strove to meet booming global demand and to maintain high standards; Mk 2s center and left, Mk Xs on the right.

November 28, 1951, is a date with very little "ring" in the annals of Jaguar. It didn't concern an exciting new car or a heroic race victory. As that month was especially dark, cold, and wet in Britain, with twice the average rainfall, industrial Warwickshire must have looked particularly grim late that day as buses splashed through the streets and news vendors yelled out the arrival of that night's *Coventry Evening Telegraph*.

For Jaguar, the day saw the completion of a move that would unlock its future—a process that had begun back in May as, each weekend, an entire department was uprooted. First to go was the machine shop; last was the paint shop.

The company's relocation to Browns Lane, Allesley, in Coventry's northwestern suburbs had come after its home at Holbrook Lane, Foleshill, simply could not accommodate its flourishing activities any longer, and that was even after 13 acres of adjacent land had been acquired and built on. Lyons had had his eye on the Browns Lane plant and its 1 million square feet of manufacturing space for a while. It had been built with government funding in the late 1930s as the "Number Two Shadow Factory" to produce tank engines for the impending war, with Daimler running it, but by 1950 most of it stood idle and empty. The Ministry of Supply was glad to lease the place to Jaguar, and the deal was sealed between Lyons and Whitehall's Sir Archibald Rowland, the only condition being that Jaguar would continue to produce small numbers of Meteor tank engines there.

The company boomed from the moment it arrived. Employment soared and the additional space allowed it to expand its range to take on most of Britain's five big carmaking groups that accounted for 90 percent of the nation's output. At least two of those, Standard-Triumph and the Rootes Group, were also Coventry based, so the city was about as close as anywhere outside the US could be to Detroit's Motown (although the local culture was more medieval and Shakespearean than it was soulful). This concentration of manufacturing meant that when the British car industry banded together to open a state-of-the-art research and development center in 1954, the Motor Industry Research Association picked a site at Nuneaton, Warwickshire, for the test tracks and laboratories. The new facilities, therefore, were right on Jaguar's doorstep.

In the New Year's Honours list issued in 1956, Lyons received a knighthood for his services to British industry and, in particular, the astounding export success of Jaguar Cars Ltd. He was fifty-five. No one could have been more deserving. The title was, it could be presumed, a happy moment after the tragedy of the previous year, when his only son, John, was killed in a car crash while driving through France on his way to the 24 Hours of Le Mans; he was just twenty-five. The normally reserved Sir William is beaming in photos and newsreels that capture the visit to Browns Lane paid by the Queen and the Duke of Edinburgh in March 1956, where the technology-mad Prince Philip was clearly in his element, watching the new 2.4-liter being manufactured and poring over the D-type on proud display.

Many of the crucial people behind Jaguar had been there at the start, Blackpool workers like purchasing manager (later purchasing director) Harry Teather and machine shop manager Jack Beardsley, who became company linchpins. Still others had been recruited by Lyons and William Heynes with their instincts for fine talent.

The people who were the final links in the chain between the factory and the customer were the distributors and dealers. Many of these were personally appointed by Lyons, usually on the strength of his instinct and a gentlemen's agreement, and remained concessionaires for decades. As a successful car salesman himself in his youth, Jaguar's owner immediately recognized the people who could sell the cars he had created. In the States, Max Hoffman in New York was one such person, looking after the East Coast from his glamorous base on Manhattan's Park Avenue, where his Jaguar emporium was designed by leading architect Frank Lloyd Wright. On the West Coast, Lyons had picked Charles H. "Chuck" Hornburg Jr. from Los Angeles after meeting him in England at the XK120's unveiling. Hornburg's personal charisma and plans for a showroom on Sunset Boulevard were impressive; the fact that he reputedly said, "I'll take them all," and then generated two thousand advance orders from an engine-less demonstration car made him crucial to Jaguar's early US success. Legend has it that he tossed a coin between Clark Gable and publisher Hastings Harcourt to decide who got the first XK120 (Gable won).

Norwegian-American Kjell Qvale was another character Lyons trusted to sell hundreds of Jaguars a year in San Francisco. "It was a handshake deal with William Lyons," Qvale said in 2005. "The first Jaguar I sold was a Mk V convertible to Reeder

The Daimler Conquest Century of 1954–1958 was the kind of middling-ability prestige British saloon that was overshadowed by the dynamism of Jaguar's products, the 1955 2.4-liter Mk 1 in particular.

This gigantic brick edifice is Daimler's Radford plant—seen here on the occasion in 1938 of a royal visit, naturally enough in a fleet of Daimlers built here. Jaguar snapped it up in 1960 and turned it into its engine factory.

Sir Williams Lyons (right) assures a mayor of Coventry that Daimler, the city's oldest carmaker, is in safe hands. The pair is astride an 1898 Daimler 4 hp Phaeton.

The Daimler SP250 had some merit as a fast roadster—seen here as one of a handful of police pursuit cars—but Lyons had little time for its weird looks and plastic body.

BMC's former corporate flagship, this Vanden Plas 4-liter R with Rolls-Royce engine, was a casualty of its merger with Jaguar, as Lyons made sure he extinguished anything that trespassed on Jaguar's luxury car ground.

Butterfield, one of my most loyal customers, and I've continued selling Jaguar cars ever since." These and other appointees made Jaguar, briefly, the biggest-selling imported car brand in the US in 1953, just before the Volkswagen phenomenon exploded.

In Jaguar's home market, nominated regional distributors supplied a dealer network. The first had been Henlys in London, but many other appointments stretched right back to the early days of SS. Roland Bellamy, for example, held the distributorship for the large county of Lincolnshire. A Morris agent in Grimsby, he first met Lyons in 1923 after ordering several special-bodied cars for customers from Swallow's Blackpool coachworks. On one visit to collect a car, Bellamy was shown the SS 1 prototype and offered sage advice on improving its chassis. His son, Richard Bellamy, recalled:

It led to my family becoming Jaguar distributors from 1934 until 1978. We were one of about twenty; Henlys was the biggest, with the south. In 1959, our new showroom was due to be opened by Mike Hawthorn, but a week beforehand he was killed. William Lyons always declined such ceremonies but, in these circumstances, he stepped in.

On the outside wall of the two-storey, brick-built block we had a special sign: half a Jaguar 3.4 Mk 1 bolted through the wall about twenty feet up. Jaguar gave us the car. It had been crashed near the factory gates, entirely destroying one side. It was illuminated by neon, the wheels revolved, and our mechanics even cut a new grille and bumpers in half to fit. It was a real local landmark.

Lyons's secret was that he carefully controlled deliveries. He used to say one car too few was fantastic, but one car too many was a glut.

Even in the 1950s, Jaguar had a fine-tuned yet surprisingly informal approach to sales partnerships. RA Creamer & Son of London's Kensington was an intriguing example. Syd Creamer, the son, was a mechanic in the family garage down a quiet cobbled mews and a budding racing driver when he got to know Jaguar's Lofty England in the thriving British motor racing scene of 1954–1955. England asked if he'd like to become an agent. Syd recalled, "I asked 'What do I have to do?' and he said, 'Oh, just carry on as you are.' I went up to the factory in Coventry and they found me some old signs in a shed. I screwed them on to the front of my showroom and that was it. I suppose it was a bit of a coup, but I didn't realize it at the time."

Creamer remained a dealer until his death more than fifty years later, expanding and even serving the Royal Family at nearby Kensington Palace, earning two royal warrants. It was a very personal business. "I like to walk into any pub in Kensington and not worry about meeting a disenchanted customer," he said.

Individual feedback sometimes proved very valuable. One regular customer was a Helena Rubinstein cosmetics executive who told Creamer he wanted "a beige car that would also glitter." "I said Jaguar didn't do such a color. He just told me to get them to tip a tin of silver paint in with beige, and eventually that's how Jaguar created its Opalescent Golden Sand color, a unique metallic paint that became a must-have on Mk 2s and E-types in the late 1960s."

In 1959, with output soaring thanks to high demand for its compact cars and with the Mk 2 versions just about to come onstream, Jaguar was able to buy the freehold of its Browns Lane home. Yet with the company's rate of growth, even that spacious complex was starting to feel cramped. Any ideas of expanding on nearby land were fraught with political difficulties; government policy was for new car factories to be built in areas of economic deprivation or high unemployment and these—like Ford's plant on Merseyside and Rootes's new factory outside Glasgow—were all a long way from Coventry. Lyons was adamant he didn't want to do that. There was, though, a third way—and an audacious one.

The Daimler Company was, in effect, the foundation stone of the British motor industry, having been established in Coventry in 1896 and producing the nation's first automobile in January the year after. Because of the Royal Family's patronage, large and regal Daimler cars were emblematic of Britain itself. The company also turned its hand to trucks, buses, and military vehicles. In 1910 Daimler became part of the Birmingham Small Arms (BSA) company, which had itself turned from making guns to motorbikes. Daimler enjoyed buoyant fortunes in World War II but once the conflict ceased, it seemed to blunder along in a confused manner. This could be pinpointed to the moment when, in 1944, the controlling business owner Dudley Docker passed away and leadership was handed over to his only son, Bernard. His unique mix of incompetence and indulgence in a lavish lifestyle as managing director meant Daimler cars suffered, with a haphazard approach to investment and even to understanding what people wanted to buy. They were once the choice of the wealthy professional classes, but Jaguar took many of those customers, and then the House of Windsor switched its allegiance to Rolls-Royce. Docker was sacked in 1956, and although new BSA boss Jack Sangster sanctioned an excellent range of V-8 engines, the decline continued. Nutty ideas, such as using one of these engines in a Vauxhall Cresta bodyshell, hinted at the malaise.

The excellent V-8 engine from the SP250 found a happy home in the Mk 2–based Daimler V-8 250, launched in 1962 as a compact luxury car with all the trimmings, automatic transmission, and power steering.

The timing for Lyons was ideal and he began negotiations with a relieved Sangster for a takeover of Daimler, the perpetual money loser in the BSA group. The talks were conducted in complete secrecy; when Jaguar announced on May 26, 1960, that it was paying £3.1 million for Daimler, many senior Jaguar staff, even directors, were caught by surprise. The most exciting carmaker in Britain was now swallowing up the oldest. The agreement covered the sale of the Daimler Company itself, commercial vehicles subsidiary Transport Vehicles (Daimler) Ltd., and the whole sprawling Daimler factory in Radford, Coventry, its home since 1937.

While it was no doubt satisfying to become the custodian of the Daimler marque and heritage, that was a minor consideration compared to the potential and usefulness of the fully equipped Radford facilities. It would soon become home to all of Jaguar's engine and component manufacture —a forbiddingly vast metallurgy and engineering complex—while car assembly was either marginalized or carefully integrated into the Jaguar way of doing things.

In 1962, for example, the Daimler 2.5 V-8 was launched, a beautifully resolved marriage of the Jaguar Mk 2 car with the 2.5-liter V-8 engine used in Daimler's SP250 (a sports car with a plastic body that neither the market nor Lyons had any affection for). It came with its own Daimler insignia, luxury interior, unique colors inside and out, and Borg Warner automatic transmission as standard. The engine was lighter and more compact than the usual XK, and the 2.5 V-8 was a superb compact luxury car, making excellent use of all the resources Jaguar had at its disposal. With a small revamp in 1967, when a manual gearbox was also finally offered, it became the best-selling single Daimler of all time—ironically yet another accolade for Jaguar!

Another strange byproduct of the takeover was that Jaguar found itself in the bus business. Daimler already had an established market in chassis for single- and double-deckers sold all over the UK and abroad, and now the new owners approved plans for the Daimler Fleetline, introduced in 1962. With its rear engine, front door, and low floor, it could be operated by a driver who also took fares. It was a great success, in London and elsewhere, and some 7,000 were built at Radford up to 1973.

Daimler's commercial vehicles operation opened Lyons's eyes to markets he had never thought of before. The Jaguar Group began to take shape. Opportunistic purchases included Wolverhampton truck maker Guy Motors in 1961 from administrators for £800,000, and then forklift truck and racing engine manufacturer Coventry Climax in 1963. The final major purchase was engine and gearbox company Henry Meadows Ltd., Wolverhampton neighbors to Guy, in 1964. All these engineering businesses benefited from the close attention the Jaguar board applied, and the focus on specific new activities. It got results, too: Jaguar Group profits quadrupled between 1955 and 1964 to £2.5 million.

But while Jaguar and its divisions could now produce all manner of mechanical components and made a vast range of vehicles (military ones included) that could compensate for the fickle consumer car market, a new threat had arisen. In 1965, the British Motor Corporation (BMC) had bought the Pressed Steel Company, supplier of Jaguar's car bodies since 1950. As BMC's most luxurious Wolseley and Vanden Plas models were in direct competition with some of Jaguar's range, there emerged the alarming prospect of Jaguar's destiny being in the hands of a bitter rival.

Lyons was almost sixty-five. It would be right to question Jaguar's early-1960s dalliance with trucks and industrial engines when self-sufficiency in body stampings might have been more prescient. Could the prudent yet shrewd Lyons have finally stumbled? Perhaps in a company he hadn't controlled through ownership of voting shares and so been able to rule with a courtly but total autocracy, decisions might have been different.

At this point, Lyons did the only sensible thing he could. He agreed to a merger of his cherished Jaguar Cars Ltd. with BMC. They came together in December 1966 under the British Motor Holdings umbrella. In effect BMC bought Jaguar, but it was more accurately the coming together of two very needy partners. BMC, run by Sir George Harriman, was a big and wasteful organization that generated wafer-thin profits on the 900,000 cars it made annually, and now struggled internationally against competitors like Volkswagen and Toyota. Jaguar, run by Lyons, was a small and lean company making a good return on its 30,000 cars sold annually, with a lucrative export market in the US. Lyons, of course, wanted to secure body supplies, but because of his fantastic reputation and track record he was also able to leverage an incredible amount of autonomy. He would still be very much in charge of Jaguar, and BMC could perhaps learn from his skillful methods.

As events turned out, British Motor Holdings would exist for a little over one year. In January 1968, the company was forced into a full-blown merger with Leyland Motors to form BLMC. The impetus came from a British government anxious—with some justification—to consolidate the country's indigenous motor industry into one megagroup that could square up to the huge American multinationals General Motors, Ford, and Chrysler; rapidly growing new contenders Nissan and Toyota from Japan; and the five European giants: Volkswagen, Renault, Peugeot, Citroën, and Fiat.

The merger negotiations were fraught with problems, especially because Leyland's Sir Donald Stokes expected to lead the massive new company; he was viewed by the British government as the dynamic rescuer of the lackluster BMC. Lyons was, of course, closely involved and helped to clear the way for Stokes's rise to the top job by tactfully and gently easing Harriman out of the way (he was not in the best of health anyway), his biggest fear being that the merger would be abandoned and Leyland would mount a hostile takeover. Of course, Lyons's number one priority was the greatest possible operating independence for Jaguar inside the new group, with executive control vested in Lyons alone. Along the way, the wily and august Jaguar founder, from his seat on the main BLMC board, could veto anything that challenged the supremacy of his precious feline pet. The Jaguar 420G-based Daimler limousine replaced the creaky Austin Princess, a Rolls-Royce–engined Austin-Healey got no further than a prototype, and Rover's two-seater mid-engine sports car project and its Jaguar-rivaling P8 luxury saloon were torpedoed. How the man managed to balance all of this skullduggery in his head as he carried on beyond pensionable age quite defies belief. On top of it all, he was about to astonish the luxury car world all over again.

An S-type body shell receiving careful attention prior to painting to ensure a gleaming finish. The issue of bodywork supplies in the 1960s was troubling for Jaguar, eventually forcing it into a merger with the British Motor Corporation.

Lyons hobnobs with customers at the opening of Roland C. Bellamy's showrooms in Lincolnshire in the mid 1960s; many of Jaguar's long-term sales partnerships were founded on close personal bonds with the revered company head.

Axed: Lyons negotiated a highly influential position for himself within British Leyland, formed in 1968, and this enabled him to veto anything upcoming within the group that threatened Jaguar's position; this Rover P8 large executive car was one of several casualties.

Chapter Twelve

THE WORLD BEATERS

XJ6 & XJS: The wonderful XJ saloon becomes the pinnacle of Jaguar's achievements, with a second coming in the 1980s. Along the way the XJ12 makes its mark as a unique luxury car and the XJS, while controversial, is startlingly different—and amazing long lived.

The gorgeous XJ6 opened a new era for Jaguar, setting dazzling new standards for the compromise between ride comfort and roadholding, and replacing four outgoing models in one fell swoop.

PHP 42G

The best car in the world. A very bold statement, indeed, but one that was widely repeated by every fortunate soul who had any contact with the Jaguar XJ6 in 1968 and 1969. Sir William Lyons, featured in the XJ6 TV commercial, quietly stated that he thought it was the finest Jaguar ever; independent critics were overawed by the big saloon's cocktail of fantastic road manners, spectacular refinement, sporty luxury, and uniquely fashionable aura. The judging panel of the influential European Car of the Year award, as ever, refused to give their precious 1969 accolade to something so upmarket, and instead it went to the worthy yet uninspiring Peugeot 504. But Britain's *Car* magazine was so blown away that it had its own trophy designed and declared the XJ6 its unsurpassed Car of the Year. "To my mind the Jaguar is not merely remarkable for what it is," wrote the magazine's erudite L. J. K. Setright, "but also because it makes redundant all cars that cost more."

The XJ6 was replacing no fewer than five cars: the Mk 2–style 240/340, the Daimler V8-250, the S-type, the 420, and the 420G. At once it served as the successor to Jaguar's popular compacts and its harder-to-love big limo, which was a very tall order. Prodigious thought and care, naturally, was poured into its development. Work had begun on Project XJ4 as far back as 1963, the hardpoints being a wheelbase of 9 feet 3/4 inch (2.76 meters), track front and back of 4 feet 10 inches (1.47 meters), and an engine bay big enough to house Jaguar's upcoming V-12 powerplant. An all-new structure with immense torsional strength was originally planned to carry bodywork that was a curious mix of four-door saloon with an E-type fastback, fronted by the familiar four-round-headlamp nose of the Mk X and 420.

Carefully taped up to disguise its identity prior to launch, a prototype XJ6 kicks up the dust as it undergoes a vigorous test schedule, part of its £6 million development program.

The cavernous trunk space of the XJ6, thanks partly to twin fuel tanks inside the tapering rear wings.

Eventually Lyons and his staff worked their way through seven different back-end treatments until settling on the gracefully tapering line of the trunk and giving the super-sleek XJ6 matching gently flared wheel arches front and back and a pronounced, muscular "hip" above the rear ones that emphasized its lithe, feline form. They felt it was so manifestly and distinctively a Jaguar, so unlike all its competitors, that "Jaguar" appeared nowhere on the car itself. The chromed leaping cat mascot on the hood was ditched as well.

The first prototype was running in May 1966 with a 4.2-liter XK engine, and nine months later there were two more, with one used extensively to test an air-conditioning system. Although Lyons and technical director William Heynes were intimately involved in the design parameters and overall concept—in a way that few board-level executives would be these days—the finessing and fine-tuning was overseen by senior Jaguar engineer Bob Knight, as fastidious and painstaking an individual as anyone could hope to encounter. Knight had been central to Jaguar's superb chassis frame, disc brake, and independent rear suspension innovations in the 1950s, and XJ4 encompassed all of them. But now he set about designing the car's anti-dive front suspension geometry that would dramatically cut roll while cornering and meant the final car could be hurled around without losing road adhesion. He also collaborated once again with Dunlop to design the super-wide ER70 VR15 tires to fit 6-inch-wide (15.2-centimeter) rims specially for the car. These featured an irregular tread pattern designed to prevent continuous booms or shudders from being relayed to the car's interior.

Knight went all out to banish noise, vibration, and harshness and so create the most refined car possible. "The idea that development towards the ultimate should ever stop is anathema to Bob Knight," wrote Jaguar chronicler Andrew Whyte. "He never failed to use every last available moment to perfect some detail." The only bumps along the XJ6 design road were corporate ones. Jaguar had set itself a hugely ambitious goal, and it was lucky to have the financial security of its buyout by BMC behind it as costs escalated (the final bill was some £6 million). And, for reasons of economic peaks and dips, demand for its current production cars fluctuated wildly. The new XJ6 couldn't arrive a moment too soon, but something had to give, and the Jaguar board agreed with the greatest reluctance in May 1968 that their plans to introduce the car with the all-new V-12 engine—and a proposed V-8 stable mate—would have to be abandoned.

Car magazine was so incensed at the European Car of the Year jury's refusal to recognize the XJ6 that it organized its own award for the car, commissioning Aston Martin stylist William Towns to design this trophy.

For a three-day visit to Mauritius in 1972, Jaguar supplied this open-topped XJ6 parade car for the use of Her Majesty the Queen and Prince Philip. The company has enjoyed a cordial relationship with Buckingham Palace since the 1950s.

Jaguar's astonishing 5.3-liter V-12 engine in its intended home, under the hood of the original XJ12, which went on sale in 1972 . . . and was immediately blighted by a labor dispute.

The ergonomics, driving position, and comfort were exemplary in the XJ6, with an elegant clarity to its dashboard and an aircraft-like transmission lever. This being a Series II, all the instruments are directly in front of the driver.

The XJ6 (a Series II shown here) was one of the most beautiful and timeless four-door saloons in the world at its launch. It would remain so throughout the ups and downs of its very long production run.

This was no great hardship for the XJ6 to endure because the standard 4.2-liter XK engine offered superb performance and was very much a reliable known quantity. Announced in September 1968 and on show to the public a month later amid widespread acclaim at the London Motor Show, the car cost from £2,253 to £2,498 for a deluxe automatic. A comparable car from Mercedes-Benz, a 300SEL, cost a huge £6,795, to give an idea of the exceptional value offered by Jaguar. But the range actually started with a £1,797 2.8-liter (2,792cc) model. The latter, restricted-capacity engine was principally intended for European markets where tax brackets made it attractive as a BMW or Mercedes-Benz rival. Yet the XJ6 itself challenged Rolls-Royce for hushed refinement while being as involving and exciting for the driver as an Italian supercar. *Autocar* enthused, "Unbelievable value. The best there is ... If Jaguar were to double the price of the XJ6 and bill it as the best car in the world, we would be right behind them ... As it stands at the moment, dynamically, it has no equal regardless of price, which explains those 12-month delivery quotes from dealers ... A tremendous advance guaranteed to put it ahead for several years at least."

In addition to the performance, there were the superb ergonomics, with Connolly leather-faced, posture-sprung seats containing body-hugging cushions developed with mattress manufacturer Slumberland; so much better than the impressive, but slippery, leather sofas in the older Jag saloons.

Jaguar made every effort in 1969 to meet the unprecedented demand, starting its first-ever night shift in February, and even seemingly adding to its backlog burden by introducing a Daimler Sovereign edition of the 4.2 in October as a slightly more sober luxury option. It built 13,769 XJ6 cars, the most of a single model since the Mk 2 in 1962. This all bode well for the first year of an exciting new decade, and the somewhat farcical "demo" by Swiss buyers outside the British Leyland London HQ in 1970, fuming at the long waiting list, delighted the newspapers. Behind the headlines, though, severe industrial turmoil at the Browns Lane factory and its suppliers was the real reason for lengthening delays in delivering to eager owners. The car set new boundaries, but the processes and organization that put it into customers' hands were cracking up under the strain (see chapter 13).

In 1970 Jaguar produced 21,833 XJs, helped a tiny bit by quietly dropping the big old 420G, and a year later it was up again to a record-busting 27,517 XJ/Sovereigns, which meant some 650 cars were departing the factory every week.

The XJ12 made its much-delayed debut in July 1972. It was unquestionably the pinnacle of everything Sir William had worked for: a combination of the most accomplished luxury saloon car available, given the world's only mass-produced V-12 engine, whose silence, smoothness, and responsiveness outshone all comers—Rolls-Royce, Mercedes-Benz, and the best that Detroit could muster. The 5,343cc engine (265 bhp at 5,850 rpm), with automatic transmission only, was a quantum leap over even the finest of the world's V-8s for silken mechanical excellence, with vibration from the powerplant virtually undetectable inside the car. With a top speed in excess of 140 miles per hour (225 kilometers per hour), the £3,226 XJ12 was the fastest four-seater car in the world. It was, naturally, extremely thirsty. Fuel efficiency might have been improved had the planned fuel injection system been ready in time; as it was, gasoline was ingested through four Zenith Stromberg side-draft carbs, and the best overall fuel consumption the car could muster was 11.9 mpg.

Not, of course, that potential buyers had thrift paramount on their priority lists. Indeed, for high rollers, a Daimler Double Six edition was offered in August 1972 at £3,849, and mere weeks afterward the XJ's only small deficiency—tight rear legroom—was addressed with a 4-inch (10-centimeter) wheelbase extension on the Double Six Vanden Plas, which boasted an exceptionally luxurious interior crafted at the famous North London coachbuilding emporium. Soon the long-wheelbase bodywork was offered across the whole lineup, and in 1975 the shorter option was deleted altogether.

September 1973 saw the arrival of a much-revised Series II range whose bumpers, raised to 16 inches (41 centimeters) above road surface level, were an indication of safety requirements in Jaguar's key US market, as were the unseen side-impact beams in the doors. Modifying an existing, cohesive car design in this way was always going to be tricky, but fortunately there was a beautiful-looking new derivative to distract the attention: a two-door pillarless hardtop XJC. Long feted as Lyons's personal favorite of the series yet, supremely handsome as it was, it was a troubling car for Jaguar. The body was extensively modified from a standard four-door, short-wheelbase shell, with specially fabricated, elongated front doors. Because of problems with window seals and the whispering intrusion of wind noise around the frameless side windows, it would be two long years before it came on the market, and even then every example had a roof section covered in black vinyl to hide cracks in the paintwork caused by the weakened, pillarless body flexing slightly under pressure. It was a crafty fix but lacked the standards by which Mercedes-Benz operated. It was only in the range for a couple of years.

The XJ12 was planned from the outset as the world's ultimate luxury saloon and, indeed, it was the only four-door car made anywhere with a 12-cylinder engine, Germany and the US included.

This XJ12L Series II is a long-wheelbase V-12–powered car, made to US specification with left-hand drive, whitewall tires, and extended bumpers for that crucial export market.

The Series II XJ range included for a time this elegant two-door coupe. This one is to the rare Daimler Double Six specification, and behind it is its Double Six namesake, a 1931 relic from Daimler's glory days.

Other changes in 1975 included dropping the slow-selling and little-liked 2.8 and replacing it with a new 3.4-liter XK with 161 bhp on tap for a top speed of 117 miles per hour (188 kilometers per hour); the 4.2 had a nearly identical maximum speed and acceleration figures but was much more flexible in the midrange, while the XJ12 finally received Bosch-Lucas fuel injection to hoist power to 285 bhp.

The late 1970s were, in many ways, lost years. Lyons had retired in 1972, and in the following period Jaguar's cherished independence was imperiled within the crisis-hit British Leyland; the company was bankrupt by 1975 and nationalized by the Labour government to ensure its survival. The decision to return to factory-backed racing was taken at corporate head office level, with the XJC cars to run in Leyland Cars livery in the European Touring Car Championship where BMWs and Ford Capris ruled the grids.

The enterprise was farmed out to the private team Broadspeed and was a notable disaster despite the participation of top drivers like Le Mans legend Derek Bell. In the old days, factory engineers turned their cars into racers using all their intimate knowledge of the vehicles' strengths and foibles. In this case, and with history as the judge, it was the wrong car with the wrong people.

Even sadder in a way was the decision, for reasons of Jaguar's inadequate resources, to hand over the stylistic revamp of the 1979 Series III to Italy's Pininfarina. For a marque built on its instinctive flair for great design, this was the ultimate post-Lyons travesty. Nonetheless, Pininfarina did a highly polished job of carefully reshaping the XJ6's roofline, imperceptibly lifting it by 3 inches (7.6 centimeters), and boosting its glass areas to make it feel considerably roomier inside, in the back especially. The wraparound, energy-absorbing bumpers, flush-fitting door handles, and fully revised interior were also deftly handled. Overall it was remarkable how well the ten-year-old shape was wearing with these subtle tweaks.

Tipping the familiar trunk forward revealed more worthwhile upgrades. Jaguar's outdated four-speed manual gearbox had been ousted for the LT77 five-speeder from the Rover SD1 (a good move), and adding Lucas/Bosch L-Jetronic fuel-injection to the now-205-bhp 4.2-liter engine meant that the 3.4 became the only Jag (and the last) with good old-fashioned carburetors.

The final significant technical development of the Series III came in September 1981. The XJ12 was now struggling to find buyers in the aftermath of the second major recession in its lifetime, and something had to be done to address its gluttony for gasoline. The solution came from the work of Swiss consulting engineer Michael May, who designed his so-called "Fireball" high-compression cylinder head for the V-12. Jaguar spent five years evaluating his work before adopting it. The vastly improved gas flow boosted ultimate power to 299 bhp at 5,000 rpm, provided greater torque, and most importantly gave an overall fuel consumption improvement of some 25 percent, at 15.6 mpg. If driven with a light

For the Series III of 1979, a diminished Jaguar was forced to call in Italy's Pininfarina to handle the careful redesign work, which included a cleverly raised roofline to give much-improved rear headroom. There were multiple improvements to the interior too.

The more substantial bumpers on the Series III—this is an XJ6 4.2—didn't spoil the svelte lines of the car too much.

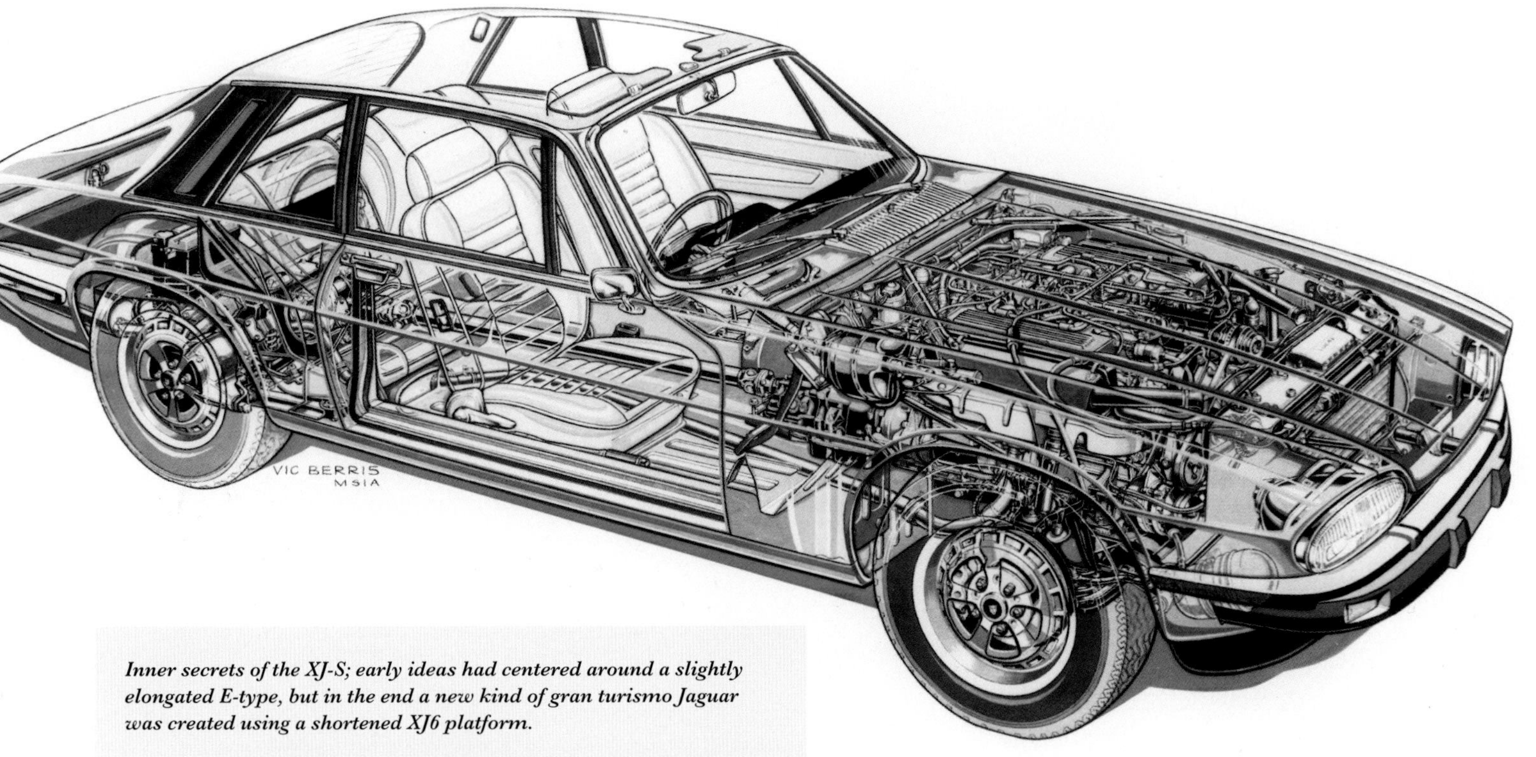

Inner secrets of the XJ-S; early ideas had centered around a slightly elongated E-type, but in the end a new kind of gran turismo Jaguar was created using a shortened XJ6 platform.

The broad and stylish lines of the XJ-S were a departure for Jaguar, and the large oval headlights and prominent rubber bumpers only highlighted the shock of the new; that livery on the door salutes the Queen's Silver Jubilee celebrations in 1977, when this one was made.

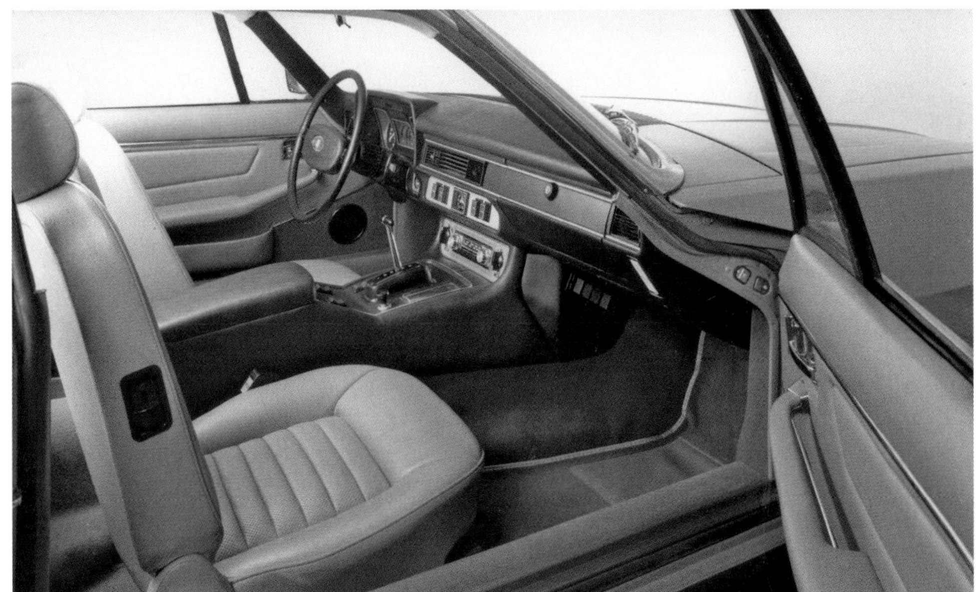

The XJ-S's functional and sporty two-plus-two interior was leather lined but free from wood trim, and air-conditioning was standard equipment.

right foot, this made the V-12 HE (for "high efficiency") no less thirsty than an automatic six-cylinder XJ6 4.2.

This car and the rest of the range dragged Jaguar away from the edge of collapse, once incoming boss John Egan had extricated Jaguar Cars Ltd. from the rest of the troubled British Leyland empire and used his newfound autonomy to radically overhaul the business. His hands-on approach saw quality levels soar, which led to a resurgence of demand from the US, where the "Jaguar is back!" battle cry was enthusiastically received. Every year from 1982 to the end of its life, sales of the XJ6 Series III continued to rise as annual output of the vastly improved cars soared. In just two years, from 1983 to 1985, the Browns Lane workforce went from making 27,331 to 38,500; the XJ6 Series III was available until May 1987, well after its XJ40 replacement had arrived, but the sumptuous Series III XJ12 continued to be available, rather incredibly, for a further five years. The final car built was a Daimler Double Six edition, and it set the seal on a total production run of 400,732.

Another Jaguar that enjoyed a late-1980s high point in popularity was the XJ-S. Such was the XJ-S's desperate plight early on that it nearly didn't make the booming 1980s yuppie period at all. But by 1989, fourteen years after the car first hit the market, an incredible 11,207 examples of the luxury GT and convertible had been sold.

Replacing the world-famous E-type would never be easy, and part of the onerous task fell to Jaguar's brilliant aerodynamicist Malcolm Sayer, beginning in 1966–1967. His earliest thoughts focused on a comprehensive E-type revamp, codenamed XJ21, intended to run a new V-8 engine derived from the V-12, but by 1968 Sayer and Lyons had decided once and for all that the new car was going to be a two-door grand tourer based on the upcoming XJ, as it was the only financially viable way forward; a sporty luxury car was particularly likely to generate healthy profits as a British alternative to German and Italian models, and sharing parts made good sense. The duo—one of the world's leading automotive theorists and the industry's canniest sage of aspirant consumer tastes—were about to work their magic again. Sayer said he wanted "a low, wide, high-speed car at least as

Jaguar's fuel-injected V-12, squeezed under the low, flat hood of the XJ-S, provided magnificent acceleration and performance, and uncanny refinement, although it would be a brave owner who took a wrench to this complex power unit.

From the XJ-SC it was a short hop to a full XJ-S convertible in 1988, complete with power-operated top. German soft-top specialist Karmann supplied the expertise it had used on the Volkswagen Golf/Rabbit cabriolet, and the choice of engine was restricted to the V-12 to produce one of the most desirable open cars of the late 1980s. This US-spec car has four round headlights.

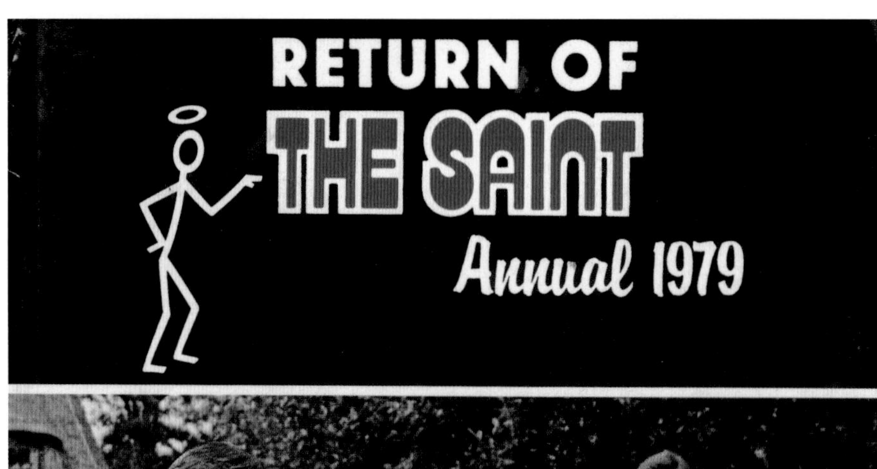

The XJ-S stormed into living rooms around the world in the 1978–1979 TV series Return of the Saint, *driven by Ian Ogilvy as Simon Templar, also enlivening merchandise like this big-selling gift annual.*

Almost given up for dead, the XJ-S was revived in this HE—for High Efficiency —iteration in 1981, with both fuel economy and build quality vastly improved; sales started to climb as the by-now seven-year-old car was reborn.

Jaguar couldn't resist the pent-up demand for open-air thrills any longer, concocting this XJ-SC cabriolet (in partnership with Coventry contractor Tickford) with fixed side windows in 1983, initially with the all-new 3.6-liter AJ6 engine.

eye-catching as those the Italians will produce." Lyons, meanwhile, with delightful understatement, said, "I took my influence as far as I could without interfering with his basic aerodynamic requirements and he and I worked on the first styling models together."

In 1978, three years after the launch of the XJ-S, Jaguar executive Bob Berry highlighted a model of a mid-engined, two-seater road car Sayer had created in the late 1960s:

It is devoid of airdams, spoilers, wings and other excrescences of the modern high-speed competition car, yet the shape was designed and developed to be aerodynamically stable at speeds well in excess of 200MPH and in all conditions likely to be met on the road. At the time we believed the car had considerable potential . . . and it failed to materialise only because the barrier impact test levels then being proposed presented substantial problems with regard to the location of the engine and the occupants, and secondly the marketing people decided that the main sales requirement was for a four-seat coupé. As a result, the far more practical but inevitably less visually exciting XJ-S design was evolved, one of the few features carried over being the treatment of the rear window and surrounding panelwork.

Motorsports were another key part of the XJ-S's renaissance: It took on BMW, Land Rover, and Volvo in European touring car races with some excellent results. This is the Brno Grand Prix in Czechoslovakia in 1983, where the big coupes finished 1-2-3.

These "flying buttresses" became the controversial hallmark of the XJ-S; nevertheless, they were a proven aid to stability and structural integrity. Sayer, a heavy smoker, died early in 1970 at the age of fifty-four, but the look of the XJ-S with its broad, low hood and oval headlights, remains a cathedral to his talents. It was more wind cheating than any E-type.

The XJ-S used an XJ6 floor pan shortened by 6 inches (15.2 centimeters), and the 5.3-liter V-12 from the XJ12, fuel injected by Lucas to a Bosch design for 285 bhp. Unveiled in 1975, it dismayed a few Jaguar sports car fanatics with its unashamed luxury and, for example, a Connolly leather-lined interior with no woodwork decor. It was also offered only as a coupe with air-conditioning as standard equipment, having been designed in an era when US legislators were threatening to make new open-top cars illegal on the grounds of occupant safety in the event of a rollover (a law never actually enacted). Potential buyers were startled and intrigued by this radical machine, and people who couldn't afford one were impressed at Jaguar's confident new direction. It was simply the company's great misfortune that the XJ-S arrived just as a terrible fuel squeeze gripped the global economy. This was a 15-mpg gas guzzler, even though its refinement was more impressive than that of the XJ12. Still, at £8,900, it comfortably undercut the V-8 Mercedes-Benz 450SLC at £11,271.

The XJ-S was very fast. With the short-lived four-speed manual gearbox, it could reach 153 miles per hour (246 kilometers per hour) and sprint 0–60 in 6.9 seconds. Even the automatic (the only option after 1979) had impressive corresponding figures of 146 miles per hour (235 kilometers per hour) and 7.5 seconds. In order to reduce emissions in the US market, however, engine modifications slapped down output to 244 bhp.

Poor demand and numerous quality and reliability problems meant that, when Egan took control of the Jaguar factory in 1980, XJ-S manufacture had all but ground to a halt. That year, little more than a thousand examples were built. Egan could have easily axed the failing XJ-S, despite its recent star turn in the *Return of the Saint* TV series and undoubted allure with the car-buying public. Instead he made the gung-ho decision to give it one last chance. The more fuel-efficient High Efficiency V-12 engine from the XJ12 was installed, while a mild revamp involved new alloy wheels, a pinstripe along the flanks, and some wood veneer in the cabin. The price for the resulting XJ-S HE was reduced to £19,187 and the car was again on its way. A combination of vastly increased quality, a possible 27 mpg if driven like a saint at a steady 56 miles per hour (90 kilometers per hour), and a patriotic, favorable reception from critics also made a big difference. People loved it and sales leapt to 3,111 in 1982.

Jaguar had a new six-cylinder engine on the stocks, the AJ6, an all-aluminum unit on which the company's power-unit guru Harry Mundy had been working since 1976. It was almost one-third lighter than the venerable XK it was intended to supplant. XJ-Ss had been used as mobile testbeds for it, piling on the miles around the West Midlands as it was thoroughly evaluated in advance of Jaguar's all-new saloon range scheduled for 1986. But in what had become a Coventry custom, it would reach the market first in a sports car, or at least a *sporty* car: the 221-bhp XJ-S 3.6 in 1983. It was paired with a Getrag five-speed manual gearbox, and there was also the option for open-air motoring at last. The XJ-SC cabriolet was a conversion of the existing bodyshell with a fixed roll cage, folding roof at the back, and lift-out roof panels above the

With enlarged engines and some deft visual uplifts from Jaguar styling chief Geoff Lawson, the XJ-S became the XJS in 1992 to keep the car fresh for a new decade. It was aging gracefully.

two seats (the rear ones making way for the folded canvas). It was a compromised design using outside contractors, but it was a first step back to convertible Jag enjoyment. A V-12 version, added in 1985, was then offered in North America, giving exasperated US dealers the convertible they'd wanted for years. In fact, Jaguar Cars North America Inc. became so desperate for a full convertible version that it commissioned Cincinnati, Ohio, coachbuilder Hess & Eisenhardt to open up new metal-topped cars. The first of 838 units was completed in 1986.

Jaguar's own full convertible, once again, needed external expertise to finesse, and the company called in German soft-top specialist Karmann, world renowned for its Volkswagen Beetle and Golf/Rabbit cabriolets, to tackle the design. The final car weighed only 100 pounds (45 kilograms) more than the XJ-S coupe despite all the hefty yet unseen body reinforcements, but the finished car, with an electrically operated, fully lined roof, finally looked super-glamorous for a life cruising along sun-kissed coastal roads. It also boasted the little-noticed innovation of a heated-glass rear screen incorporated into the fabric roof. To reinforce the upmarket image, the 146 mile-per-hour (235 kilometer-per-hour) car came only with the V-12 engine. Who could have guessed that, in 1989, the fifteen-year-old XJ-S would be more desirable than ever?

Another model that stoked desire was the 1988 XJR-S, essentially a standard V-12 car with a reasonably tasteful, body-colored body kit and new alloy wheels, created to cash in on Jaguar's victory at Le Mans that year. At first the engine was the same as the one used in normal editions, but the final products, offered with a 6-liter V-12 engine, were packing 333 bhp.

By 1992, a raft of changes had overhauled the big GT series that now lost its hyphen to become the XJS. Engines became a 4.0-liter 223-bhp AJ6 with five-speed manual or four-speed automatic transmission or a 6-liter 308-bhp V-12 auto. The man in charge of Jaguar's all-important styling department, Geoff Lawson, reshaped the car's side window surrounds and rear light clusters to refresh the original, and the cabin was comprehensively revised. The car was aging, though pretty gracefully, and with a few more annual modifications sales purred along until 1996. The car had become a classic in its own lifetime. The final tally was 115,413 cars sold, making it one of the marque's most perennially popular models ever, despite a decidedly checkered career.

These 4-liter "Celebration" editions of the XJ-S were unveiled in 1995—when the basic car was a full 20 years old—shortly before manufacture ended.

MOC 214P
MOC 208P
LOP 383P
JVC 481N
LOE 89P

Chapter Thirteen

WILDERNESS

A nadir in the 1970s:
Despite Lyons's carefully negotiated semi-independence for the company he'd built from scratch, it suffers hugely in the 1970s and through British Leyland's bankruptcy. The old hands retire and it is cast adrift.

This arresting photo, taken in 1976, illustrates the incredible diversity of vehicles made by British Leyland, which one year earlier had been rescued from insolvency by the British government. The front row shows the newest jewels in the troubled company's crown (left to right): Triumph TR7, Rover 3500, and Jaguar XJ-S, while an XJ6 is hemmed in at the center of the sixth row.

Jaguar worked around the clock to meet the enormous demand for its acclaimed XJ6—literally, since in February 1969 the Coventry plant introduced its first-ever night shift. Everything, from the most complex lathes in the machine shops to the simplest tea urns in the canteen, was running red hot. Even hiccups at suppliers couldn't interrupt the assembly of new cars; customers were so itching to get their hands on them that, when a minor industrial dispute in June at a firm making the diecast XJ6 grilles resulted in a halt in deliveries, Jaguar dispatched the cars with temporary wire mesh covers and a promise that the UK dealers would fit the parts later. All very courteous stuff.

Good omens: Lyons accepts a Car of the Year award in 1969 for his XJ6 from Car *magazine, which should have helped catapult the car to the top of the motoring tree in the 1970s, as waiting lists grew.*

When strikes started to prevent major components from reaching the production line, though, the effects were devastating. In July 1970, for example, a strike at Lucas Industries meant no cars could be built for nine days, and in January 1972, one hundred machinists at Jaguar's Radford plant put down their tools, resulting in another two-week standstill.

The strikes, big and small, both inside Jaguar and in its supply network, bedeviled production in the first years of the 1970s. The tense battle lines were drawn between workforce and management and, while there was certainly plenty of political agitation in the unions, many of the disputes were about the ironically named Industrial Relations Bill introduced by the new Conservative government, something to which Sir William Lyons, possibly unwisely, had lent his public support. Jaguar was simply a typical example of the contemporary malaise afflicting the whole of British manufacturing.

Production still rose, from 21,833 Jaguar XJs in 1970 to 27,517 a year later. Yet the often-stated intention of doubling production to 50,000 cars a year seemed to be constantly frustrated. A generous soul might have cut the exasperated Browns Lane assembly workers some slack. Many of them, working on the piecework system, could be laid off if there were insufficient parts to complete the cars, and working conditions in the cramped buildings were increasingly grim. Jaguar had long been driven by the priorities of design, engineering, and marketing, and while money was poured into these areas there was very little investment in the plant itself. The paint shop, for instance, hadn't been updated for over twenty years, and it didn't help that unpainted bodies,

The British Leyland stand at the May 1970 New York Auto Show at The Coliseum convention center (just ignore the distracting orange BMW in the foreground) drawing the crowds to admire the new XJ6, a lineup of E-types, and a selection of MGs drawn from the recently formed corporation's vast range.

A ghosted image of the Jaguar XJ 5.3C, the two-door derivative briefly offered between 1973 and 1975; the frameless windows should have made it a superior, pillar-less cruiser, yet instead they were hard to seal and just added another headache to Jaguar's 1970s malaise.

when they arrived from the Pressed Steel factory in Castle Bromwich, were blemished with rust. Buyers expecting a top-quality luxury car delivered on time shouldn't have had to suffer for their loyalty. A new low came in June 1972 when a ten-week strike across the whole company utterly crippled the supply of Jaguar XJ12s and Daimler Double Sixes just as their excited owners should have been receiving the first deliveries of these awe-inspiring new super-saloons.

Jaguar's old guard was changing. Company founder and driving force Lyons, now seventy-one, retired in March 1972 (his close ally William Heynes had already gone in 1969). Lofty England replaced him as chairman and chief executive. Around the same time, chief engineer Wally Hassan was pensioned off and replaced by Bob Knight, a board member since 1969 and a lifelong Jaguar stalwart.

The advent of the new Series II range of Jaguar XJ saloons in September 1973 should have been a joyous occasion, and plans were finally underway to expand the Browns Lane buildings to cope with global demand that, in some cases, was restricted by waiting lists that stretched into many months. Unfortunately, though, quality took a serious nosedive and the sixty-two-year old Lofty England seemed incapable of fixing things. That autumn, the British Leyland head office parachuted in thirty-four-year old Geoffrey Robinson—fresh from running carmaker Innocenti in Italy—to shake things up and, hopefully, boost morale. The sidelined England left shortly afterward. Robinson barely had time to replan the factory layout, though, much less cement his reputation as a turnaround guy, when on December 6, 1974, government minister Tony Benn announced the government was stepping in to guarantee British Leyland's capital. The gigantic company, Jaguar included, was effectively being nationalized and the British government now owned 99.8 percent of a business that was basically insolvent.

Due to a dizzying number of build-quality rejects and rectification work under warranty on shoddily built customers' cars, Jaguar was unviable in ways that differed from other parts of the fallen empire, such as Austin-Morris and Leyland Trucks. By March 1975, Robinson's plans to make a thousand cars a week were in tatters, and unsold XJs were stockpiled on windswept airfields nearby. The prevailing fuel crisis, of course, severely dampened demand for the thirsty V-12 cars. Production and jobs were cut, a new paint shop remained in abeyance, and Geoffrey Robinson himself was axed; he had strongly objected to Jaguar's total loss of independence as all the carmaking parts of the crisis-stricken business were rolled into one corporate entity: Leyland Cars.

This meant that 1975 was an inauspicious year for the new and exciting XJ-S to make its debut. The company was in the doldrums, and running it now fell to Bob Knight, the gifted engineer who had joined SS Cars in 1944 and created the chassis for the Mk V and C-type, disc brakes for racing and road cars, the independent suspension system on the E-type, and the exceptional road manners of the XJ6.

Dogged doesn't begin to describe Knight. The story is told of his completing the independent suspension system design in twenty-seven days to win a £5 bet from Lyons, who wagered that it couldn't be done in a month. He had begun work on the XJ6's successor, codenamed project XJ40, in 1972–1973, and was accustomed to operating on slender resources linked by short chains of command to produce engineering alchemy. Now Knight found himself virtually alone defending the Jaguar modus operandi. He was an unlikely streetfighter, but he now did everything in his power to resist the dilution of Jaguar's engineering base by Leyland Cars chief Derek Whittaker who, corporate hatchet in hand, sought to fold it into Rover or Triumph. Knight resolutely held Jaguar's independent nucleus together—its tight-knit engineering and design teams operating on absolute shoestrings—while British Leyland seemed hellbent on destroying the company's soul. History has proved him to be Jaguar's unsung hero—a chain-smoking procrastinator who drove colleagues crazy with his quest for perfection. Now, with work on XJ40 almost a spare-time indulgence, most of his energy went into, as one observer put it, "a protracted campaign of non-cooperation and stubborn refusal" in order to keep Browns Lane's sparse design and engineering facilities intact.

Under British Leyland, the place was reclassified in comical Soviet style as "Large Car Plant No 2." Knight, though, kept the increasingly ragged Jaguar Cars Ltd. flag flying. In 1976, a decision was made on the urgent paint shop issue, and it was not music to Knight's ears. Instead of replacing the facility at Browns Lane, the £15.5 million new paint shop would be relocated at the Castle Bromwich body plant. This former aircraft factory also produced the shells for the new Rover 3500 SD1 and had plenty of its own problems, both from a quality viewpoint and in labor disputes. For some time in the late 1970s, the only paint colors the plant could manage were red, white, and yellow, with no ability to produce any metallics. Quality issues were so troubling that the launch of the XJ Series III range had to be postponed for several months until standards improved. New thermoplastic paints chipped easily, and there was no "hospital facility" to fix paintwork issues, all of which had to be done in the decrepit old paint shop back at Browns Lane; it simply couldn't cope with the volume of faults and imperfections.

Meanwhile, the ill-starred Leyland Cars division of British Leyland was no more by 1978, and Jaguar was bound up with the corporation's two other upmarket brands to form the equally short-lived Jaguar-Rover-Triumph. Bob Knight, his skills newly recognized with a CBE honor, was now Jaguar's official managing director, tasked with steering his beloved company through another storm as the second energy crisis of the 1970s took its toll on sales in 1979–1980. A rare bright spot was that the Castle Bromwich body plant was to come under complete Jaguar control. Still, with everything stacked up against the firm, how could it possibly hope to survive, let alone thrive, into the 1980s?

There were some benefits to being part of British Leyland for Jaguar: This ride simulator was among various facilities developed by BL Technology at its Gaydon test center, here pounding the suspension on an XJ Series II to expose flaws.

Here is the XJ Series III in 1979, still looking great after eleven years; this model should have been the best yet, but Britain's industrial decline was taking its depressing toll on quality, as inadequate management went up against restive workers in decrepit factories.

Chapter Fourteen

INDEPENDENT SPIRIT

Revival, 1980s: John Egan arrives to save Jaguar in 1980, just in the nick of time. He steers it toward a stock market flotation and resurging fortunes in the important US market. The XJ40 of 1986 becomes his legacy in keeping Jaguar's great traditions alive.

The gorgeous XJ6 opened a new era for Jaguar, setting dazzling new standards for the compromise between ride comfort and roadholding, and replacing four outgoing models in one fell swoop.

JAGUAR

On the day in April 1980 that John Egan arrived at Jaguar Cars as its new chief executive, he found restive workers milling around the gates of the Browns Lane plant, pondering an all-out strike. Once inside, Egan came across Jaguar managing director Bob Knight, chain-smoking his way through another dismal day at the firm where he'd helped create the D-type, E-type, and XJ6. The dynamic new boss told Knight he needed him to shepherd the new XJ40 range into production while Egan turned the firm around. Knight promptly resigned.

"He was a very fine and meticulous engineer, but he was deeply pessimistic," said Egan. "He must have thought I was just another agent of the devil, like the others. The sales director Bob Berry buggered off too. Some of the old Jaguar people had been fighting this rearguard action for years. They just didn't think we'd make it. Bob had been forced to put up with all kinds of nonsense from his superiors. He was tired of fighting in Jaguar's corner."

Egan already had an excellent track record in the automotive industry with Unipart and then Massey Ferguson. For this new challenge, he'd only agreed to tackle Jaguar if the company was a totally separate entity from the rest of British Leyland. In July 1980, therefore, Jaguar-Rover-Triumph was summarily dissolved, Jaguar Cars Ltd. regained its independence, and Egan assumed his joint role of chairman and chief executive. The first move he had to oversee was brutal: the layoff of 1,600 employees, including 500 at Jaguar's Browns Lane site, where the Coventry paint shop closed and the work transferred to its Castle Bromwich body plant; the remainder were let go as a result of a dramatic slump in demand for luxury cars due to the prevailing recession. Voluntary resignations made up most, if not all, of the layoffs.

Much more positive was the formation, in September 1980, of a quality taskforce to grapple with the myriad problems that made modern Jaguars second rate when compared to their German rivals. It quickly turned into a crusade against the poor processes and inferior components that blighted the finished cars, and within two months seven of the twenty most pressing issues had been resolved. Egan immediately tackled matters at Castle Bromwich, vastly improving quality standards of the XJ bodies. Just making the windscreen and doors fit properly, he told the author, saved the company £20 million.

Reject rates were sometimes as high as 50 percent, which contributed to the cars' unreliability. To address this, Egan adopted a strategy used by Mercedes-Benz: a forensic approach to the quality of bought-in components, assessing a batch and imposing tough financial penalties on the supplier if there was a failure rate of more than 1.5 percent. By July 1981, 1,700 suppliers, including Lucas and Adwest, were being told to clean up their act or lose Jaguar's business altogether. The subsequent improvements were dramatic and immediate. As Egan recalled: "Everything was subject to quality and productivity improvements as we went along. People had to work smarter. We did it with the enthusiasm and support of the workforce. The shop stewards were telling [the workers]: 'You're crazy; follow us and we'll get you more money for doing less work.' We were saying: 'You've got to put some effort into it.' I wondered what people had been doing all these years. It was mystifying."

Egan would regularly pick a car off the production line and drive it home, returning the following morning and triggering an "action day" to fix an issue he'd discovered. "Quality circles" were formed involving every level of factory staff and problems were quickly and collectively ironed out. The company also worked with its suppliers to help them adjust. "The chief executive today won't need to concern himself with things like this," Egan said, "but I did then. It was me saying yes, we can do all this stuff." The XJ6 was prone to overheating. It had desperately needed an extra engine fan for years, and Egan ordered one fitted. "BL wouldn't allow it because it was losing so much money."

When I saw the Pininfarina-facelifted XJ6, I knew that car could sell … if we could just make it work. And the XJ-S! I presumed they were still building them, but they'd not made one for years. It had more problems than the XJ6, so even the unsold stock was pretty unsaleable. Other British-made cars had faults too, so Jaguar wasn't unique, just a lot worse. It would take a dealer half a day to make the cars saleable, with twenty or thirty faults to fix. And then he was going to get eighteen faults in the first year of warranty.

The man-hours needed to build an XJ6 fell from a virtually bespoke seven hundred to just three hundred. Jaguar made much of its quality and productivity gains, and sales started to pick up briskly, especially in

John Egan (center, with his management team) arrived at Jaguar in the nick of time in 1980 to save the marque from oblivion; in his first few years he made a hands-on drive for quality his main priority.

Germany and the US, and the firm began to take on more workers once again to work night shifts.

Another area where Jaguar started to show its renewed competitiveness was on the racetrack. Back in the late 1970s, the US team Group 44 had seen surprising success campaigning a much-modified XJ-S in Trans-Am racing. In 1978 Jaguar won the manufacturers' championship, having been runner-up the year before, and team principal Bob Tullius won the driver's championship in both years. Now Tom Walkinshaw Racing (TWR) in the UK was engaged to take the XJ-S racing again in the European Touring Car Championship, and it enjoyed a storming first season in 1982, with compelling wins in the round in Brno, Czechoslovakia and in the 24 Hours of Spa, and a one-two in the Tourist Trophy at Silverstone. More excellent results followed in 1983 and 1984, and Tom Walkinshaw scooped the drivers' championship in the XJ-S in the latter, too. Jaguar enjoyed five victories to BMW's six with its 635 CSi. The reliability and power of the 5.3-liter V-12 engine was amply demonstrated, adding a halo effect to XJ-S road car sales.

In 1984, though, the Jaguar name assumed a very high profile for a significantly different reason. The UK government had decided that Jaguar Cars would be the first part of the calamitous BL empire to be returned to the private sector, and it chose a public offering for shares in the same way it had been selling off many of the country's utilities. The allure of the Jaguar name was much easier for the public to grasp than a regional water board, and the level of interest was enormous. Once the last contractual links had been severed with BL in March 1984, the buildup to the high-profile sale began; despite doubts from the Labour opposition, applications for the 177,880,000 shares were 8.3 times oversubscribed. The shares began trading on the London Stock Exchange in early August 1984 at £1.65 each, which resulted in BL securing a much-needed cash windfall that valued Jaguar Cars PLC at a juicy £294 million. It immediately joined the FTSE Index as one of the UK's one hundred largest public companies. Within two years, the shares were worth £5.22 apiece, and some doubters claimed this meant the company had been sold off too cheaply. As its youngest product, though, the XJ-S, was nine years old at the time of privatization, and its factories were continually in need of urgent investment, the debate about Jaguar's true value involved a cacophony of factors and opinions.

One person who was said to be immensely proud at the company's newfound independence was Lyons himself. Although he had officially retired twelve years earlier to enjoy life at his imposing Wappenbury Hall mansion and breed Suffolk sheep and Jersey cattle on his farm in Devon, he had tenaciously retained his Jaguar links. "For a while, Grandpa was really quite depressed about what had happened to his company, and his health declined," recalled his grandson Michael Quinn.

He had seen the writing on the wall with the rise of Japan, and much improved American cars. Jaguar couldn't remain independent and they had to share costs.

He and Lofty [England] did manage to keep Jaguar separate for a while, sticking to the agreement Grandpa had with BMC's George Harriman that he would continue running Jaguar in an autocratic way as "his" business, not always following official policy. That relationship started to suffer when Leyland and Lord Stokes arrived. It must have been horrendous, really. Decisions started to be taken over his head, and he realized his position was untenable.

The darkest hour was before the dawn, and just as Jaguar seemed to be in terminal decline, John Egan arrived. One of the first things he did was contact Lyons. "Egan got him on the phone and said, 'We'd love to have you back as honorary president,'" recalled Michael Quinn. "Grandpa said, 'Very kind of you but, actually, I already am.' Egan was absolutely shocked that,

Under Egan, Jaguar was able to take full control of the Castle Bromwich body plant—where this Series III is being painted—and once it did, standards of finish were quickly raised.

Early 1980s Jaguars took a quantum leap in customer satisfaction, especially in the key US market, and wealthy buyers flocked back to enjoy the characterful ownership experience with most of the heartache removed!

Several cost-effective partnerships with outsiders enabled Jaguar to reestablish itself in the 1980s, including entrusting Tom Walkinshaw Racing with running the XJS HE campaign; here the car is holding off BMW and Rover rivals from its lead in the Donington 500 European Touring Car race in 1982.

despite that, he'd been ignored for five years, although [Jaguar styling chief] Keith Helfet told me Grandpa had been sneaking into Browns Lane almost weekly. He could never totally let go."

For the five years until his death at eighty-three on February 8, 1985, Sir William reveled in seeing Jaguar Cars Ltd. reformed and supporting its new management.

"He was very, very happy that the thing was beginning to look as though it was going to survive," Egan told the author. "He was a joy to work with. I could puzzle things out with Bill. I had a very rough relationship with the rest of BL, so it was nice to have someone like that who wasn't trying to kick me in the balls all the time!"

There was, of course, a tremendous amount to do to get Jaguar's all-new saloon car range into production. Can there be an individual model anywhere that ever had such a long gestation period? Design work began in earnest in 1972 on "XJ40" but was soon sidelined when British Leyland and Lord Stokes decided Jaguar could manage without a new car for a good long while. Chief engineer Bob Knight had then tersely refused the "opportunity" to install the Rover V-8 engine in his XJ40 (British Leyland top brass were told it simply would not fit in the engine compartment, and no outsider ever asked to check). Finally, in late summer 1980, the go-ahead on the XJ40 project was sanctioned once again, and eighteen months later a running prototype was taking its first tentative steps on the road, thanks to an agreed £80 million development budget.

The styling had been a worrying eight years in deliberation, during which time proposals from Italy's Pininfarina had been commissioned and rejected, and any radical ideas about the vital new car's final form had been put aside in favor of a

The V-12–engined XJ-SC joined the range in 1985, helping broaden the appeal in particular as an alternative to the Mercedes-Benz 500SL. Careful final checks are made to a car as it nears the end of the assembly process at Browns Lane.

The rejuvenated and expanded 1985 Jaguar range photographed at Lyons's home at Wappenbury Hall, Leamington Spa, in 1985.

John Egan and Sir William Lyons established a great bond in the five years before the company founder's passing in 1985. "He was a joy to work with," said Egan. "I could puzzle things out with Bill."

The abandoned Chrysler UK/Talbot design studios at Whitley were transformed into Jaguar's much-needed new design and engineering center, which opened in 1988.

Another masterpiece begins: designers sculpting the full-size model of a future Jaguar inside the design studios at Whitley, Coventry. All kinds of cars had been created at the site, from the Chrysler Alpine and Dodge Omni to initial designs for the Renault Espace.

Any revolutionary thoughts were set aside during the painfully long genesis of the XJ40, as a cautious update of the XJ6 was deemed right for Jaguar's established clientele.

cautious evolution calculated to appeal strongly to the existing Jaguar sales demographic. It was crucial, indeed, to preserve that Jaguar look as sales of the aging XJ6/12 were snowballing year on year. John Egan was so keen to extract all the sales and goodwill he could from their success that the XJ40 launch date was bumped forward yet again, now scheduled for 1986.

Design and development of the AJ6 straight six, successor to the evergreen XK, had been initiated by longtime (but now retired) engine expert Harry Mundy, and the all-aluminum power unit was brought into production under the eyes of Jaguar engineering director Jim Randle and power-units chief Trevor Crisp. Some felt, perhaps, that it was not a new paragon of refinement, but it was gutsy and robust; for the three years leading up to the XJ40's debut, it had given pretty good service in the XJ-S.

For the new saloon range there would be a smaller, 12-valve, single-overhead-camshaft 165-bhp 2.9-liter version alongside the 24-valve, double-overhead-camshaft 225-bhp 3.6-liter AJ6. In a series of prototypes, examples of these engines covered more than 5.5 million miles (8.9 million kilometers) of testing in all weather. But there was no place in the new range for a V-12, for which sales in the existing XJ12 were very slack. Transmission choices were a ZF four-speed automatic or a Getrag five-speed manual.

The new car received its public unveiling at the 1986 British Motor Show at Birmingham's National Exhibition Centre to an especially rousing reception. The entry-level XJ6 model came with cloth upholstery and lacked air-conditioning, alloy wheels, and antilock brakes so that it could furnish a basic Jaguar at £16,945, slightly less than a top-of-the-range Rover Sterling. The Sovereign trim option then offered most of the true opulence expected on a luxury Jag, plus more modern-looking rectangular headlights that, nonetheless, set many Jaguar fans grumbling at the disharmonious chasing of automotive fashions. The most expensive of the XJ40 variants available was the Daimler 3.6-liter, at £28,495. Sales in 1987 and 1988 pulled ahead encouragingly, up to 39,432 in the latter year. Positivity seemed to gush from the creaking gates of Browns Lane along with all the XJ6s, alongside a few of the old-style XJ12/Daimler Double Six cars that were still being built.

The media gave the new range rave reviews, with the usual applause for the uncanny refinement in ride comfort and sticky roadholding they offered, and much approval for an interior that now epitomized "traditional British" with its walnut or rosewood dashboard and trim and cosseting leather upholstery.

JaguarSport was a joint venture with TWR aimed at bringing some of the excitement of the 1988 XJR-9 Le Mans win to the road car range, by way of sharpened handling and body-styling kits.

Early examples of the XJ40 featured digital instruments; as they displeased owners and proved somewhat less than reliable, after four years they were replaced by these traditional analog dials.

This is *Autocar* in October 1986 on the £18,495 XJ6 3.6-liter: "Arguably the most important launch of 1986, the new XJ6 may not look significantly different from its predecessor. Don't be fooled: it's a completely new car from the ground up with a nearly magical ride and handling compromise."

Shortly afterward, the hard-driving boss was ennobled as Sir John Egan. In the real world of actual ownership, though, the early years of XJ40 were unhappy ones. The antediluvian nature of the Coventry assembly line, which some sources state used mostly secondhand equipment that Jaguar had installed in the early 1950s, plus the cocktail of new parts, brought unwelcome gremlins surging back. There were issues with several mechanical components, but most frustrating for the customer were mystifying electronic maladies often associated with the car's gimmicky digital instruments. It soon got around the car trade that the XJ40, impressive though it appeared, was more of an unpredictable dog than a sleek big cat.

Annual production fell back dramatically to 32,833 in 1989 as a new wave of crisis management took hold. Even more ominous for Jaguar was the arrival that year of Toyota's exceptional super-saloon, the Lexus LS400 (it too had a digital dashboard—one that functioned perfectly). By 1990, seeking to buff up its tarnished reputation, the XJ6 fought back. The engines were uprated from 2.9-liter to 3.2-liter and 3.6-liter to 4.0-liter to boost power and torque while keeping abreast of tougher catalytic converter standards demanded by US emissions rules. There was now no Jaguar or Daimler in the range offering less than 200 bhp; on top of that, the substitution of analog instruments in the dashboard brought a much-needed return of dependability. Relentlessly upbeat public relations did an assured job of distracting attention away from the company's internal struggles and, with the share price buoyed by the good news, profits were plowed back into the business.

The company had been able to pick up the abandoned Talbot design studio complex in Whitley, Coventry, for a song, and then spent £52 million turning it into a brand-new product engineering center that opened in May 1988, into which Jaguar's expanded ranks of designers and engineers were relieved to decamp from the poky and decrepit facilities at Browns Lane.

As the 1980s came to a close, though, Jaguar was in many ways back at square one, where it gasped for life at the start of that decade. The company offered cars with a unique character and great potential, produced in facilities that were far behind the times. It was perpetually short on investment capital, and once again facing a severe economic downturn. Another chapter ends on a strangely familiar cliffhanger ...

A Jaguar XJ40 body is installed in the roof assembly jig at Castle Bromwich in 1986 as the structure of the car takes shape.

In the end the XJ40—this is an XJ6 Sovereign—became a good car that worked very well, but the teething troubles weighed heavily on Jaguar's progress after its star-spangled debut on the London Stock Exchange.

Rectangular headlights might have been deemed the height of modernity when the XJ40 was first considered—back in the mid-1970s—but many marque aficionados thought they were ill suited to the car when it was finally launched; this is a 1992 4.0.

PEBBLE BEACH
02-06
Tour d'Elegance

Chapter Fifteen

JAGUARS AND OUTSIDERS

Jags and not Jags: Jaguars had been interpreted and modified by outside designers, with mixed results. Group 44 and TWR partner it back to racing dominance, and external collaboration make the astounding XJ220 a reality. Classic Jaguars are flattered by imitation and cherished by owners, reinforcing their iconic status.

Trying to design an XK120 better than the Jaguar original was always a tall order, but as there was no GT model in the range, Pininfarina had a go in 1954 with this one-off, allegedly built for New York dealer Max Hoffman.

Jaguar was born with the principle of improving the products of others with a keen eye for style, proportion, and image. The early SS cars were striking, coachbuilt enhancements of existing vehicles with an individuality all their own, while the 1935 SS Jaguar saloon had aimed to become a rather blatant "budget Bentley." Of course, as long as a car had a separate chassis frame, replacing the bodywork was always going to be a matter of nuts, bolts, and imagination. Yet it was a brave designer who tried to beat Sir William Lyons at his own accomplished game. Before World War II, a few dozen SS cars had been delivered in bare-chassis form to outside coachbuilders—especially in Switzerland—to receive mostly four-seater drop-head coupe bodywork. It seems the Swiss firm of Beutler was the first to give an XK120 its individual treatment. As a rather heavy-looking two-seater cabriolet, it was certainly striking but no competition for the standard roadster.

In Italy, Stabilimenti Farina was the first to body a Jaguar XK120 (and two Mk VIIs), in this instance filling the specific order from a Jaguar dealer in Belgium in 1951. But the first Italian Jaguar to truly make an impact was the XK120 Supersonic from Carrozzeria Ghia in 1954, a gleaming red exhibit at the 1954 London Motor Show where its rocket-influenced form, fastback roof, and jet-age tailfins really drew the crowds. Six months later, Pininfarina's racy rendition of an XK120 SE, allegedly built at the request of New York Jaguar distributor Max Hoffman, similarly showed where the future direction for a more modern gran turismo Jaguar might lie. Although neither car went into production, both have survived in glorious restored order to show what might have been.

This is the 1954 Ghia Supersonic, a radical Italian interpretation of an ultramodern Jaguar XK120 GT; rear end styling around the lights and tail-fins drew on imagery of the unfolding era of jet-fighter aircraft.

The wildly futuristic XK140 created by industrial design legend Raymond Loewy; it spent a year being driven around Paris before going to the US, where it was briefly owned, as here, by boxing champ Archie Moore, who'd paid £25,000 for it. At the end of 1957 it was destroyed in a fire.

American industrial design guru Raymond Loewy was obsessed with cars and designed his own radical wedge-shaped coupe using an XK140 as its basis. He had it built by Boano Lavorazioni in Turin and drove it around Paris in 1955 to slack jaws everywhere. Shocking in its pointy, avant-garde lines, some of its themes fed into Loewy's later work on the Studebaker Avanti. There were other XK140s and 150s, too, from renowned Italian designers such as Bertone, Zagato, and Allemano. One of them, Giovanni Michelotti, even turned a Jaguar D-type into a low and broad road-going GT. However, with the arrival of the E-type and Mk X in 1961, Jaguars ceased to have separate chassis, and set a design pace that even the Italians struggled to match. Whenever a designer in Turin tried his hand at modifying an E-type, as Pietro Frua did in 1966, few liked the result.

Jaguar didn't offer a wagon, or "estate car," until 2002, when the company was eighty years old. Long before that, though, people thought they should. Acclaimed Jaguar racing drivers Mike Hawthorn and Duncan Hamilton came up with a scheme for a sporty Mk 2 estate in 1958 and worked with motoring artist Roy Nockolds on the design. They simply could not persuade Lyons that there would be a market for it, and the nascent venture lost impetus after Hawthorn's death. A single prototype *was* built, however, with a 3.8-liter engine, and was often used by the Coventry factory to carry backup parts to race meetings in Europe.

Another designer, Tony Stevens, created a commodious estate version of the XJ Series III in 1980, and, although a few cars were converted, it was far too ugly to be a Jaguar original: the need to accommodate the twin gas tanks meant the filler caps were mounted halfway up the rear roof pillars, although there was no disputing the practicality of the lift-up tailgate and folding back seats. Only when Lynx Engineering came up with its sporty and beautifully proportioned Eventer three-door sports estate version of the XJS in 1982 did an outside specialist get it right, though fewer than one hundred expensively handmade units were sold.

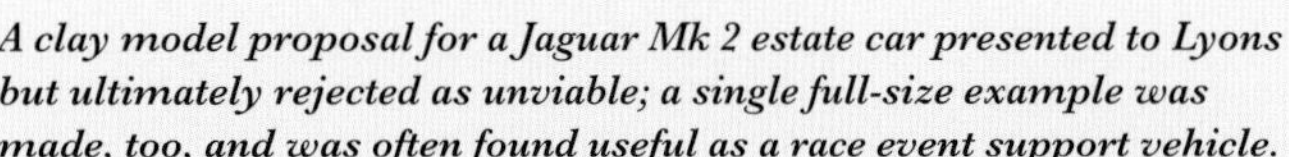

A clay model proposal for a Jaguar Mk 2 estate car presented to Lyons but ultimately rejected as unviable; a single full-size example was made, too, and was often found useful as a race event support vehicle.

Perhaps this estate car conversion by Ladbroke Avon of the Series III XJ6 in 1980 amply justifies Jaguar's dislike of the genre. It was the design work of Tony Stevens. Clearly, there was a great deal of luggage room, but elegance took a back seat.

In the mid-1960s, Jaguar's resolutely curvaceous styling was looking a little old-fashioned, and Italian design house Bertone tried three times to interest the company in its immense contemporary design skills, each sharp-edged car stepping ever further away from the traditional Jag look. First came the S-type-based FT two-door sports saloon in 1966, and then a year later *The Daily Telegraph* commissioned the Pirana as a modern rendering of the E-type. Jaguar treated it with disdain, but the car inspired the Lamborghini Espada. Finally, in 1977, Bertone revealed its ultra-wedge-shaped Ascot show car based on the XJS. As with the F-Type, this left Jaguar HQ unmoved.

Mention of the Espada brings to mind another Jaguar-based car: the 1973 Owen Sedanca. Offered at £8,600 by London's H. R. Owen dealer chain and penned by designer Chris Humberstone, the Sedanca aimed to provide a bespoke super-luxury GT car with four full seats inside its aluminum bodyshell, which was built up using a standard XJ6 floorpan and scuttle structure.

One station wagon–type rethink of a Jaguar really did work stylistically: the XJS-based Lynx Eventer of 1982. The proud owner here is the former leader of the British political party the Liberal Democrats, David (later Lord) Steel.

Italian design house Bertone seemed hell-bent on snaring Jaguar as a client. This is the S-type 3.8 FT of 1966, a two-door, four-seater reinterpretation of Coventry's big-selling saloon in typically crisp contemporary European style.

The Pirana was an E-type, ultra-modernized by Bertone for a **Daily Telegraph** *display at the London Motor Show in 1967, where it caused a huge stir. A development of the design reappeared later as the Lamborghini Espada.*

Dozens of orders fizzled out, leaving just three units built in the teeth of the sudden global energy crisis.

Notwithstanding the economic challenges, the early 1970s saw the passion for desirable vintage and classic cars rising everywhere, and historic Jaguars such as the SS 100 and D-type started to change hands among collectors, connoisseurs, auctioneers, and dealers for increasingly substantial sums. These cars, together with the XK120, are some of the foundation stones of the entire classic car movement, and it was the richness of the Jaguar story that gave them their mystique. That and the undimmed thrills of driving them on roads that were faster and smoother than when the cars were new.

Old cars, though, require heavy maintenance and skilled handling. What if one could have all the low-to-the-ground, open-topped fun of an SS 100 with none of the drawbacks of the engine, gearbox, brakes, and steering in a forty-year-old relic? It was this concept that persuaded former clothing manufacturer Robert Jankel to turn carmaker in 1972 with his Panther J72, a newly built evocation of the vintage original but with Jaguar's latest 4.2-liter straight six XK or 5.3-liter V-12 under its long, hand-beaten hood. The J72 "replicar" proved a surprise hit, and Jankel quickly followed it with his Deville, also using Jaguar power in a showily opulent re-creation of a 1930s Bugatti-type limousine. It certainly had its fans, rock star Elton John and hell-raising actor Oliver Reed among them.

Many old 1950s Jaguar C- and D-types were brought out of retirement and onto the grids of the growing historic racing scene in the 1970s. There were, obviously, only a limited number of vehicles to go around, and in 1973 engineer Bryan Wingfield decided to build a replica, which he named the Dee-Type, as faithful in every detail as he could make it. The body was lovingly re-created in aluminum and the XK engine was still being made, so using one for authenticity was easy. The Dee-Type was unveiled in 1975 and would be the first of many replicas; some were amateurish, but others, such as those built by Lynx Engineering, were all but indistinguishable from the originals. They also kept time-honored panel-beating skills going in what became a lucrative cottage industry. Any suspected fakery among what then purported to be the genuine article would only add to the need to establish provenance in genuine cars that, today, could be valued in the tens of millions of pounds.

Aston Martin Lagonda designer William Towns twice tried to work his magic on Jaguars. The owner of a Yorkshire engineering business sponsored the first one, the Guyson E12, in 1974. It was a dramatic rebody of an E-type Series III V-12 in the wedge-shaped idiom of the time. In 1989, he took the XJS convertible and went in the opposite direction for the Railton Fairmile and Claremont, rebodying the cars with svelte aerodynamic coachwork, including faired-in rear

The 1970s "wedge" trend seemed to leave Jaguar, and its XJS, completely untouched, but Bertone redid the big Jag coupe in that idiom anyway for this show car in 1977, dubbing it the Ascot.

This is the 1973 Owen Sedanca, a British attempt at a large four-seater luxury GT that was hand-built around a Jaguar XJ12 mechanical package and inner structure. It was poised for great success when a tough fuel crisis broke out, and almost all orders were cancelled.

wheels, that utterly transformed the aging original. In both cases, just a pair of cars were made.

The 1980s would see myriad customizing and tuning companies use Jaguars as a basis for their craft. The XJS, for example, was subjected to a 10-inch (25-centimeter) wheelbase stretch and a sharply truncated roofline by Glenfrome of Bristol in 1990 to create a version of the car that could seat four adults in proper comfort. Lister in the UK and Arden in Germany coaxed huge power outputs from the cars' V-12 engines and fitted super-wide tires covered by flared-out, boy-racer-style bodywork extensions. They fed a limited demand for a Jaguar that was almost certain to be pulled over by the police, if only so they could marvel at the hot rod makeover.

Stretch limousine conversions of the XJ6/12 ranged from the harmonious Guy Salmon Twenty-Six, which Lyons might have quietly approved of, to the top-heavy Melbros that definitely would have made him frown. Then, after the Daimler DS420 limousine itself was finally retired in 1992 after twenty-four years, both old-style XJs and the newer XJ40 saloons became default starting points when motoring formality was essential, as for extended limousines and hearses—all a world away from Silverstone, Laguna Seca, or Le Mans.

When, in October 1956, Lyons said that the official Jaguar works racing team would cease to exist, citing the "heavy burden on the technical and research branch of the Engineering division," it was a glum day for all concerned. Yet the name was destined to remain in top-class sports car racing for years to come, partly due to the efforts of privateers who had their own Jaguar D-types, and partly due to fairly obscure independent constructor Brian Lister, based in Cambridge. Operating from his family ironworks company, he'd been providing

Vintage cars were getting fashionable by the 1970s, but owning and driving one was strictly for devotees. Panther guessed astutely that people yearned for an SS 100 but wanted modern comfort and reliability, which is what the handmade J72 offered.

Jaguar D-type replica by Lynx Engineering, mid-1980s. There simply weren't enough of the originals to go around among fans of the Le Mans–wining icon, so these faithfully recreated copies fulfilled a need.

wealthy amateurs with efficient and fast single-seaters and sports-racing cars for several years. Now, thanks to sponsor Shell-Mex, which was keen to be involved with a successful British car, he was brought together with Jaguar, which agreed to supply the engines and transmissions for a new machine.

The product of this partnership was the Lister-Jaguar, nicknamed the "Knobbly" for the curved appendages of the slim body that covered its wheels.

With its own special tubular chassis frame, the Lister-Jaguar made its debut in February 1958. It was unfeasibly quick, able to accelerate from rest to 100 miles per hour (161 kilometers per hour) in 11.2 seconds. Driven by the disabled racer Archie Scott-Brown, it immediately won the 1957 British Empire Trophy race before a slew of other excellent showings. It wasn't strictly a Jaguar, but the fire

Known for his work with Aston Martin, independent designer William Towns brought the E-type up to date for Yorkshire engineering company Guyson. This rendering led to two examples being made, one of which Guyson still owns.

The Railton Fairmile of the late 1980s was another William Towns project, one that gave a sleek new identity to the by-then venerable XJS with a new set of body panels.

The Glenfrome company of Bristol had a go at stretching the XJS into a full four-seater by putting 10 inches into its wheelbase and squaring up the cabin for comfortable rear headroom for this one-off—offering pragmatic answers to questions that hardly anybody had asked.

The resurrected Lister marque in the 1980s stood for extensively modified Jaguar XJ-S cars with widened bodywork, fatter tires, wind-cheating details, and boosted horsepower. This Le Mans model was at the more extreme end of what it offered.

in its belly came straight from the D-type, ensuring its position in the marque's fantastically rich and diverse motorsport heritage.

For many years afterward, Jaguar's racing honors were upheld by individuals outside the company. The highest-profile name throughout the 1970s had been American Bob Tullius who, with his team Group 44, campaigned first the E-type V-12 and then the XJS in US sports car events with some very tidy results as they beat Porsches and Corvettes. As a result, the Coventry factory gave its approval in late 1982 for Tullius to build his own sports car around a Jaguar V-12 drivetrain to contest International Motor Sport Association sports car races in North America. In spirit it was somewhat akin to a revival of the late lamented XJ13 in that the engine was midmounted, but it was installed as a stressed member of the chassis, supporting the rear suspension, in an aluminum honeycomb monocoque structure. This XJR-5 (XJR-4 had been Tullius's heavily modified XJS) adopted Group 44's striking green-on-white livery and finished third in its race debut at Road Atlanta in 1982. A year later, the car won the same event. In 1984 it went to the 24 Hours of Le Mans, dropping out with transmission failure, but was back the following year, winning its class and coming in thirteenth overall in a credible finish.

These successes, together with the XJS's powerful showing in European Touring Car races, reawakened Jaguar's belief in motor racing as a way to top its image with a competitive halo. There was, however, no way the company could join the grid on its own; instead, it called in Tom Walkinshaw Racing to design a state-of-the-art sports-racing car and then turn it into a winner. It was never going to be easy beating Porsche at its game, but genius race engineer Tony Southgate began design work on the XJR-6 with that in mind. Meanwhile, Group 44's revamped

Since the demise of the Daimler DS420 limousine in 1992, standard Jaguar saloons have been subject to numerous stretch-limo attempts. This one, called the Twenty-Six after the number of extra inches cut into its middle, was marketed by long-established Jaguar dealer Guy Salmon.

XJR-7 was doing consistently sterling work on the tracks, chalking up a string of second and fourth places in 1986.

The Southgate-TWR car, renamed XJR-8, came into its own in 1987, winning eight of the ten World Sports Car Championship fixtures to clinch the series title, but even with bodywork tweaked specially for the rigors of Le Mans, the cars failed to complete the race. The Championship itself would come Jaguar's way again, though.

And it was not long in coming. In 1988, when the new XJR-9 LM driven by Jan Lammers, Andy Wallace, and Johnny Dumfries added a sixth Le Mans victory to Jaguar's trophy cabinet, and again claimed the championship title. In 1990, the successor XJR-12 plus Lammers, Wallace, and Davy Jones scored a superb one-two in Florida's Daytona 24 Hours, and then the car enjoyed another fine one-two at Le Mans. John Nielsen, Price Cobb, and Martin Brundle won, and the Lammers/Wallace/Franz Konrad car came second. With 730 bhp from a 7-liter version of the V-12 engine, and hitting the scales at 900 kilograms (1,984 pounds), the power-to-weight ratio was incredible, and the two cars beat off a ferociously competitive field, including nineteen Porsches and seven Nissans. The average speed throughout the whole race for the victorious car was more than 126 miles per hour (203 kilometers per hour), and at one point it hit 219 miles per hour (352 kilometers per hour).

There was a second place in the World Sports Prototype Championship that year, but the new XJR-14 (now with a Ford-Cosworth V-8 in place of the V-12) took the whole thing again for Jaguar in 1991, after which point the marque's renewed racing era started to wind down. Le Mans

American team Group 44, headed by the enthusiastic and talented Bob Tullius, brought an XJ13-style car to life on a shoestring with its XJR-5, which proved highly competitive from its very first IMSA race in 1982.

The Jaguar XJR-9 on its way to winning the 24 Hours of Le Mans in 1988, the driving shared by Jan Lammers, Andy Wallace, and Johnny Dumfries; that made it Jaguar's sixth victory there.

Stirling Moss in a Lister Jaguar "Knobbly" at Silverstone in 1958; Brian Lister's phenomenally fast cars kept the Jaguar flag flying in international sports car racing for years after the factory officially quit motorsports.

The Jaguar XJR-6 was designed in the UK by TWR and Tony Southgate, and was the first step in reestablishing factory-backed racing in the mid-1980s. Surely close to a high point for tobacco advertising in sport as well.

went to a rotary-powered Mazda, but XJR-14s were second, third, and fourth.

The notion of a "concept car"—a nonrunning showstopper intended to pull in big crowds at motor shows, to hawk for media exposure, and to generally give the impression that a carmaker is forward looking and imaginative—had never held much appeal for Jaguar. It had tended to display exciting, irresistible cars and actually put them in customers' hands shortly afterward, avoiding vague pledges about future dates. For the revitalized company in the 1980s, however, it was crucial to keep testing boundaries, and engineering director Jim Randle nursed a secret desire to return to the time when Jaguar could create high-tech sports cars in-house that were eminently raceworthy but could also be savored on the road. It was Christmas 1987 and, while Jaguar's currency was rising on the world's race circuits, the XJR series hosted pure, raw racers that few members of the public would ever get close to, let alone drive. Randle made some sketches and basic models of what he wanted and, to tap into the gray matter of twelve of his like-minded colleagues—and because there was no budget—he set up The Saturday Club to build something special in their spare time. Jaguar suppliers were invited to contribute too.

Once the ambitious scope of the new car got noticed internally, things suddenly gathered momentum when it was realized that here was something as sensational as anything Ferrari or Lamborghini could conjure. It manifested itself as an aerodynamic two-seater with a midmounted 48-valve, 6.2-liter Jaguar V-12 engine and drive to all four wheels via a special 4x4 transmission system from FF Developments. Jaguar decided the car would be the centerpiece of its exhibit at the 1988 British Motor Show at Birmingham's National Exhibition Centre, and the rush to prepare XJ220 (named in honor of its notional top speed) was so intense that Randle's crew were still putting the finishing touches on it a matter of hours before the unveiling.

The reception was rather more than rapturous. The XJ220 was the star of the show, easily outshining Aston Martin's new Virage. A production model had never been seriously contemplated, but in December 1989, the company boldly decided to offer the car for sale to the public, announcing a £290,000 price tag in January 1990 for one of the limited run of 350 examples. Jaguar had perhaps been guided by the frenzy for other exciting, limited-production supercars such as the Ferrari F40 and Porsche 959, for which a clamor in the heady days of the late 1980s created huge demand, with people willing to pay well over the astronomical list prices to bag one. Some 1,400 potential XJ220 buyers frantically waved their £50,000 deposit checks.

So far, so exciting. But then came the considerable problems of transforming an untried show vehicle into a road car that had to match up to its promises. Jaguar turned once again to its entrepreneur-partner Tom Walkinshaw for help. Through an existing joint venture, his TWR had already devised and built a range of uprated JaguarSport versions of the XJS and XJ6 for the public, but the XJ220 was something else entirely. Everything apart from the basic V-12 engine would need to be designed, tested, and manufactured specially for it. Even the motor itself would be challenging because its considerable age would require much attention to get it to meet ever more stringent emissions rules.

In fact, the engine itself was quickly jettisoned and in its place TWR installed a 3.5-liter V-6 that had originally been created for the MG Metro 6R4 rally car and used more recently in the Jaguar XJR-10 and XJR-11 race cars. With twin turbochargers there was much more engine power (542 bhp) and torque (475 lb-ft) than the concept, and its far more compact dimensions meant the XJ220's wheelbase could be shortened by 7.9 inches (20 centimeters), thus trimming its weight significantly. The chances

The Jaguar team of XJR-9s pleasing the crowds at Le Mans in 1988; the marque's success finally interrupted a seven-year unbroken run of wins for Porsche.

The XJR-14 took the World Sports Car Championship for Jaguar in 1991, although by that time the firm's V-12 engine had been replaced by a Cosworth V-8.

Mid-engined XJR-15 gave super-wealthy sportsmen the opportunity to drive a limited-production Le Mans–style sports car in a dedicated race series; this JaguarSport project was a TWR brainwave, at arm's length from the Coventry factory.

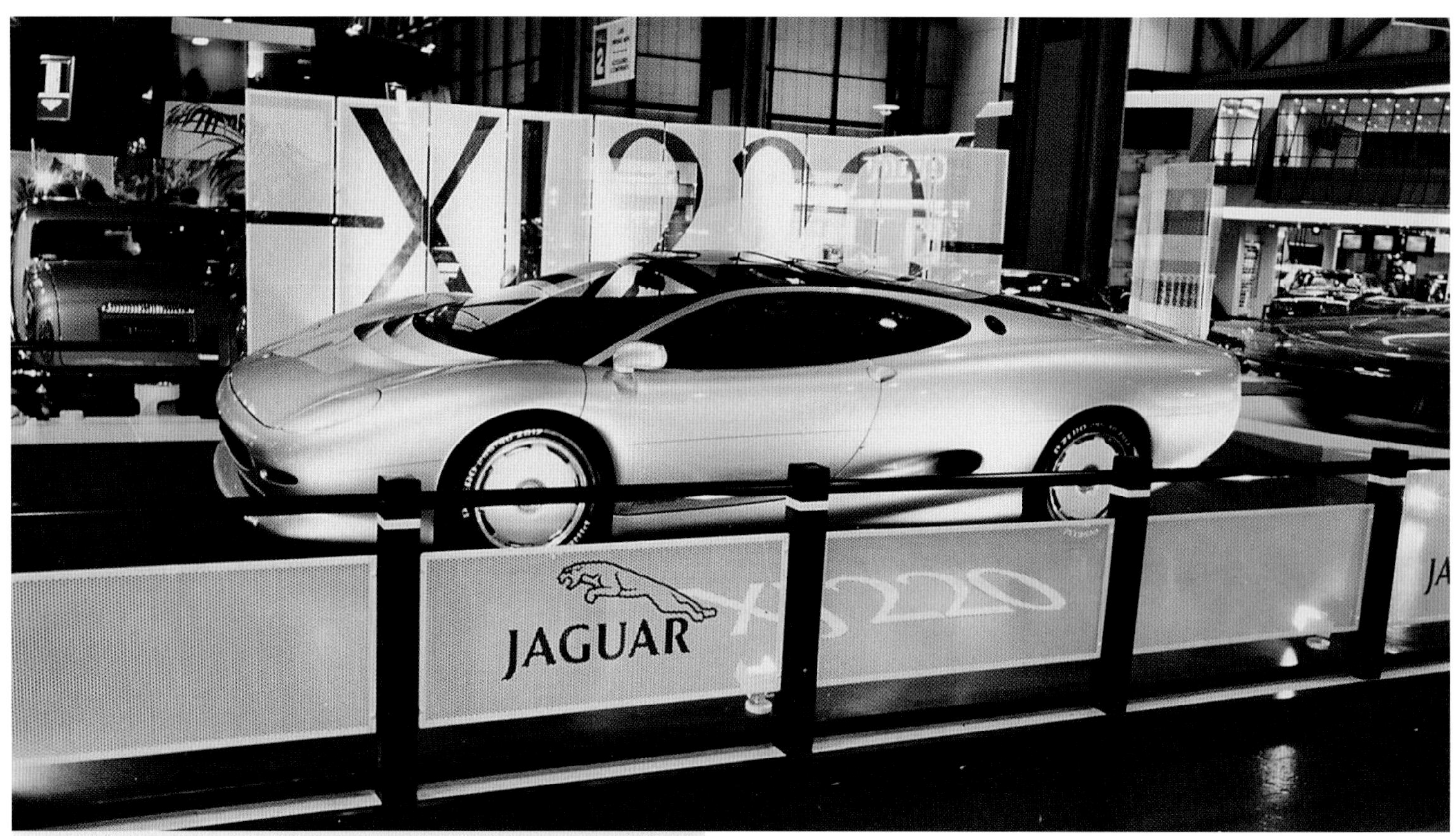

Taking the 1988 British Motor Show at Birmingham's National Exhibition Centre by storm, the XJ220 show car was bursting with high-tech thinking, including a four-wheel-drive transmission system.

of making the complex four-wheel-drive system function properly looked too risky, so the production car was rear-wheel-drive only like all other Jaguars. Finally, although the show machine had featured Lamborghini-style scissor-type doors, conventionally hinged ones were used for production, which was to take place in a dedicated TWR factory at Bloxham, Oxfordshire.

Jaguar's Le Mans hero Martin Brundle powered the eventual XJ220 into the record books as the fastest production car on the planet in March 1992 at the Nardò circuit in Italy, and its 217 mile-per-hour (349 kilometer-per-hour) top speed ensured its hold on that particular crown for five years. Not quite 220 miles per hour (354 kilometers per hour), yet still sensational. *Autocar & Motor* backed this up with an independent 213 miles per hour (343kilometers per hour) in its road test, and were in vocal reverence of every aspect of this incredible car, not least its savagely animalistic acceleration. The XJ220's place as an all-time great was assured.

The car's rosy future evaporated within a few short years, and the passage of time between the 1988 debut and the first deliveries in 1991 proved disastrous. Jaguar had shrewdly index linked the purchase contracts, and this had led to the asking price spiralling to £403,000—a rise of more than £100,000. That still might have been okay, but the euphoria around costly supercars had dissipated with the economic crash that occurred in this period. Other people who had ordered the cars were irate that half the cylinders, drive to two of the wheels, and a genuine Jaguar engine were all absent! Many buyers, particularly if they'd had speculation on their minds when they reserved theirs, now did everything they could to wriggle out of their orders. Production was abruptly curtailed after 281 cars; some of those remained unsold and the final one was not disposed of, it's said, until 1997, at just £127,500.

With a trio of specially prepared XJ220C cars, Jaguar was back at Le Mans in 1993, contesting a new Grand Touring class, which it might have won had the car not been disqualified on a technicality. Meanwhile, TWR also built a parallel small run of XJR-15 cars that were, in fact, tamed and restyled versions of the XJR-9 Le Mans winner. With a price tag of £500,000, the XJR-15 was the first road car with a chassis and body made from a carbon-fiber and Kevlar composite. Along with the cars themselves was a specific one-make race series—three races supporting Formula 1 Grands Prix at Monaco, Silverstone, and Spa-Francorchamps—to be pitted against each other; as they featured Jaguar V-12 engines, many of the marque's super-wealthy devotees approved, albeit the Coventry factory held this venture very much at arm's length.

Jaguar lost plenty of money on the controversial XJ220 at a time, perhaps, when it could least afford to. Jaguar also learned some valuable lessons about hubris. But it gained untold kudos for the sensational machine that emerged from the troubled process.

The production version of the XJ220, costing £403,000, was ready by 1991—a shorter, lighter car with two-wheel drive and a 3.5-liter, twin-turbo V-6 engine.

The Nardò test track in Italy was the arena where the XJ220 proved to be the fastest new car on the market, after it achieved 217 mph in the steady hands of Jaguar's Le Mans driver Martin Brundle.

Chapter Sixteen

16

RICH UNCLE HENRY

Ford-era expansion: Ford acquires Jaguar in 1990 to add to its carmaking inventory. Never an easy fit with Detroit's methods, Jaguar's fully funded expansion includes controversial sharing of Ford parts and a conflicted philosophy as the S-Type and X-Type polarize opinions.

A speeding XK8 in 2000; a supercharged edition was also introduced in 1998 with 370 bhp on tap, called the XKR.

Jaguar enjoyed a mere five years as an independent entity until, in February 1990, a full takeover by the Ford Motor Company was sealed. The American giant had agreed to do this only on the basis that Jaguar's board, headed by Sir John Egan, was completely receptive to the offer, and it paid an eye-watering £1.6 billion for the privilege. That valued each share at £8.50, which meant that anyone who had clung on to their stock since privatization now saw a juicy return on their faith in Jaguar.

In Nick Scheele's brief stint as Jaguar chief, it was his duty in 1992 to see the final XJ Series III off the production line and into Jaguar history, after 403,000 examples had been produced.

Car industry leaders were impressed by its achievements, including BMW boss Eberhard von Kuenheim, according to Egan. "I think he wanted to buy the company. But when I told him that I might not come with it, he got nervous," he told the author. Although he had certainly delivered value to shareholders, Egan revealed in 2015 that he was unhappy at the prospect of insensitive Ford ownership, despite the promise of autonomy for Jaguar.

"You've got to add sizzle to the sausage with Jaguar, and I don't think they understood what to do with this company. We left them a beautiful chance with the F-Type and the supercharged V-8 engine to go with it. That was a terrific car. And the XJ8, by the time they finished with it, was also a good car. But I knew that if I stayed I couldn't keep them off my back with the recession coming. There were hard times ahead, and they would seize complete control."

Egan departed not long after the takeover. Perhaps it was Ford's realization of the true state of Jaguar that hastened his departure. By March 1990 it was said that Ford calculated the asset value of Jaguar at about £320 million, so the company had paid a 500 percent premium on that to make sure that no rival got its hands on the marque. At the time, some £1.3 billion for a brand name was an awful lot of money.

The timing was certainly tough. In 1990, for example, Jaguar made 30,862 of its core XJ saloons, but in the following year that number collapsed to 17,190 in the teeth of one of the severe economic recessions that had periodically pummeled the company since the late 1960s. But it was the state of affairs at the Browns Lane plant that really shocked new chief executive and lifetime Ford man Bill Hayden. The facilities and manufacturing processes caused him to compare the place with backward factories behind the old Iron Curtain. "Apart from some Soviet factories in the Russian city of Gorky, Jaguar's British factory was the worst I'd seen," he told *The Independent*.

Having undoubtedly paid more than the company was worth, Ford now had to come to grips with Jaguar. For a start, the most ambitious new venture then on the roster—a successor to the Jaguar E-type—was axed almost immediately. This long-running project had begun its meandering path in 1982. The car, the "F-Type" referred to earlier by a supportive John Egan—and the final Jaguar with any Lyons influence—drew some initial inspiration from Pininfarina's XJS Spider show car of 1978, but soon went its own way as the XJ41 hatchback coupe and the XJ42 convertible. With so much design work already undertaken, it looked set for production but would have undoubtedly been a colossal undertaking had the button been pressed.

Another long-delayed car did get the go-ahead, however, and in 1993 the V-12 engine, now in 318-bhp 6-liter form, made its belated debut in a modified and improved XJ40 as the new XJ12/Daimler Double Six. Jaguar's venerable engine in a car where, finally, most of the blights had been banished began the marque's fight back. *Autocar & Motor* declared

The beautiful Pininfarina XJS Spider (left) was a 1978 show car that started the clamor for an "F-Type" Jaguar; by 1987 the motoring press (right) had gotten wind of the fact that the car was being planned in secret, but it was an immediate casualty of Ford's takeover in 1990.

Ford's first move on the new product front was to usher the new XJ12 into production in 1993, marrying the XJ40 body with Jaguar's 6-liter V-12 engine; delays and indecision would henceforth be no more.

that the engine brought life to the XJ40 when it tested the Daimler Double Six: "Release the brake on a XJ12 and you'll feel pulled forward by a vast bungee that's attached to the horizon you're heading towards at a not inconsiderable speed. It's pure Browns Lane." There was high praise for the sumptuous interior, the mechanical refinement, and the £54,000 price—a substantial £20,000 less than the top Mercedes-Benz S-Class. Standard transmission was a General Motors–supplied four-speed automatic, and as fuel consumption could be as low as 12 mpg, the car was only for the deep-pocketed customer.

Early on in its ownership, Ford decided to bite the bullet and completely overhaul Jaguar's saloon range. Ford was accustomed to replacing its cars every five years; there would be no more dragging out of new car programs over decades, as cash-starved Jaguar had done in its recent past. The results of the £200 million investment in Project X300 were revealed at the Paris Motor Show in October 1994: a very comprehensive update of the XJ40 with, as its crown jewel, a 326-bhp supercharged 4.0-liter engine in an electrifying XJR sports saloon version. This was

A new overhead conveyor system was installed at Browns Lane, inaugurated by Her Majesty The Queen in 1994 and playing its part in hauling the plant up from standards that were on a parallel with Soviet truck factories.

The X300 Jaguar saloon range arrived in 1994, a smart but still cautious update of the XJ40 led from the front by a new XJR model packing a 326 bhp 4-liter straight six boosted with supercharging.

In 1996 Jaguar's more formal sub-brand, Daimler, celebrated its centenary with an especially lustrous Century model and much respect for having in itself founded British car making. A unique show car, the Corsica convertible was also built for the occasion—the only open-topped XJ-type derivative ever to have emerged from the factory.

the world's first supercharged six-cylinder engine in a mass-produced car, giving Jaguar a proud new boast. The supercharger led pressure-fed waste exhaust gases back into the engine for added power, providing such a boost that this large four-door saloon could sprint to 60 mph (97 km/h) from standstill in 5.7 seconds, and on to 100 mph (161 km/h) in 15 seconds. Top speed was limited for decency to 155 mph (250 km/h), in line with most German high-performance cars, but *Autocar* put its finger on the true selling proposition of the £45,450 XJR: "The supercharged engine's monstrous mid-range torque endows the XJR with wondrous overtaking ability."

You still got an awful lot of car with the bottom-of-the-range XJ6, though, and at £17,000 less. Assembly quality also took a quantum leap thanks to big improvements in working practices at Browns Lane, especially a new £8.5 million overhead conveyor system—installed over three weeks in an extended August holiday shutdown—to replace the creaky 1940s-style assembly line. The Queen paid the second visit of her long reign to the factory to see it crank into action in summer 1994. The leaps in efficiency were credited to Bill Hayden, something of a manufacturing guru within Ford and the perfect man for the Herculean task of bringing Jaguar into the modern industrial world. He was, however, only in his post for two years before handing over the baton to another British ex-Ford executive, Nick Scheele.

The XJ40 benefited hugely from the new assembly line, but the stage was also set for the next-generation Jaguar saloon when the final example rolled off the track in June 1994. Just as with the original XJ40, consumer clinics had confirmed that Jaguar's customers, both existing and potential, were partial to what was now the "traditional" look, which led to the conservative design evolution of the X300. The well-loved overall profile was the same but, at the front, this new XJ reinstated the four round headlights of the original 1968 XJ, with a gracefully sculpted hood to match. Jaguar had taken heed of what its biggest fans wanted: a return to elegant curves and a characterful ownership experience. It was necessarily planning something very different from the alternatives offered by Mercedes-Benz, BMW, and Lexus, all of which sold vastly more cars in up to six ranges.

More soberly presented Daimler editions continued to be offered of both the six- and twelve-cylinder XJs (with long-wheelbase options added in 1995), and these came to brief prominence in 1996 when Britain's motor industry celebrated its centenary. The first British car of all had been a Daimler, and the historic occasion was marked by a Daimler Century limited edition with its distinctive chrome wheels, unique dark blue paint, and electrically adjustable rear seats. Jaguar also built the first, and only, XJ convertible, a short-wheelbase, open four-seater named the Daimler Corsica, which did a tour of events in 1996 to celebrate the company's links to the country's motoring roots.

Much more significant for Jaguar's future, however, was another new car launched in 1996: the XK8. Ford had done a laudable job in keeping the venerable XJS going for its first six years in charge, but here was an exciting new two-seater luxury GT and convertible as its replacement. What's more, there was a totally new power unit under its hood: the AJ-V8, Jaguar's first ever V-8 engine.

Geoff Lawson had been appointed Jaguar's director of styling in 1984, but this was the first whole, original car to emerge under his authority, with its well-balanced proportions, low, tapered nose, and, in the case of the coupe, shapely fastback. Inside the two-plus-two interior, the ellipses of the walnut dashboard and center-console surround matched the smooth exterior contours. In fact, to cut development costs and take advantage of well-proven componentry, the basis of the car was a carefully repurposed XJS floorpan and running gear. The unusual position of the handbrake, as seen on the XJS, between the driver's seat and the door, was the only external giveaway.

In 1996 Jaguar's more formal sub-brand, Daimler, celebrated its centenary with an especially lustrous Century model and much respect for having in itself founded British car making. A unique show car, the Corsica convertible was also built for the occasion—the only open-topped XJ-type derivative ever to have emerged from the factory.

An early photo of the XK8, launched in 1996. In addition to the lithe shape, under the hood was Jaguar's all-new 4-liter V-8 engine to give this impressive new GT the legs to go with the looks.

Michael Owen came out of nowhere to become the new young star of English soccer, so Jaguar was more than happy to put him in the supportive leather driving seat of his own XK8.

The deliciously inviting interior of the XK8 convertible, this car being a 2000 model. The eagle-eyed will note the handbrake lever in its unusual position between the driver's seat and the door, a legacy of the repurposed XJ-S heritage of the car's structure.

The V-8 engine, though, was an all-new piece of Jaguar engineering, designed at Whitley, made entirely from aluminum, and offering a very different kind of beating heart in a "big cat," with smooth power, excellent refinement, and yet a throaty growl that couldn't fail to excite each time the throttle was blipped with gusto. It was, in truth, the engine the company had wanted and needed for many years. Whereas the ever-thirsty V-12 was uncannily quiet, the six-cylinder AJ6 seemed coarser, and the 4.0-liter V-8 in the impressive new Lexus LS400—a car representing the biggest existential threat to Jaguar's appeal in the early 1990s—had set a new benchmark in whispering refinement. Now Jaguar had a decent response, a 4.0-liter, 290-bhp, 32-valve, quad-cam V-8 marking its arrival in the XK8 as it was unveiled in Geneva in March 1996 and, very shortly afterward, at the New York Auto Show. It was allied to a standard five-speed automatic transmission to stake out the car's sports-luxury aspirations. A so-called Computer Active Technology Suspension (CATS) setup aimed to tip the XK8 slightly more toward tenacious roadholding than limo-like ride quality.

The new engine was in the vanguard of a house revolution at Jaguar. In 1997 it made its appearance in the XJ saloon range too, in 3.2- and 4.0-liter forms. The subtly restyled cars were now appropriately retitled the XJ8 series, and by June 1997

The AJ-V8 engine found its next home under the hood of the XJ in 1997, which was promptly retitled the XJ8; Jaguar's engines were now all manufactured for it by Ford ay Bridgend, Wales, and the Radford plant in Coventry was closed.

both the AJ6 and V-12 engine series were consigned to history. Going with them was Jaguar's aging engine plant at Radford Coventry (the old home of Daimler, acquired thirty-seven years earlier); henceforth all AJ-V8 motors would be produced by Ford at its engine production complex in Bridgend, Wales.

It took just twenty-eight months to usher the new XJ8 (Project X308) from initiation to the first cars rolling off the production line—unheard-of speed for Jaguar by historic measures. That also included a new supercharged XJR with huge BBS alloy wheels and similarly large Brembo brakes, all to cope with scorching 0–60 acceleration in 5.6 seconds. The term "muscle car" had been coined to describe Detroit's high-performance V-8s of the 1960s and 1970s; now Jaguar was offering its own slingshot in the same tradition. And with more than 15,000 examples ordered, it became a very successful model indeed.

The constant vitality and currency of Jaguar meant that its rich heritage, while never exactly disregarded, rarely occupied much management time at the company. A Jaguar Drivers' Club had been formed independently in 1956 with other clubs, varying from owners' collectives to fully commercial

This image of the high-performance XJR in 2000 clearly shows how the forms and profile of the original XJ6 had survived for three decades, and many owners loved that very longevity.

Long-time styling chief Geoff Lawson spent the 1990s as part of the team that stabilized and revived Jaguar, although radical ideas were largely eschewed by Ford. His untimely death came in 1999.

Plenty of people thought it high time Jaguar returned to the territory of a modern-day Mk 2—a rival to the hugely popular BMW 5 Series. This proposal along those lines came from Italdesign in 1990, and was called the Jaguar Kensington, but it got the usual cold shoulder from Coventry.

Super V-8 was the rather dull title for the Daimler versions of the V-8–powered Jag saloons, invariably ordered in sober, long-wheelbase form biased toward sumptuous rear-seat comfort as the chauffeur up front attended to the taxing business of driving.

The 1998 S-Type answered the call for a more compact Jaguar executive saloon; the look was deliberately retro, which split opinions, and some parts were shared with Ford cars, but its excellent performance was never in doubt.

operations, popping up later. In addition, the preservation of older Jaguars had fostered a veritable cottage industry of restorers and specialists committed to rescuing and maintaining them. In 1983, though, and with founder Lyons still alive, Jaguar Cars established the Jaguar Daimler Heritage Trust as a registered charity to protect the vintage and classic examples of the marque kept in the ad hoc factory collection and to carefully preserve company records, artifacts, and archives. Under Ford control, these efforts were taken even more seriously, and in September 1998 an official Jaguar museum was opened at Browns Lane to display some of the firm's most prized possessions. This group was also responsible for the preservation and promotion of Swallow, SS, Daimler, and Lanchester history.

So much for Jaguar's past. Ford now mapped out an ambitious vision of Jaguar's future, one where the

The luxurious interior of a 2000 S-Type, an interesting amalgam of the latest ergonomics and safety features, traditional materials and eye-catching curves.

Holy smoke: The S-Type R drew its supercar-baiting urgency from a supercharged 4.2-liter V-8, and at a stroke became the fastest-accelerating standard Jaguar yet . . . probably also eating its way through tires quicker than most.

Fresh from the car designer's imagination, this was an early rendering of how a Jaguar competitor to the BMW 3 Series might look.

company could offer a far wider range of cars in line with its German and Japanese competitors. Offering steppingstones within a lineup was the proven way to attract and retain customers, and there had been rumblings for many years, both inside Jaguar and in the motoring press, about the desirability of a new car in the mold of the Mk 2, to be a British sports saloon alternative to the BMW 5-Series. Some observers had even pinpointed specific new models, such as the sophisticated-looking Mazda Xedos 6, as precisely the kind of car that could bring the Jaguar experience to a wider audience. Indeed, Italian consultancy Ital Design—whose principal Giorgetto Giugiaro had been responsible for many famous shapes, Volkswagen Golf and Fiat Punto included—came up with the svelte Jaguar Kensington styling exercise, along similar lines. Now, with Ford's huge global resources on tap, that new car was about to happen. Compromises, however, would be required.

The new Jaguar S-Type that made its highly trumpeted debut in Birmingham in 1998 gave the marque a brand-new entree on par with the Mercedes-Benz E-Class, Lexus GS300, perhaps the Alfa Romeo 166 and Saab 9-5, and definitely the BMW 5-Series. The range started with a 2.5-liter V-6 gasoline engine and culminated in a 4.0-liter V-8, all driving the rear wheels. A 2.7-liter turbodiesel would follow.

It wasn't just the name that harked back to the mid-1960s. The Geoff Lawson styling, too, with its reprise of an upright oval grille flanked by four sculpturally incorporated headlights and a gathering of the bodylines in a tapered tail treatment, aimed to recapture something of past glories. In doing so, it was very much a splitter of opinions: some liked its retro themes, but others were lukewarm, and a few were positively hostile. Did it really look like a "dead cod," according to one influential source? The acclaim was not the rapture and applause that customarily greeted a new Jaguar.

The styling had required approval in Detroit by executives who, perhaps, held quaint ideas about Jaguars and—indeed, like many potential buyers—some odd expectations fixed in the stasis of a past era. It was the price Jaguar had to pay for sharing a platform. Logical economies of scale dictated that the S-Type use the same underpinnings as Ford's Lincoln LS and Thunderbird and, in the case of the smaller engines, Ford Duratorq–based power units, which, with variable valve timing added, became the Jaguar AJ-V6. These parameters notwithstanding, the entire car was developed at Jaguar's full-fledged Whitley design center, which accounted for half of the £400 million budget. The other half went to constructing a new assembly hall for the S-Type next to the Castle Bromwich body plant, starting from scratch and avoiding all the irreconcilable difficulties of trying to squeeze any more out of Browns Lane. It wouldn't really have mattered to owners receiving the first cars in March 1999, but this was, at the time, the biggest brownfield site redevelopment anywhere in Europe.

The S-Type received extremely positive notices in independent road test assessments. *Autocar* rated it as one of the ultimate cars in its class after trying the £37,500 4.0-liter V-8 and reveling in its "delicious blend of noises on full throttle yet [it] remains almost silent under a light load." A few years after launch, the base engine increased in size to a 3.0-liter and the V-8 to a 4.2, which, when supercharged, made this potent 400-bhp fire-breather the fastest-accelerating production Jag ever—0–60 in 5.3 seconds—and very purposeful with its huge wheels and wire mesh grille. There was a mild makeover in 2004 to boost interest in the S-Type, although coming from a strong start, customer enthusiasm proved hard to sustain. The controversial looks, and perhaps even the substantial Ford input, didn't help.

But if the Ford factor lay in a difficult-to-shake preconception in the premium car world, then the next new Jaguar was driving further into the minefield of intangibles that make people pay extra for a car beyond the bald sum of its parts. Ford had decided next to splash £600 million on a Jaguar to rival the top-selling BMW 3-Series compact sports saloon. The codename was X400.

There was no room at any of the existing inns, but it was still deemed essential that the baby Jag be British built. This led to a plan for Jaguar to take command of Ford's Halewood factory on

Designers working hard on a full-size clay model of the upcoming X-Type in Jaguar's high-security styling studios.

An X-Type working prototype wears heavy camouflage to deter prying eyes as it undertakes pulverizing tests on its suspension system.

Merseyside in the northwest of the country. It had been home to the top-selling Ford Escort for generations, but that car would soon be discontinued, replaced by the Ford Focus, and Halewood was running out of work. The team from Coventry moved in in 1999 and the transformation got underway, even though the final Escort did not depart the factory gates until July 2000.

The car itself, called the X-Type, made its official debut seven months later. Once again, taking cost-sharing advantage of existing Ford resources was vital to the new car's genesis, and its running gear was borrowed from the then-new second-generation Ford Mondeo. This meant transverse-mounted engines—Ford V-6s of 2.5 and 3.0 liters—although the X-Type range was unusual in initially boasting four-wheel drive across every model. When in 2002 an economical 2.0-liter V-6 model joined the lineup with front-wheel drive only and priced at below £20,000, however, the accusations that this was essentially a fancy Ford were harder to contest. Nonetheless, only about a fifth of the parts in the two cars were fully interchangeable.

The outer styling was the swan song of Geoff Lawson, who died at age fifty-four in 1999. It was another reminder of how Jaguar was, to a significant degree, held hostage by its past. Any kind of new design direction had been roundly shunned, and in its place an attempt was made to shrink the elegant XJ character down to Ford Mondeo–sized proportions. It was, if anything, even more divisive than the S-Type. Taken on its own, and with a snug but comfortable interior, the X-Type was a very good car, the four-wheel drive bestowing excellent handling and superb grip in all weathers. The cars were well built too. In 2003 came a capacious and pleasingly stylish X-Type estate and a 2-liter (later 2.2-liter and 152 bhp) V-6 diesel, both absolute firsts for Jaguar and aspects that were found in both the Mercedes-Benz C Class and BMW 3-Series ranges, direct rivals.

X-Type goals called for annual sales of 100,000, but in its best year, 2003, it only achieved half of that lofty aim while, of course, still

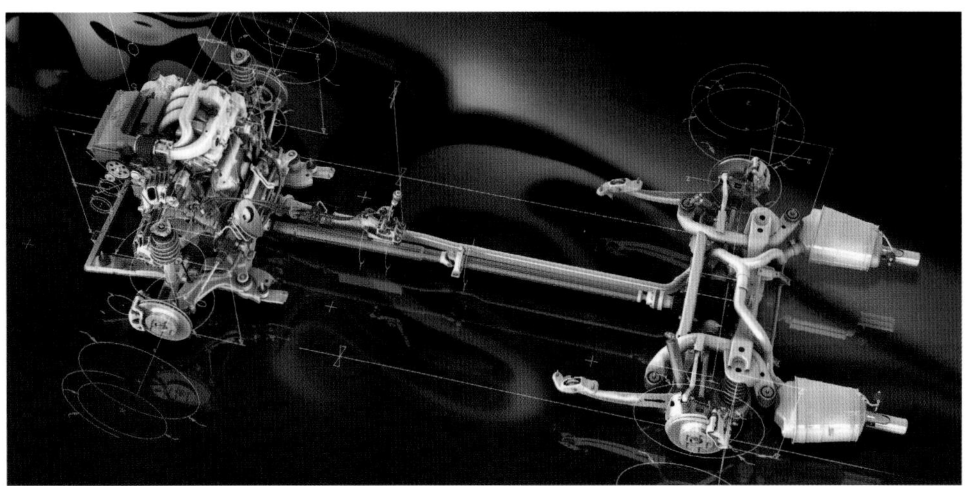

The four-wheel-drive system in the X-Type was a major talking point and was at first offered across every model in the range in tandem with V-6 engines.

This ghosted image lets the observer in on the X-Type's structural secrets, but you need a truly expert eye to spot all the similarities to the Ford Mondeo MKII from which the car was derived.

The X-Type was an excellent car in all conditions, thanks to its four-wheel drive; most people who drove it fully approved, although the cabin was on the snug side.

Jaguar's R1 car placed the marque into the Formula 1 arena in 2001 for the first time ever, but all attempts to muscle its way to the front of the grid were thwarted. Nice try, though.

assuming the mantle of Jaguar's bestseller. In the early part of the new century it was a pity that Jaguar's two crucial new cars, while intrinsically more than competent in themselves, somehow failed to attract enough interest to justify the £1 billion spent. The S-Type R, especially, was an extremely fast performance car and the X-Type estate a very neat and stylish package.

Adding to the prevailing disappointment was the poor showing of the Jaguar name in its first appearance on the Formula 1 grid. This was another Ford initiative involving the company's longtime collaborator, Jackie Stewart, whose Stewart Grand Prix team was rebranded as Jaguar Racing in January 2000 after Ford bought the Jaguar marque and business. There was driving talent aplenty, with Eddie Irvine and Johnny Herbert on board, and while the first season with the R1 car saw the team struggling to get into its stride, by May 2001 it finally clinched its first championship points and a podium finish at the Monaco GP after Irvine brought the R2 home in third place. By season's end, Jaguar F1 was joint ninth place in the F1 leader board with seventeen points.

Sadly, that proved a high point. Despite recruiting the legendary Niki Lauda as team manager, the evolutionary R3 car experienced handling problems and the subsequent R4 fared little better. In 2004, the whole outfit, including the promising new R5, was sold to Red Bull Racing and Jaguar's Formula 1 foray was over, with precious little to show for the many millions expended, although it had been good to see this evocative British name contesting motorsport's top echelon.

Regardless, what an amazing transformation Jaguar had undergone in ten years under Ford's wing: a portfolio of four strong models, three production plants, quality and reliability levels at or above industry benchmarks, billions invested. A brand-new Jaguar was now available to the widest base of customers in the marque's illustrious history. For once, the infrastructure and financial stability matched the aspirations to produce desirable cars. Jaguar was fortunate to have Ford's backing. Now all it needed was some fresh inspiration.

Lyons would have been 100 in 2001, so Jaguar built the 500 XJR 100 and 50 XKR (coupe and convertible) editions in his honor. As the pinnacle of each type, these supercharged peaches came in metallic black with red-stitched charcoal leather, bird's-eye maple veneer, heated seats in front and back, and "100" emblems.

The estate was, to many, the best of the controversial X-Type bunch, for its looks (it was the first Jaguar with Ian Callum's design involvement) and its versatility. Here was Jaguar's first-ever station wagon.

Chapter Seventeen

17

GETTING ITS MOJO BACK

A new era: In the early part of the twenty-first century, Jaguar reevaluates itself, with new design chief Ian Callum fronting a fresh direction. The beautiful new XK arrives in 2004 and, below the skin, aluminum structures and safety features put Jaguar back at the technical cutting edge.

The open and closed XKR high-octane twins arrived in 2007 with supercharged V-8 engines of 4.2 liters, updated a couple of years later to 5-liter.

Like so many small boys in the 1950s and 1960s, Ian Callum was obsessed with modern sports cars. Growing up in Dumfries, Scotland, he had a close bond with his grandfather, who would help him identify a Porsche 356 when it roared past his house or take him to Glasgow to press up against the plate-glass window of the city's Jaguar showroom and ogle the gleaming E-type inside. His teachers belittled his doodles (drawing was an abiding passion), but by 1968, at age fourteen, Ian knew for sure that he wanted to design the real thing. The problem was, he had no idea how to go about it, so he handwrote a letter to William Heynes, Jaguar's managing director, with sketches enclosed, asking for advice. He was overjoyed to get a prompt reply, although somewhat less excited by its contents, well meaning though they were.

"He wrote: 'You have to join Jaguar at a young age, become an apprentice, work through the factory and then we can train you to do technical drawing and you can go into the technical office,'" Callum recalled in a 2019 *Auto Express* interview. "I wrote back again and said, 'No, you don't understand. I want to design the shapes of the cars,' which, basically, was Lyons's job—that's what he did."

Callum did find a way to follow his dreams through trial and error, trying various courses before spending three years studying industrial design in Glasgow. Then he won a scholarship offered by Ford, allowing him to complete the vehicle design course at London's prestigious Royal College of Art. His first design when subsequently joining Ford of Europe in 1979 was a wing mirror for the Transit van.

But opportunities within the multinational company for a talented young designer were virtually limitless, and he worked at Ford outposts all over the world. After eleven whirlwind years, though, mild disillusionment set in and Callum changed tack, working for Tom Walkinshaw's tightly run TWR Automotive on numerous ventures.

Being closely allied to Jaguar in multiple ways, TWR served as its race team contractor, upgrader of production models to sporty specification, and builder of the spectacular XJ220. And with the XJ220 coming to its controversially premature end, there was a fully equipped carmaking facility at Bloxham, Oxfordshire, looking for a new use. "I thought I'd end up in this massive, super palace of a place," he said. "But it was Kidlington Industrial Estate. An industrial estate with tin sheds."

As a little boy, Ian Callum used to press his nose up against Jaguar showroom windows in rapture. In the spring of 1999, his dream finally came true: to be the shaper of Jaguar's design destiny. Here he is with his own Mk 2 subtly updated in a highly personal way.

Things are going to be different around here: Callum's urbane R-Coupe concept car of 2001 kickstarted a serious change of emphasis, where traces of Jaguar's heritage became more dinner jacket than straitjacket.

The arrival of diesel engines in production models was celebrated in 2003 by Callum's R-D6 concept, a startling—for Jaguar—five-door hatchback that indicated from then on almost nothing need be off limits.

The 2005 Advanced Lightweight Coupe began a new release strategy—previewing new production cars with a showpiece that was very close to the customer-ready car to follow. In this case, that was the new XK.

Walkinshaw was never short on ideas. Having prepared and raced Jaguar XJSs on a lean budget with some excellent results in the early 1980s, he knew the big Jag coupe inside out. Now his plan was to take the aging XJS platform and design a stylish new body for it, to which Callum was hastily assigned. In a bizarre twist, though, Jaguar rejected the idea, and the car was instead taken up by Aston Martin, which, like Jaguar, was wholly owned by Ford. So Callum found the first car for which he could take full and total design credit was the XJS-derived 1993 Aston Martin DB7. The car won widespread acclaim for its beauty and became one of Aston Martin's all-time bestsellers. Ian next designed the Aston Martin Vanquish and was closely involved with early work on the DB9 and V-8 Vantage. He puts his success in helping rejuvenate the veteran British supercar company down to "Simplicity. I think I learnt very early on just to not overdo things. And also, I always looked for a way that things looked strong."

Cutting-edge indeed: The X350 XJ launched in 2003 boasted an innovative all-aluminium structure craftily riveted and glued together. Bigger in every direction than the outgoing X300, it was still substantially lighter.

In April 1999, Jaguar and Aston Martin were drawn together more formally than ever when Ford formed its Premier Automotive Group (PAG). This division, headquartered in a trendy new building in London's Soho, allowed the Detroit behemoth to unite all the upmarket brands it had acquired during its huge 1990s spending spree. These included Land Rover and Volvo in addition to Jaguar and Aston Martin, together with Ford's established luxury Lincoln brand that it had owned since 1922. The new group vice president was former BMW product guru Wolfgang Reitzle, who was also announced as the new chairman of Jaguar Cars Ltd.; the overall head of design was the American J Mays.

Even some Jaguar aficionados might be unaware of the importance of Mike Beasley, here chatting with Anne, Princess Royal, at the inauguration of a new railhead at the Castle Bromwich factory. Toiling behind the scenes for years, Beasley had seen Jaguar through many sticky patches before a brief spell as managing director.

Under Ford's conservative aegis, the new X350 XJ adhered faithfully to the shape that had defined Jaguar's large saloons for 35 years, masking the revolution going on within.

There was a Daimler Super Eight edition of the new XJ, shown here, but not for very long. In 2008 the marque was quietly dropped, and in truth no one kicked up a fuss about that.

For the team working away at Jaguar, this may have seemed distant corporate stuff with little impact on their activities. But two months later, Jaguar's chief designer Geoff Lawson died suddenly. Mays wasted no time in offering the job to Ian Callum ... quite literally the culmination of a life's dream for the car-mad Scot whose reverence for the work of Lyons was stitched into his very soul.

"I was actually quite shocked because I didn't think I was ready for it," he recounted to *Auto Express*. "I remember standing in front of my team in the studio here, my second day, there was 100 people. I was handed this bloody lollipop mic and was asked to speak to them. And I just was standing there completely ... I mean, my hands were shaking. I blurted out some pathetic sentences, saying, 'This is going to be the most dynamic 10 years of this company,' and all that sort of stuff."

The long-wheelbase version of the XJ made it surely one of the most sumptuous ways to travel as a fortunate back-seat passenger, and it had a mature elegance just perfect for a grand entrance.

The interior of the X350 long-wheelbase XJ could be specified with more electronic equipment than any previous Jaguar, to complement the wide choice of trim and upholstery options.

It was too late for Callum to even tweak the X-Type, which launched in 2001, although the first Jaguar he had a hand in shaping was the handsome estate car adaptation, the better looking by a considerable margin. The S-Type, too, was set on its unswervable product cycle track, and Callum's 2005 facelift struggled to revive much interest in a strange-looking car that was gradually overlooked in the market despite its many excellent attributes. For the Frankfurt Motor Show, however, he made an emphatic design statement with the R-Coupe concept car: henceforth it would not be business as usual.

Purely a one-off, the Concept Eight was an XJ specially equipped with this full-length glass roof as the main feature of a super-stylish makeover.

Along the right lines: Early concept sketches helped extrapolate the key themes for the new XK, with subtle but never slavish influences from the E-type. In more expressive XK artwork (below), Ian Callum's team started to give the XK an edgy look, something Callum admitted took him out of his comfort zone.

The XK was the second new Jaguar to embrace all-aluminum construction, and this ghosted overhead view easily conveys the unseen strength that was built in.

The so-called pop-up hood on the XK was a major industry innovation in passive safety, cushioning the impact for any pedestrian involved in an accidental collision.

A muscular and substantial-looking two-door, full four-seater coupe—in the spirit, perhaps, of the short-lived XJC of the mid 1970s—the R-Coupe reworked the vertical grille frontage of the S-Type and the tapered window line of numerous older Jaguars as part of a bold but not unrealistic future vision. Its base design was notionally the 4.2-liter supercharged XKR, though the show car was a nonrunner. It was followed exactly two years later by the concept R-D6, marking the introduction of new diesel-powered Jaguars. With a V-6 twin-turbo for power (in theory), this time the style was a bit more startling for a Jaguar: a roomy five-door hatchback with rear-hinged back doors like the Mazda RX-8, and a side-hinged tailgate like the original E-type.

That year, 2003, would be pivotal for Jaguar on several fronts. The least well known was probably the retirement of one Michael Beasley, managing director. Beasley's immense contribution to keeping Jaguar going through thick and (mainly) thin stretched back to 1974, and he was director of all manufacturing between 1978 and 1985, during which time he became, in the words of John Egan, ". . . part of the gang that saved the company; his contribution was immense. . . . He just stuck to his task. He was a real hardworking, straightforward guy." Entirely typical of his can-do approach, and utter lack of pretension, was his organization of a convoy of Land Rovers and trucks to collect automatic transmissions from the Borg Warner factory in Wales after a heavy snowfall threatened to halt deliveries and bring the Jaguar factory to a halt.

An engineer to his core, a man who collected antique cameras and built a 200-yard (220-meter) model railway in his garden in his spare time, Beasley was still on retainer to recruit new engineers when he departed Jaguar, leaving behind a renewed legacy of automotive innovation. This was laid bare in 2003 with the public unveiling of X350, the all-new XJ large saloon range, in whose preparation Beasley would have been closely involved.

Claims that this was the first all-aluminum monocoque body-chassis to reach mass production could be clearly contested by Audi with its A2 and A8 cars. But what X350 did usher in was the first industrial use of a new rivet-bonded joining technique, with self-pierce rivets and epoxy structural adhesive joining together the many aluminum pressings, castings, and extrusions to form the structure onto which the alloy panels attached. Despite being

The all-new XK was not only a major step forward for Jaguar: it also instantly became one of the most desirable luxury GTs available when it appeared in 2006.

longer, wider, and taller than the outgoing model, and more spacious inside, this new XJ was a full 200 pounds (90 kilograms) lighter thanks to structural steel used only for the front and rear subframes that cradled the new self-leveling adaptive air-suspension system, with Jaguar's time-served independent rear-suspension setup now retired after forty-two years. The bare bodyshell was 40 percent lighter, yet 50 percent stiffer than the old steel one. Here was a whole new manufacturing process for the Browns Lane workforce to apply.

The car saw the glad return of the XJ6 nameplate as a 3.0-liter V-6 gasoline option joined the two V-8s, now in 3.5- and 4.2-liter forms, the latter in standard 300-bhp XJ8 and supercharged 400-bhp XJR forms. Six-speed automatics were standard across the board. By 2005 V-6 diesel, adult-orientated Daimler models, and long-wheelbase options were also available.

Technically, this new XJ was as exciting and cutting edge as Jaguar's many other historic high points. To consider its construction

Alongside the XK Coupe was a two-plus-two convertible that exuded an air of expensive luxury.

The first XK comes to life at the Castle Bromwich plant after it had been hugely expanded in one of Europe's biggest industrial redevelopment projects.

methods and engineering was to explore the unfolding trend for mass-produced cars of the future. In terms of appearance, however, it underwhelmed. Its look, both outside and within the sumptuously appointed cabin, was old-school Jag, still reeking of the first XJ6 first seen thirty-five years before. *BBC Top Gear* magazine summed up the problem: "The current XJ is a world-beater wrapped in a very old-fashioned body that doesn't appeal to where America is right now. It has not one square centimetre of 'bling.'"

It is ironic to think of Ford top brass insisting that the old-fashioned Jaguar design be retained and the conservative opinions of the upper-middle-aged and lower-elderly Jaguar faithful being noted during customer research sessions. Ian Callum could only watch the predestined introduction process rumble on, just as for the X-Type. "I really didn't have much warmth for either of them," he said later, "because they were too traditional. But I went through it all. I did all of my PR stuff, talked them up."

With the last of the trio of Jaguar's early 2000s concept cars, though, no rictus grin was required. The Advanced Lightweight Coupe (ALC) first appeared at the 2005 North American International Auto Show in Detroit and immediately won Jaguar multiple plaudits for being absolutely back in form, taking just enough inspiration from the E-type while presenting a confident, beautiful new form as a 2+2 luxury GT. Callum handled the exterior, Giles Taylor the interior, while the all-aluminum construction was derived straight from the new XJ and the supercharged V-8 powertrain came from the XKR. The tan leather interior had shiny aluminum insert highlights and the gearshift used paddles mounted on the steering column.

Unlike the R-Coupe and R-D6, though, the ALC was an exciting new Jaguar that was ready for customers, in very slightly modified form, just one year later. The all-new XK was offered from the start as both a hatchback fastback and a convertible. Callum commented, "The priority was to get the nose up

A brushed-aluminum effect replaced what might normally have been a lot of black plastic on the dashboard, along with minor controls and surrounding trim inside the XK to give a pleasing "machined" ambience.

and give the car tighter lines, so I decided to give it edges. It was my first Jag and I was nervous, especially since I was being watched by the Jaguar executive committee. But it worked."

The reason for the raised nose profile was a key technical innovation heralded by the new XK: the Pyrotechnic Pedestrian Deployable Bonnet system designed to reduce the severity of pedestrian injuries in an accident. The hood would pop up in a collision to create a cushioning effect between the engine and the hood, drastically softening the impact.

The new XK became the first Jaguar never seen inside the historic Browns Lane plant because it joined the S-Type—and also now the big XJ—in the vastly more modern Castle Bromwich assembly facility, where its bonded/riveted all-alloy construction took place. Finally, the Coventry production lines fell silent, with only the genius ghosts of Messrs. Lyons, Heynes, England, Sayer, and Knight prowling around the spiritual home of their XK120, D-type, E-type, and XJ6. Lyons's grandson Michael Quinn, though, soon to be appointed patron of the Jaguar Daimler Heritage Trust, reckoned the removal of Jaguar assembly out of Browns Lane wouldn't have upset the old man in the slightest. "I think he would have been sad to break with Coventry but, from a bricks-and-mortar viewpoint, he'd have wanted to move on," he told the author.

With 0–60 acceleration of 4.2 seconds and a 196 mph maximum speed, the full-production XKR-S joined the range in 2011 to put down new Jaguar performance markers yet again.

Three years later, the main site was sold off and soon bulldozed for redevelopment. When the Trust moved out of its museum building in 2012, the last bit of Jaguar sped off to its new future.

The full-length tailgate on the new XK was a big leap in practicality over the outgoing model, with no detriment to the car's looks.

Chapter Eighteen

TOTAL RENEWAL

XF onwards: Jaguar's new mainstream executive car arrives in 2007, receiving a rapturous reception and starting another epoch; the impressive all-new XJ follows, and then the F-Type, a new sports car at last.

Thanks to a role in the 2015 James Bond movie Spectre, the C-X75 did at least come to the attention of an intrigued worldwide audience.

This pair of design proposals show that, right from the start, the replacement for the sometimes unloved S-Type was going to tear up the rule book of Jaguar aesthetics.

It's wrong to describe the XF as a "big leap" for Jaguar, tempting though it may be to equate the brand with the South American predator at the top of the food chain. But what it *did* represent was the first time that all the stars were in total alignment for a new car: state-of-the-art, high-quality manufacturing; a stimulating experience for owners of a car at or very close to the top of its class; and a design that was at once ultramodern yet distinctive enough that it couldn't be mistaken for anything else.

The first glimpse of the XF was provided by a C-XF preview show car in spring 2007, followed by the ready-to-go production version at Frankfurt in autumn that year. Sales of the medium-sized executive sports saloon to supplant the ill-fated S-Type began in spring 2008.

Ian Callum has stated that this car had to get Jaguar back to the forefront of its sector. "My job was to move from the past to the present, and XF's the car that did that," he explained. "It was a lovely car and it still is a lovely car. We said, 'This is the new face of Jaguar.' I think we wowed the world with it. People got it."

Here is the C-XF, the muscular-looking concept car that previewed the new executive saloon in the spring of 2007.

For the XF, the steel S-Type platform was reused in thoroughly reworked form to bring the car to market as quickly as possible; an aluminum hood was fitted.

The overall coupe-like shape, the feline treatment of the headlights, and a prominent, chrome-edged wire mesh grille redolent of the first XJ6 all helped to define the XF. The sumptuous interior, meanwhile, used simple, bold forms for uncannily clean lines (by class standards), with all controls and vents flush fitting and a custom-designed Bowers & Wilkins 500-watt audio system. The cabin included a particular piece of theatre called the JaguarDrive Selector, a beautifully weighted popup circular drum that enabled the driver to select the six speeds of the standard automatic transmission (there was no manual, initially) by fingertip rotation. The engine range at first consisted of a 3.0-liter V-6 gasoline, 2.7-liter V-6 turbodiesel, and 4.2-liter V-8s with or without supercharger. This lineup would be constantly adjusted throughout the XF's eight-year life: a smaller-capacity, Ford-based four-cylinder gasoline and diesel introduced for better fuel economy, the 3.0-liter gasoline V-6 gaining a supercharger, and the V-8s increasing to 5.0 liters; the supercharged edition in the XFR fire-breather produced 503 bhp and 561 lb-ft of torque. Still more was available in the limited-production XFR-S, which was delimited to attain a heady top speed of 186 miles per hour (300 kilometers per hour) reached via a 4.4-second 0–60 sprint time on huge 20-inch alloy wheels. Later came a rear-biased all-wheel-drive option for added traction on slippery asphalt.

Had Jaguar stuck to its original plan to build the XF with an all-aluminum bonded construction like its XJ and XK siblings, the old S-Type would have had to hold the fort for at least another eighteen months. There was no time to waste, though, so the XF had to use a modified version of the Ford DEW98 platform from the old S-Type/Thunderbird. That meant remaining all steel, apart from an aluminum hood, plus continuing to sport its shapely front and rear plastic bumper sections.

The front of the new XF exuded a feline aura with a bold new grille treatment that would soon become the established face of Jaguar saloon cars.

Coupe-like contours of the XF sought to bring visual dynamism to a market sector where the "three-box" saloon was the norm. There was also universal praise for the car's handling and poise.

From the start the new car was showered with consumer media awards, and a slew of "best executive car" medals notably highlighted the excellent 2.7 turbodiesel model whose engine could also be found in the car's Premier Automotive Group stablemate, the third-generation Land Rover Discovery. Sales were strong and the car received a proper image boost when a highly modified example (a precursor to the XFR-S) set a new world speed record for a Jaguar when Paul Gentilozzi hit 225.675 mph (363.189 km/h)—8 mph (12.9 km/h) faster than the fastest-timed XJ220—at the Bonneville Salt Flats in Utah. Jaguar had scored a direct hit, it seemed, and would go on to sell more than 200,000 examples of this important turnaround car.

Jaguar wasted no time tailoring the XF for niche purposes. Mk 2s and S-types had been popular as high-speed patrol and pursuit cars among Britain's police forces in the 1960s, and in 2009 Coventry started to court the cops seriously again with a turbodiesel-powered XF specification specially tailored to law enforcement, garlanded with flashing LED lights on its roof bar, bodysides, and grille.

Subtle and moody interior lighting helped to emphasize, at night, the close attention paid to the design of the inner door panels on this characterful executive express.

"Refined simplicity" was the watchword for the dashboard, with sparing use of wood trim to accentuate the luxury aura.

The rotary gear selector, which retracted into the center console, was a novelty, beautifully weighted for effortless fingertip control.

For cargo-heavy civilians, meanwhile, Jaguar launched an estate car in 2012, called the Sportsbrake. Like the BMW 5-Series Touring or Mercedes-Benz CLS Shooting Brake, its 2,084 cubic feet (59 cubic meters) of space and one-touch folding back seat targeted wealthy customers who might need room for a big dog or outsize luggage, but who didn't want to sacrifice sporty driving for the van-like ignominy of an SUV.

By this time, Daimler had been quietly retired. In 2008 Jaguar reached an agreement with DaimlerChrysler that it could have exclusive use of the trademark (it promptly retitled itself Daimler AG) and, after forty-eight years, the name vanished from the most luxurious of Jaguar models. No one seemed to notice, much less care.

In 2012 the Jaguar XF 2.2D swept the board to become the overall winner of the Tow Car Awards, with similar accolades—plus many other trophies—in subsequent years. Here it is manfully hauling an Airstream trailer caravan.

Jaguar spotted a good potential market for the XF with British police forces and created a dedicated specification to tailor the car as an ideal high-speed patrol or pursuit vehicle.

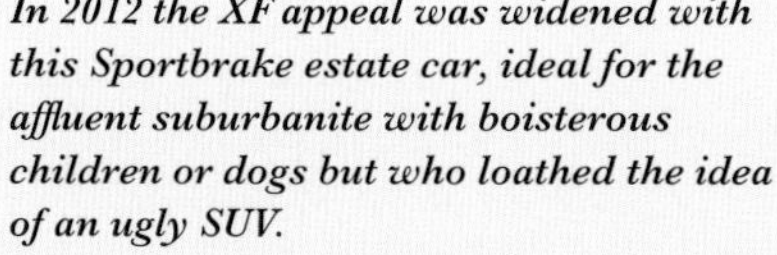

In 2012 the XF appeal was widened with this Sportbrake estate car, ideal for the affluent suburbanite with boisterous children or dogs but who loathed the idea of an ugly SUV.

In 2010, Jaguar could finally address the rapidly fading appeal of its XJ large executive car with an imposing all-new model. The innovative aluminum platform was carried over largely unchanged, and the stylistic rulebook was tossed away as Ian Callum and his team strove to create a completely new look. He recalled briefing his team, telling Steve Cropley of *Autocar*, "I said: 'Look, we've raised the game here [with the XF]. We're going to do it again. I don't want you just to do a copycat. I want to go to another level. In 20 years' time they'll think, 'Wow, this is special.' But there was a lot of pushback internally at the time."

The new family "face" that had been established with the XF was adopted, featuring a prominent and powerful-looking front grille with slinky headlights, but the rest of the car was penned in a dramatic fastback idiom. The full-length glass sunroof arched over the passenger compartment and tapered to a substantially overhanging trunk, with black three-quarter pillars emphasizing the powerful, sweptback stance. The vertical "cat's claw" taillights were a controversial touch. Inside, the feeling of a luxury speedboat was conjured up in the so-called "Riva loop" design motif that ran from one front door to another along the "prow" of the dashboard.

The engine range offered the by-now familiar 3.0-liter V-6 turbodiesel and the 5.0-liter V-8 with power outputs eventually spanning 470 to 550 bhp for the 174-mile-per-hour (280-kilometer-per-hour) XJR. In 2013 there was also a 3.0-liter gasoline supercharged V-6. Transmissions were six-speed automatics across the board, with shift paddles on the steering column for more direct driver involvement. Indeed, the most noteworthy technical alteration from the obsolete X350 to this X351 model was probably the reinstatement of a coil-sprung front suspension, leaving the air-suspension rear end unaltered. There were myriad ways to personalize the new XJ: the car's permutations, in either standard- or long-wheelbase models, were extensive to start with and proliferated hugely during its nine-year production run.

Callum stated that his bold new XJ exuded "a rebellious edge." It was certainly true that the car managed to look simultaneously elegant and aggressive. But it was still a Jaguar intended for affluent grownups rather than punky upstarts, as illustrated by the fact that incoming British Prime Minister David Cameron added the first of two gray ones to his Downing Street fleet in 2010; both of his vehicles would be discreetly armor plated according to Jaguar's "Sentinel" high-security specification. Cameron's successors, Theresa May and Boris Johnson, have continued to occupy its wide and cosseting back seat.

But the reenergized Jaguar Cars still had not adequately addressed the elephant in the room: the lack of a proper Jaguar sports car in its range. Unabashed hedonism had been absent, in fact, since 1975 and the final E-type, or maybe since the 1992 XJ220 supercar. One possible route forward was examined in 2010 with the C-X75, a highly aerodynamic two-seater design exercise with a daring hybrid drivetrain. The car's 780 bhp was delivered via a 194-bhp electric motor at each wheel, drawing power from a battery pack. Two small diesel gas-turbine engines, made by Bladon Jets, replenished the batteries' energy and in doing so gave a range of 559 miles (900 kilometers), although the car could also cover 68 miles (109 kilometers) in its pure electric mode. Apart from monumental torque via its vectored four-wheel-drive system of 1,180 lb-ft, and the potential for a 0–60 acceleration of 2.9 seconds, the car

The XFR was Jaguar's answer to the BMW M5, with a massive 503 bhp on tap to make it perhaps Britain's most accomplished super-sports saloon.

had the credentials to produce a paltry 28 g of CO_2 per kilometer on the EU emissions test cycle. Advanced aerodynamics played a big part in its efficiency, with a diffuser and active airfoil under the car's beautiful lines to suck it down to the road.

There was elation when the company announced it would build a limited run of 250 between 2013 and 2015, albeit with a more conventional gasoline recharging unit rather than the miniature jet engines. The announced plan was for the Williams Formula 1 team to collaborate on the venture (as they had done on the design itself), but after eighteen months the C-X75 was canceled as the fallout from the 2008 financial crash showed little sign of making it viable, even at an estimated £900,000 per car.

It remains one of the tantalizing few Jaguar might-have-beens, and Ian Callum's biggest regret. Nonetheless, five impressive working prototypes were constructed, including one, backed by a fleet of six C-X75 lookalikes, that found eternal fame after being featured in the 2015 James Bond film *Spectre*.

In 2012, however, the definitive Jaguar F-Type was unveiled. The E-type's spiritual successor had finally arrived. Although the car depended on a modified version of the XK's glued-and-bonded aluminum structure, this time it was purely a two-seater. There were some echoes of an F-Type concept car that had done the motor show rounds in 2000, the work of designers Keith Helfet and Geoff Lawson, but this production F-Type was Callum's amalgam of design cues from the XK, XJ, and C-X75 infused with just a hint of the dartlike E-type to its profile to salute the golden era of fifty years earlier.

With an all-new double-wishbone front- and rear-suspension system featuring adaptive dampers and

The all-new XJ's long tail and swept-back roof produced a distinctive new alternative to the BMW 7 Series/Mercedes S-Class; UK Prime Minister David Cameron was among the first to receive one.

The supportive driving position of the new XJ offers a sea of twinkling details on the dashboard in this version, given the Autobiography personalization treatment.

The "cat's claw" rear light clusters ensured that, while controversial, the 2010–2019 XJ was unmistakable for any other large luxury saloon.

adjustable settings, the F-Type could be tweaked across twenty-five driving modes programmed for varying road conditions and driving characteristics, making this, in one respect, the most driver-focused Jaguar ever. The standard eight-speed automatic gearbox had steering column paddles for switchblade manual operation override.

The 3.0-liter V-6 supercharged engine was powerful enough, at 335 bhp, to allow this very lightweight sports car to attain 171 miles per hour (275 kilometers per hour), while the 488-bhp supercharged 5.0-liter V-8 created a 186-mile-per-hour (300-kilometer-per-hour) machine (artificially limited to protect all involved). The snug cockpit featured a prominent aluminum rail around the center console on the passenger side that seemed to cradle the driver's control center.

A 2014 model-year XJ showing the fold-out laptop tables and optional TV screens available for rear-seat passengers.

The F-Type roadster became available in 2013, followed a year later by a matching coupe. The company was convinced the open car would be a bestseller; in fact, the coupe soon proved more popular and Jaguar was delighted to discover that three-quarters of F-Type buyers were newcomers to its dealer showrooms. It was galling to think how all this pent-up demand had previously been funneled away to Porsche, BMW, Audi, perhaps Alfa Romeo and Nissan, possibly TVR, or maybe even to secondhand Aston Martins, when all along customers were really after a twenty-first-century E-type. Now Jaguar had just the car, and within two years it was outselling the Porsche Boxster and Cayman in the critical US market and leading the comparable sports car sales charts in the UK. It was the illustrious winner of the World Car Design of the Year award in 2013. The coupe's introduction also ushered in the ultra-high-performance F-Type R with a 567-bhp edition of the V-8 engine, good for catapulting this one—said to be the most compact Jaguar since the XK120—from 0 to 60 in a lightning-quick 4.0 seconds. Carbon "ceramic matrix" brakes and Torque Vectoring braking were technological safety harnesses included in the supercar package.

Moreover, the F-Type Project 7 "speedster" had gone some way to meeting the desire for an extra-special Jaguar now that the C-X75 had been parked firmly beyond reach. Project 7 was dreamed up by Italian-Brazilian Jaguar designer César Pieri in his spare time, its "aero haunch" recalling the signature stabilizing fin on the 1950s D-type Le Mans winners, and its fixed rear airfoil contrasting with the standard F-Type's deployable rear spoiler. Its 542-bhp supercharged V-8 marked it out as, for the time, the most powerful production Jaguar ever, although that production was strictly confined to just 250 examples, all meticulously built by hand and finished by Jaguar's Special Vehicles Operations division. The whole edition was sold in a trice, many vehicles destined to join other rare classic Jaguar sports and sports-racing cars in delectable private collections worldwide. In 2020, a mildly facelifted F-Type was introduced and offered with two versions of the supercharged V-8, a new 444 bhp edition joining the existing range-topper. The V-6 was axed while the entry-level was catered for by a turbocharged 2-liter Ingenium four-cylinder engine producing 296 bhp.

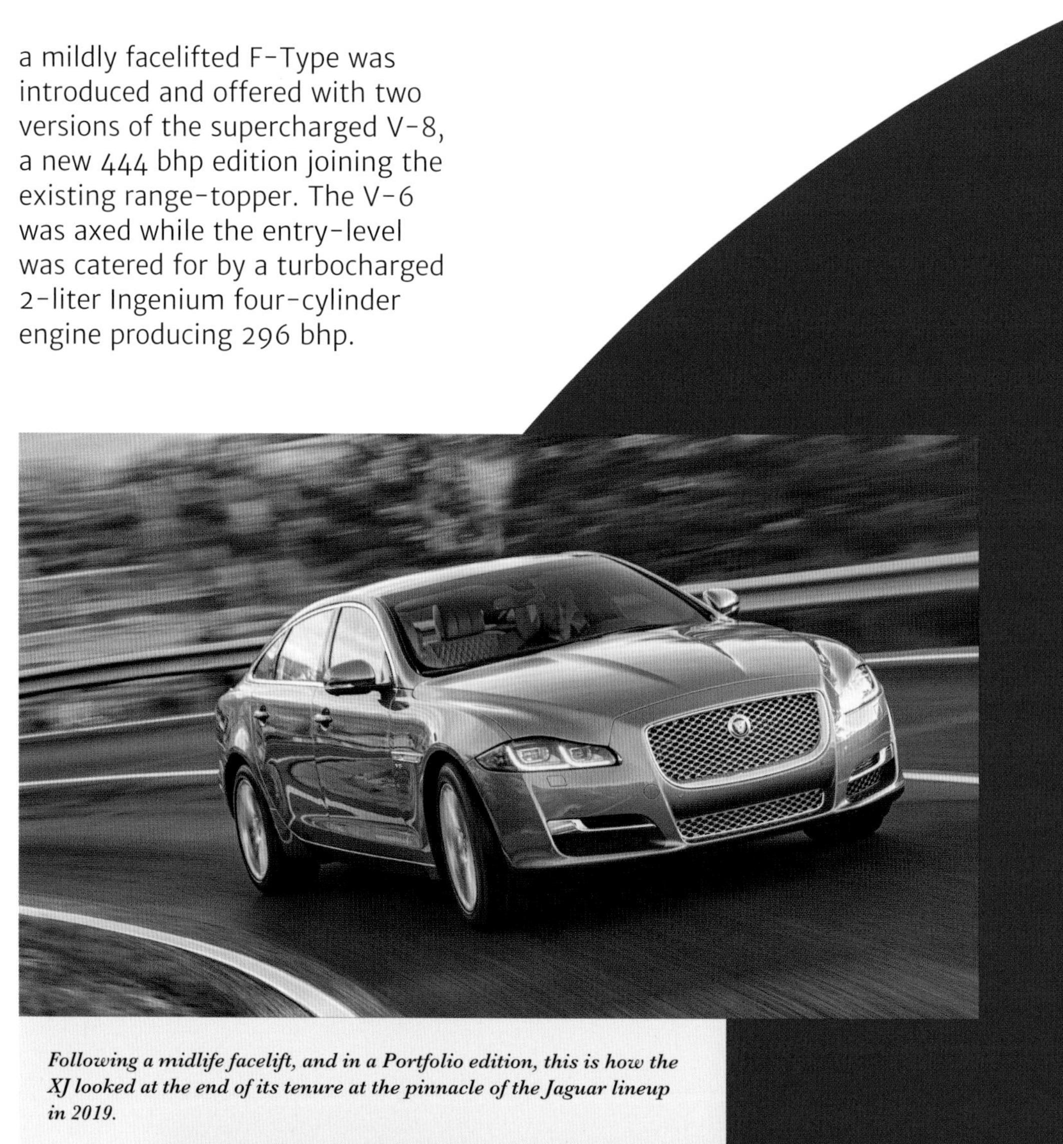

Following a midlife facelift, and in a Portfolio edition, this is how the XJ looked at the end of its tenure at the pinnacle of the Jaguar lineup in 2019.

With a hybrid-electric drivetrain and tiny gas turbine engines, as well as input from the Williams Formula 1 team, the C-X75 was as daring technically as its looks were exquisite.

The C-X75 supercar was briefly in prospect in 2013 as a production car before Jaguar backed away from the plan, perhaps wanting to avoid repeating lessons learned with the XJ220.

This E-type–style side-opening tailgate was a notable feature on the C-X16 show car, the precursor of the new F-Type, although not destined to make it to the showroom.

The twistiest of bends were no problem for an F-Type SVR equipped with four-wheel drive for unrivaled high-speed grip.

The F-Type SVR in open form, able to sprint its compact self from rest to 60 mph in 4 seconds.

By 2012, the year Britain hosted the Olympic Games, Jaguar's product renewal had been comprehensive and total, making it competitive against the world's best prestige marques in most key market categories. Behind the scenes, Jaguar's corporate status had undergone a similarly radical revolution.

A distinctive bar frames the center console in the driver-focused cockpit of the F-Type convertible.

Soccer legend David Beckham added Jaguar brand ambassador to his many roles as he was enlisted to help promote the F-Type, here in coupe form.

The F-Type burst into life in 2012, finally putting a genuine two-seater sports car back into Jaguar's world for the first time since the E-type's 1975 demise.

上海银行
Bank of Shanghai
DBS

Chapter Nineteen

THINKING BIG, AMBITIONS FULFILLED

Tata takeover: In 2008 Jaguar's destiny shifts once again when it changes hands and merges with fellow British motoring icon Land Rover. The meeting of minds and global outlook brings Jaguar into the burgeoning SUV market with the F-Pace, and the new business invests heavily in British know-how.

This striking study of the F-Pace sets it against the Shanghai skyline; soaring Chinese demand for prestigious SUVs was one of the driving factors behind the car's existence.

In the end there was only one suitor—one company with the vision to make a solid future case for Jaguar and come up with the ready money needed to keep the company standing tall. It was an industry outlier that, until March 26, 2008, was better known in the UK for its teabags than most of its other activities, despite having been in business for more than 150 years.

Ratan Tata (third from right) and his Tata conglomerate put their faith in two famous British marques, bringing Jaguar and Land Rover together as one entity. He was helped by (left to right) Cyrus Mistry, who replaced him as Tata chairman in 2012, JLR chief executive Ralf Speth, Ian Callum, Land Rover design head Gerry McGovern, and Tata vice chairman Ravi Kant, seen here at the 2012 New Delhi Auto Expo.

On that day India's Tata Group announced that it had sealed a deal with Ford to take over both Jaguar and Land Rover, paying £1.15 billion ($2.3 billion) for the privilege. Some senior staff inside the head offices of the two companies in Coventry and Solihull were not too unnerved by the announcement; the widely respected head of the holding company Tata Sons, Ratan Tata, and his team of accountants had been poring over the books since June the previous year, formulating ways that Jaguar and Land Rover could be extricated from the Ford empire while supplies of, for instance, engines, stampings, and systems could carry on seamlessly after the change of custody. But for many of the 16,000 workers at the manufacturing plants involved, the realization that they were now employed by India's biggest vehicle-making business came as quite a shock.

It seemed that all the major names in global carmaking, if they had considered bidding, decided to pass. The previous two decades had seen a merry-go-round of car manufacturer mergers and acquisitions, and several—Mercedes-Benz's takeover of Chrysler, General Motors' acquisition of Saab and Hummer, BMW's ownership of Land Rover—ultimately proved to be calamities. And while Volkswagen had successfully sponged up Bentley and Lamborghini, the Japanese manufacturers kept their respectful distance from acquiring struggling enterprises. Indeed, Tata's main competitor proved to be another firm little known or understood outside India, Mahindra & Mahindra, with competition also coming from a clutch of investment companies including One Equity and Cerberus Capital.

For many, it was bewildering to see Ford bail out of assets it had been so keen to acquire in the first place, at such a thumping loss, and after it had invested so much in new cars like the Jaguar XF, of which the first examples were being collected by eager new owners around the time

As part of a steady globalization of Jaguar, the XF was assembled at Tata's plant in Pune, India, using completely knocked down kits from the UK.

The XE was Jaguar's most accessible saloon car range since the X-Type, this time developed entirely in-house and extending the all-aluminum construction concept to a mass-market BMW 3 Series competitor.

Once the XE had touched down, it was escorted to its star-studded unveiling at Earls Court by this pair of Mk 2s in replica 1960s police livery.

of the announcement. But once Alan Mulally, the new Ford chief executive officer, took office in 2006, he had set his sights on shutting down the company's high-profile Premier Automotive Group, which had been masterminded by his predecessor Jacques Nasser. First to be sold was Aston Martin in 2007; now Jaguar and Land Rover were going to Tata; and, in 2010, with Volvo sold to China's Geely, PAG was gone in a puff of smoke. At the same time, Nasser's plans to diversify into everything from scrapyards to the Kwik-Fit tire and exhaust chain were abruptly reversed. Ford would be going back to basics, buffing up its famous "blue oval" brand on cars and trucks that appealed to the mass market.

It was a massive about-face exercised with brutal efficiency for two important reasons. Henry Ford's descendants, who still held huge stakes in the family firm, were none too pleased with Nasser's unconventional strategy. More importantly, though, implementing that strategy had cost a king's ransom, and Ford's losses were mounting at a truly horrifying rate. If businesses like Jaguar weren't

Tightly drawn contours of the XE were Jaguar through and through, offering a more compact alternative to the top-selling XF.

disposed of, no matter the humiliation as plans were so publicly shredded, there was every likelihood Ford would have gone bust. The losses just had to be cut. This was confirmed six years later by former Jaguar boss Sir Nick Scheele: "It could have turned the ship over. It was a mammoth cash drain, and in the dark times of 2008–09, cash was what was required."

Ford had decided to offer Jaguar and Land Rover only as a single package, which included three factories (with the Halewood plant near Liverpool already making both the X-Type and the Land Rover Freelander) and two design centers at Whitley and Gaydon, Warwickshire, plus three extra marque names—Daimler, Lanchester, and Rover—thrown in for good measure.

It was a sensible move because, despite its almost absurdly illustrious heritage, it was claimed at the time that Jaguar had never actually turned a profit in eighteen years of Ford ownership, while Land Rover in contrast had become consistently profitable.

A delighted Ratan Tata told the BBC: "We have enormous respect for the two brands and will endeavor to preserve and build on their heritage and competitiveness, keeping their identities intact. We aim to support their growth, while holding true to our principles of allowing the management and

The XE interior radiated sportiness, slickly executed in the Jaguar idiom of the era.

employees to bring their experience and expertise to bear on the growth of the business." Grizzled industry watchers uttered sardonic laughs at the idea that Tata was going to leave Jaguar and Land Rover management alone to run the companies. After all, a constant stream of Ford executives had come and gone during the Detroit giant's tenure at Jaguar, with their various edicts from HQ on which direction to take the company.

Yet while Tata had its own automotive ventures in its home country, notably the super-cheap Nano city car, it was true to its word. Jaguar's headquarters remained firmly anchored in the UK. Shortly after Tata assumed control, the economic meltdown of 2008 appeared as a serious threat to any future prosperity for Jaguar. The timing looked extremely unlucky. In his book, *The Jewels In The Crown*, an account of the takeover, veteran industry journalist Ray Hutton paints a different picture: British government loan guarantees of almost £800 million for what was now the nation's biggest and most important domestic car manufacturer were eschewed; instead, Tata chose to go with a £500 million loan from a consortium of Indian banks, which came with many fewer political strings attached and meant they could run the business as they wanted. This included appointing key people with excellent track records in the German prestige car industry, in particular ex-BMW executive and former PAG head Ralf Speth as chief executive in 2010. Ravi Kant, the key advisor to Tata on its new acquisition, told Hutton, "In the companies we acquire we keep management independent, but accountable. 'Hands off' is not the same as 'left alone,' it does not mean we are not involved."

Indeed, Ratan Tata got closely involved. As the all-important XF was being launched—the car that epitomized Ford's turnaround for Jaguar from which it would never derive any benefit—the charismatic Indian tycoon chartered a jet and toured the US, always Jaguar's most important market, to meet with dealers and gather horse's-mouth feedback. He did this for three years on the run, flying the Jaguar flag while, back in the UK, engineers at Whitley were beginning work on a project codenamed D7, a highly versatile and adaptable structure called "Premium Lightweight

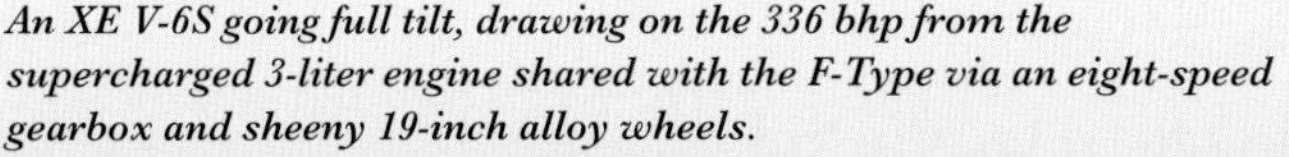

An XE V-6S going full tilt, drawing on the 336 bhp from the supercharged 3-liter engine shared with the F-Type via an eight-speed gearbox and sheeny 19-inch alloy wheels.

Jaguar's all-new Ingenium four-cylinder power unit was designed in-house and manufactured at a brand-new engine plant in Wolverhampton, West Midlands.

Architecture," which was in fact an all-aluminum set of components that would form the bedrock of both Jaguar and Land Rover cars in the years to come. It was a brave move to press ahead with this new technology in such uncertain times, but, as in Jaguar's halcyon days, genuine innovation would be the pathway to the future.

The money, the management, and the technology were all in place by the time Ratan Tata retired in 2012. The acclaimed XF was selling strongly, and the following year the momentous announcement was made that this desirable sports saloon would soon be rolling down a new Tata-owned assembly line in Pune, India, constructed from completely knocked down (CKD) kits dispatched from the UK. A few XJ6s had been built from CKD kits at British Leyland outposts from New Zealand to South Africa in the 1970s, but this was the first time a proper commitment had been made to build Jaguars abroad (alongside the Land Rover Freelander II) so they could capitalize on a growing and enthusiastic local market thousands of miles from base.

Then, also in 2013, Jaguar launched its gorgeous F-Type sports car. Enthusiasts rejoiced and Ratan Tata, in an interview in 2016, regarded the two-seater with enormous pride. "The Jaguar F-Type holds a very personal place in my heart as it is something I pushed through the company," he said. "When we acquired Jaguar, there was no true sports car in the model lineup and nothing in the future plans. My feeling was that Jaguar had such a rich racing heritage and a tradition of building great sports cars. We needed to re-create the image of Jaguar, once again, by building beautiful, fast cars. I think we achieved that with the F-Type."

A preproduction F-Pace going through its cold-weather testing program. Sharing drivetrain components with Land Rover via the D7 platform made the car a realistic proposition.

With 300 examples hand-built by Jaguar's Special Vehicle Operations, the XE Project 8 was wild in every way thanks to its 5-liter supercharged V-8 engine and widened body. Available as a two- or four-seater, in left-hand drive only, it was the fastest-ever four-door saloon car around the Nürburgring, lapping the 12.9 miles in 2019 in 7 minutes 18.3 seconds.

This was the year when Jaguar Cars Ltd. and Land Rover Ltd. finally ceased to exist as separate entities. Five years into Tata's ownership, the two marques officially became one operating unit, called Jaguar Land Rover (JLR). Their progressive integration took a major step forward in 2013 with the groundbreaking ceremony on a brand-new engine plant intended to bring the manufacture of power units back in-house for the first time in more than a decade. After much casting about, JLR picked a site in the i54 Business Park in Wolverhampton for its Engine Manufacturing Centre and booked 8.6 million square feet (800,000 square meters) of factory space. It was a huge boost of confidence for

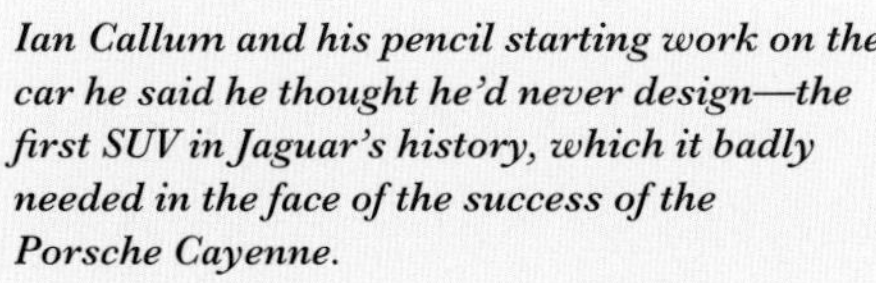

Ian Callum and his pencil starting work on the car he said he thought he'd never design—the first SUV in Jaguar's history, which it badly needed in the face of the success of the Porsche Cayenne.

An F-Pace impressing the crowds at the Goodwood Festival of Speed as part of a two-wheeled stunt display.

the company's general roots in the West Midlands area, which initially brought six hundred and eventually eight hundred jobs to the area. The £800 million investment also included £300 million for a sister plant in India intended to cope with ever more buoyant sales of locally assembled Jags and Land Rovers.

On October 30, 2014, Her Majesty the Queen (with the Duke of Edinburgh) stepped onto Jaguar territory for the third time in her reign to open the new factory and bring Jaguar engine production back home. The lines rolled into action to start making the all-new Ingenium family of engines, four-cylinder gasoline and diesel all-aluminum 2.0-liter units feeding into the company's supply chain to Halewood where, although the ill-starred yet perfectly decent X-Type had been discreetly dropped in 2009, they would find a place in the phenomenally successful Range Rover Evoque that was keeping the plant working around the clock. A central tenet of the inline engine concept was its modularity, with three-, four-, five-, and six-cylinder versions all easy to produce, and running hydraulically operated variable-valve-timing technology derived from a Fiat design for optimum performance.

The next new Jaguar would drive into a significantly changed company landscape and represent all that Tata had planned for the marque. This was the XE, unveiled at the 2014 Paris Motor Show and airlifted by helicopter over Tower Bridge and into London's Earls Court (the since-demolished exhibition center that had seen the debut of so many famous Jaguars) for a gala launch presented by singer Emeli Sandé and the Kaiser Chiefs rock band. It was quite an arrival for a car that really merited the fanfare.

The XE was just the thing Jaguar had always needed to rival the BMW 3 Series. The compact four-door sports saloon offered Ian Callum's taut, sparing, handsomely proportioned, and super-clean XF lines, now shrunken to a smaller package, with a prominent rectangular mesh grille and narrowed-eye headlights. The 2.0-liter gasoline engine was a Ford-supplied Ecoboost, tried and tested in many other cars and well liked for its dependable and eager performance. The diesel, though, was the first use of Jaguar's new Ingenium family. A brand-new subframe-mounted multilink rear suspension system was also featured for this rear-drive car. *Auto Express* covered more than 22,000 miles (35,000 kilometers)—and averaged fuel economy of nearly 50 mpg—in just such an XE in a few months and was fulsome in its praise: "The XE has delivered everything you'd want from a small Jaguar saloon. It's great to drive, looks stunning, rides nicely and has served up decent efficiency. A few niggles with quality are the only real criticism after nearly a year of hard motoring."

The final part of the new direction for Jaguar covered by the XE was behind the scenes. It was the first example of the marque to be produced at the Land Rover plant at Solihull, in the company of other long-established classics like the Range Rover and Land Rover Defender. It was also the first conventional British luxury saloon produced there since the Rover SD1 of 1976. Early sales were so brisk that a second line had to be opened at Castle Bromwich, and in its first two years the XE sold almost 70,000 units.

While the XE was new Jaguar at its confident best, the F-Pace that followed to market in 2016 was positively audacious. With this car the marque entered, extremely belatedly, the burgeoning premium sport-utility vehicle arena. Among Jaguar's peers, Porsche had been the pioneer with its 2002 Cayenne; despite unbridled hostility from Porsche traditionalists and conventionality-minded critics, it had been a runaway success, outselling Porsche sports cars within a few years and leading to

The versatile D7 platform gave life to the second-generation XF in 2016 with a subtle evolution of the XF style and 2-liter Ingenium engines in both gasoline and diesel forms.

A commanding driving position was, naturally, an important part of the F-Pace's appeal.

Along with the second-generation XF saloon came a new Sportbrake station wagon that was, if anything, even more handsome.

Porsche's latter-day prosperity. Of course, the Cayenne carried all the cachet of the Porsche brand, but took it to developing markets such as China where powerful, ritzy off-roaders were fashionable and the 911 sports car had relatively little resonance.

Now, with its D7 platform to access, the Jaguar design team could produce its response, and the four-wheel-drive drivetrain was developed in tandem with a closely related model for sister brand Land Rover, the Range Rover Velar. Jaguar's tall and roomy F-Pace was described as a "performance crossover" and presented chief designer Ian Callum with his greatest challenge to date as he sought a way to match the high-riding stance with Jaguar's athletic trademarks of sharp, bold surfaces and waistline "haunches." He declared it "the car I thought I'd never build" to *Autocar* editor-in-chief Steve Cropley: "Some say we could have launched this earlier but I believe we had to build the brand first, with models like F-Type." The engine lineup included Ingenium four-cylinder, AJV-6, and V-8 options, with an eight-speed auto and four-wheel drive across the board, plus a six-speed manual available on some diesels. Most of the mechanical drivetrain hardware was shared with the XE despite the very different natures of the two cars.

A real Jaguar? Those who had grown up with the E-type and Mk 2 may have demurred. But a reality for Jaguar in the twenty-first century it certainly was. In the years that followed, a similarly unlikely path was also followed by other hallowed names, including Lamborghini, Maserati, and Aston Martin. The F-Pace cut quite a distinctive dash, and owners loved it. In 2016 it instantly became the best-selling Jag and was a strong factor in a doubling of Jaguar Land Rover sales since Tata assumed control, with $16 billion spent on a new product bonanza and 20,000 more employees taken on.

It was an environment worlds away from the rocky times Jaguar had endured in the 1970s and 1980s. Jaguars would now be manufactured in Jiangsu, China, in a 50/50 joint venture between JLR and Chery Automobile, with a specially developed, roomier XEL long-wheelbase model expressly aimed at the corporate-executive market there, where few owners would choose to be anything other than chauffeur driven.

By this stage, too, the second-generation XF had arrived, now sharing the all-aluminum D7 structure with its stablemates and

The E-Pace was Jaguar's second SUV, launched in 2017 and built under contract in Graz, Austria; it is distantly related to the Range Rover Evoque.

adopting Ingenium engines alongside the V-6 and V-8 options. The entire one-piece bodysides were single light-alloy pressings, and when the car went into production in China—in addition to being made in the UK and assembled from kits in India—the country's unique long-wheelbase XFL model became the first aluminum-bodied car built there.

Finally, the E-Pace. Despite a title that rather gives the impression of electric power, this compact SUV was likely to be the last "conventional" new model Jaguar would ever introduce. Conventional, that is, in offering only fossil fuel–burning power units (2.0-liter Ingeniums in gasoline or diesel forms) and clinging to a much-modified version of the steel structure from the Range Rover Evoque, the so-called D8 platform with some very distant Ford ancestry. Wings, hood, doors, tailgate, and roof were all made of aluminum to cut weight and reduce fuel thirst. As a Jaguar alternative in a hugely mainstream market sector, the five-door E-Pace with four-cylinder engines and either two- or four-wheel drive made perfect sense, though aside from its by now familiar Jaguar nose treatment, the untrained eye could easily mistake it for other, similar cars. Here, too, in the spirit of JLR's stealthy globalization as it made up valuable ground against German rivals such as BMW and Mercedes-Benz, was the first Jaguar destined never to be built in Britain. With every square meter of the existing plants in Jaguar's homeland bustling with activity, a place for the E-Pace line had to be found elsewhere; the contract-manufacture premises of Magna Steyr in Graz, Austria, were selected. This move perhaps signaled the transition of Jaguar from twentieth-century marque to twenty-first-century luxury brand where domicile is unimportant. And Jaguar, of course, had never before known such popularity.

The E-Pace gave Jaguar a premium toehold in a growing area of the market and added a lot of the motifs familiar from the marque's other cars to a compact SUV form.

Chapter Twenty

PLUGGED INTO THE FUTURE

Electric era and the I-Pace: Jaguar's radical new battery-powered arrival wins the coveted European Car of the Year award for good reasons; it propels the concept of a premium electric car dramatically forward and opens an exciting new front for Jaguar in a challenging future environment.

Dispensing with an internal combustion engine meant that, possibly for the first time in Jaguar's history, the I-Pace design could be an absolutely clean-sheet exercise; this is the very start.

JAGUAR

When Jaguar's saga began in a garden shed at the British seaside a century ago, transport revolutions came along frequently. The arrival of the modern, chain-driven, human-powered bicycle as a consumer product in the 1880s was swiftly eclipsed by the motorcycle with an internal combustion engine. In the decade that followed, the same power unit brought carriages alive with horsepower that put the actual horse out to graze; motive power for commercial vehicles also lost the hoof, turning to diesel, steam, and gasoline instead. Henry Ford brought the automobile to America's drivers with his 1908 Model T, and Herbert Austin did the same for his British counterparts fourteen years later. Even after that, new concepts kept coming, including such novel movements as the secondhand car, commuting at the wheel from suburbia, the driving test, and even the two-car family.

Somewhere in the midst of all this, a couple of entrepreneurs came up with a pleasingly packaged seat-on-a-wheel that could be bolted onto a motorbike frame to foster human interaction. Where this simple product would take one of them no one could ever have foreseen, but it shows how rapidly changing times can coax out smart thinking. And so to the I-Pace, introduced in 2018: Jaguar's radical route to the zero-emission, low-carbon, technologically connected world of the future.

Jaguar's trick has always been to amalgamate recent design and engineering advances into its cars, each time adding its own enhancements and melding together the elements into something special. With twin camshafts, disc brakes, independent suspension systems, and aluminum construction methods it has been a confident leader without inventing very much. The I-Pace, though, ups the cutting-edge ante considerably.

It's probably the boldest and most convincing Jaguar ever in terms of setting dazzling new standards with available technology, and it carries with it one claim to fame with just a few codicils: it's the first all-electric sport-utility vehicle to emerge from any prestigious car manufacturer—the first car to stride into Tesla's world, and it's not from BMW or Lexus.

Actually, the electric drivetrain is quite close to what's offered by the Tesla Model S saloon and Model X SUV. It features two concentric electric motors, one for the front axle and one for the back, with permanent four-wheel drive and a single-speed gearbox with no manual function. Together they deliver 394 bhp and a relentless 513 bhp of torque, which make acceleration, well, truly electric at 4.5 seconds for 0–60 with a whir instead of a Jaguar's customary V-8 bellow.

Flat under the floor in the car's all-aluminum structure (the modified D7e version of the D7 underpinning the XE and F-Pace) is its lithium-ion battery pack, a king-size 90kWh relative of the batteries in our smartphones. It houses thirty-six modules, each containing twelve prismatic-type cells, and it accounts for 1,329 pounds (603 kilograms) of the car's overall 4,467-pound (2,026-kilogram) curb weight. The rigidity of this battery chamber has made the I-Pace skeleton considerably stiffer than its D7 cousins.

Range anxiety is dealt with thanks to the I-Pace's ability to cover up to 292 miles (470 kilometers) on a single charge, a figure backed up by the findings of the 2017 Worldwide Light Vehicle Test Procedure, under whose guidance the whole car was planned at Jaguar's Whitley design complex. Assuming an average daily commute, according to Jaguar research, of 38 miles (61 kilometers), a full recharge is needed after a little over a week of standard driving.

For anyone who grew up sloshing four-star fuel into the twin tanks of an XJ6, the shocking thing is that a visit to a gas station—except to pick up a sandwich—became a thing of the past with the I-Pace. The portal to replenish energy was a socket on the front wheel arch, and the most efficient place to do that was at a specially installed, mains-connected AC wall box fitted at home in the garage or underground parking lot. The onboard 7kW charger unit turned the AC current to DC at a rate that would put back 22 miles (35 kilometers) of range for each hour hooked up, for a total recharge in thirteen hours. Using a standard domestic electric socket over eight hours offered enough battery life for 56 miles (90 kilometers) of driving, while, for the fastest recharge, a public DC 50kW charge point would yield 168 miles (270 kilometers) of range after being plugged in for an hour. Stronger 100kW charge points, still scarce at the time of the I-Pace's introduction, promised even speedier results. Along with all that, kinetic energy generated during deceleration and braking was harvested as battery charge when on the move, and the car could even adjust its own heating and air-conditioning to be as energy efficient as possible.

The car came as standard with all the various cables needed for any of these options, and managing the recharge—including finding convenient charge points along a planned route—could be done via a smartphone app. All of it needed a little reeducation to acclimate to utter independence from gasoline—Jaguar bravely choosing a complete break rather than the hybrid electric/fossil fuel compromise—but an important upside was the unique character and design of the car itself.

Ian Callum achieved what every car designer dreams of: a shape unlike anything else that still works. "I was

Laid bare: The D7e platform for the I-Pace cradled the 36-module lithium-ion battery pack, which also acted as a stiffening element for the whole car.

A beaming Ian Callum with the I-Pace at its unveiling, the car he calls "the special one."

determined from the beginning that this would be a very different-looking car which reflected its electric architecture, but was still distinctively and unmistakably a Jaguar," he said. "Everything is new—from the ground up—so we had a great opportunity."

Callum was able to recapture some of the cab-forward stance of his much-mourned C-X75 two-seater concept show car, with a visual emphasis biased toward the front because, of course, there was no cumbersome engine to work around. "It's clearly a very defined and different profile than you would expect from an SUV," he explained. "The waistline preserves our beautiful lines but emphasized towards the front rather than the rear to exaggerate the front haunches."

Dramatic 22-inch wheels helped bridge the chasm between sports car and family practicality (the I-Pace is a notably roomy five-door with an all-glass roof panel), while minimal front and rear overhangs demonstrated the long wheelbase. Air scooped in through the grille (with no radiator behind it) is funneled straight up to the windscreen through a duct, and the suspension hunkers down by a centimeter or two at speeds above 65 miles per hour (105 kilometers per hour). Both these helped cut wind resistance and contributed to the I-Pace's slippery 0.29 drag coefficient. Crisp contours all around generally cut turbulence, while there was a luggage compartment at both front and back.

Jaguar employed acoustic expert Iain Suffield and sound designer and musician Richard Devine to create a new driving soundtrack in the absence of the usual din of internal combustion. They developed layers of hushed "refinement" to impart this electric Jag's character and stand in for eerie silence. Apparently taking cues from the look and feel of the car as it went through the design process, they also paid attention to aural craft—for instance, the stop and start sounds—to engage drivers. As one can imagine, it needs to be heard to be appreciated.

The day of the I-Pace launch was precisely half a century after Ian Callum wrote to William Heynes asking for advice on how to join the company. It was also at this point that Callum made up his mind that his work with Jaguar was done; two years later he decided to leave the company and pursue a more idiosyncratic and independent design life while remaining a consultant to the marque that's had a profound effect on his career. "We've seen such dramatic changes," Callum told *Autocar*.

The car creation process is so complex now that I don't believe anyone in the company understands the whole process—except the designers. I've had many fantastic experiences and had many amazing opportunities. One of my biggest highlights was creating the XF because it represented the beginning of a new era, moving Jaguar from tradition to contemporary design. It was a significant turning point in our story. And then, for me, the I-Pace is the special one. I came into this role with a mission to take Jaguar design back to where it deserved to be. It has taken 20 years.

Writing in the Society of Automotive Engineers' journal *Automotive Engineering* in 2018, Dan Carney declared the I-Pace a "landmark vehicle":

Where the new Jag outpaces Tesla's current S and X is in its dynamic qualities—not surprising considering Jaguar's history as a sports car company. The I-Pace's superior ride and handling are enabled by its adaptive suspension system, which offers a variety of settings to suit various conditions. But the I-Pace's unexpectedly accurate steering and neutral handling characteristics during

Buzzing hot and cold: Jaguar took I-Pace prototypes for a test on America's West Coast and through its blistering inland states to make sure it could stand up to sustained use in hot weather, then up to the Arctic Circle to sample well-below-zero reactions.

The full-length glass roof latterly become a staple Jaguar feature, and so it was incorporated into the new I-Pace too.

spirited driving (experienced both on the track and on winding mountain roads) are made even more noteworthy by its placid ride during normal highway driving. Manufacturers have claimed "car-like" handling from their crossover SUVs for a while, but it is only the most recent examples, such as the BMW X4 M40i and the I-Pace, which truly deliver twisty-road handling on par with sport sedans. Jaguar engineers employed continuously-variable shock absorbers that provide clearly discernible differences in ride and handling depending on the setting, as the shock adjusts for the road surface and driver inputs. The vehicle's lack of body roll, pitch and dive during such driving is an impressive accomplishment.

I-Pace was showered with several dozen awards, foremost among them the European Car of the Year (a Jaguar first) and World Car of the Year for 2019.

The initial list price for this technical masterpiece was £63,000 (£58,500 once British government green grants were deducted). Its top speed was limited to 124 miles

per hour (200 kilometers per hour), ample for all practical purposes. But therein lay the chief divergence from Jaguars of old: How long could it keep that up on a full charge? "A long time" was the verdict of one Jaguar engineer, but obviously it would never be the best way to get the most mileage from a night's suckling at the plug socket.

As with the E-Pace, this all-new car was assembled in Graz by contractors Magna Steyr, which had built cars for both Aston Martin and Mini, as well as the G-Wagen off-road vehicle for Mercedes-Benz.

In 2018, the year of the I-Pace's debut, Jaguar reached its first ten years under Tata ownership. Jaguar Land Rover annual sales had tripled to 600,000, with deliveries of new Jaguars alone reaching 181,000, an all-time record. The company had also sunk £3.8 billion into research and development, some of it in partnership with nearby Warwick University.

During that period, too, Jaguar had returned to its super-rich heritage in the most extraordinary way. In 2014 the company's Heritage business arm announced Jaguar would start making E-types once again. In particular, it had examined the record books to verify that, of the eighteen E-type Lightweight race cars originally planned, only a dozen of the chassis numbers allocated had been used in 1963–1964. The intention now became the creation, with painstaking authenticity, of the remaining six cars. Every last nut and bolt would be just like the originals, and 230 individual parts were digitally mapped so they could be exactly reproduced. The originals had become legendarily covetable, multimillion-pound cars, so the £1 million cost for each continuation car—with their newly handmade (at Browns Lane), all-aluminum bodies and aluminum-block 3.8-liter XK engines—didn't raise eyebrows.

There was no gearbox as such, so a selector on the I-Pace was superfluous, allowing for the creation of a different form of center console.

The spacious five-seater hatchback I-Pace was assembled by Jaguar's contractor Magna Steyr in Austria, which has an excellent reputation for quality and drivetrain technology.

They were also FIA-approved for use in historic racing events. The classic car market watchers were, however, perturbed by the move, which some dismissed as fakery; the controversial trend for such nonperiod replicas could be traced back to 1988 when four unused chassis numbers were used for four Aston Martin DB4GT Zagatos as "Sanction II" cars.

The renamed Jaguar Classic division was also ramping up its efforts as a recreator of historic cars in this decade. Now relocated to Jaguar Land Rover's Special Vehicle Operations's huge new premises at Ryton-on-Dunsmore near Coventry, the division announced its plan in 2017 to add nine more Jaguar XKSSs to the original sixteen cars produced, rounding out the series to a neat twenty-five. A year later, the in-house team of specialist engineers and technicians, aided by outside craftsman-led businesses, turned their attention to the D-type racing car, swelling the number from the original seventy-five examples with twenty-five modern iterations in a mix of 1955-style short-nose or 1956 long-nose guises.

The I-Pace came as standard with a recharging point behind a flap on the front wheel arch, plus a variety of different cables to suit the power of varying electricity-supply outlets in a continually expanding network.

Four-wheel drive, deep reserves of torque, acclaimed handling, and an artfully created internal "soundtrack" have redefined the performance Jaguar in the I-Pace.

So much for blasts from the past. In July 2019, Jaguar's future, for so many years a somewhat hazy vista, came into sharp focus. And it would be led by the I-Pace as Jaguar Land Rover announced that its sports and luxury car brand would pursue an electric strategy. The Castle Bromwich factory in Birmingham had recently become home to the XE in addition to all other non-SUV models, but a number of factors were beginning to have an impact on demand for all of them. These included the uncertainty of Britain's departure from the European Union; a sudden plunge in demand in China; the widespread demonization of diesel for false claims and increasingly unacceptable choking pollutants; and the radical announcement from the British government that sales of all new gasoline- and diesel-powered cars would be halted from 2040. (That seismic deadline has since been brought forward to 2030.)

Henceforth, new Jags would be electric cars. The impressive but slow-selling XJ was quietly retired and all work concentrated on an exciting replacement (delayed as of this writing) with a fully electric drivetrain. We are promised a car with "beautiful design, intelligent performance and revered luxury," a combination of which Sir William Lyons would surely approve if only he were still here. What has been announced, though, is something Jaguar badly needs for its plans to work: the UK's first "giga-scale" battery manufacturing facility in a partnership between startups AMTE Power and Britishvolt. "One thing is clear, if batteries go out of the UK then also the automotive production will go out of the UK," chief executive Ralf Speth had warned darkly. At the same time the Wolverhampton plant celebrated making its 1.5 millionth Ingenium engine, a new site at Hams Hall was gearing up to assemble 150,000 of the advanced electric drivetrains called for by future model plans.

The final words on Jaguar are written here at a time of great uncertainty, as the world economy reels from the impact of the COVID-19 pandemic. Jaguar Land Rover has suffered, as have all carmakers. Sales were down an unprecedented 42 percent for the period of March–May 2020, the height of lockdown and consumer malaise. In April and May it built almost no cars as its factories, offices, and dealer showrooms fell silent. Yet there were encouraging signs of things improving, especially in China and the US. Then in July 2020, and following hotly denied rumors that Tata might sell its British business to a rival, former Renault chief Thierry Bolloré was announced as Jaguar's (and Land Rover's) new chief executive officer. "It will be my privilege to lead this fantastic company through what continues to be the most testing time of our generation," he said, any trepidation well concealed.

Running Jaguar has always been a rollercoaster ride, one that began its initial steep climb when the tiny sidecar and body company SS packed its bags and moved to Coventry to join the big time. Through wonderful cars, fantastic engines, epic race wins, and boldness in every direction, it has now survived its first one hundred years. But there's plenty more life in the old cat yet.

Steve McQueen was devoted to his Jaguar XKSS, no matter how many speeding tickets it brought him. From 2017, you could buy a brand-new one and enjoy its raw excitement all over again.

Jaguar decided to revisit its past in 2014 to complete the intended run of eighteen Lightweight E-types with the six cars never built in the 1960s; here one of the painstakingly re-created all-alloy bodies is taking shape.

The "new" E-type Lightweights had to be absolutely authentic in every way, calling on skills in-house and from expert craftsmen to get them exactly right.

The FIA, motorsports' governing body, certified the new Lightweight E-type so it could be used as intended for historic motor racing events.

Interesting to see the tiny doors that were part of the original XKSS, which was based on the D-type on the newly hand-built shells for the continuation XKSS.

In 2017 Jaguar next decided to round out the tally of XKSS cars by adding nine new ones to the sixteen originals from the 1950s to make a run of twenty-five; dashboard controls are here married up with the aluminum structure.

POSTSCRIPT

Jaguar is a work in progress, even after one hundred years. Between the end of writing this book and the eve of going to press, the marque's destiny took an interesting new turn, even though the true shape of this wonderful marque's future is yet to be fully visualized.

After 2025, according to the "Reimagine" strategy led by new chief executive Thierry Bolloré, no new Jaguars will run on gasoline or diesel. Electric propulsion enabled by batteries or perhaps hydrogen fuel cells will provide all the power, while a new electric car platform could be developed with a partner or in-house for Jaguar alone. The electric reincarnation of the large XJ saloon, though, was abandoned.

And that's not all. While Bolloré would not be drawn on the fate for specific models, he indicated an exciting shift upmarket toward the ultimate—as opposed to everyday—luxury end of the car industry spectrum. Where performance and race-bred tenacity are concerned, Jaguar has long been mentioned with the same reverence as similarly august British marques Aston Martin and Bentley. From now, it seemed Jaguar perhaps would emulate their levels of opulence and exclusivity, which might mean scaling back volume to stoke desirability and derive more income-per-car sold rather than striving for BMW levels of output. "Quality over volume" was Bollore's intriguing new mantra, while at the same time stating that design would be "drop-dead gorgeous."

There were no plans to close factories, but a bold intention to make the entire Jaguar Land Rover organization a net-zero-carbon business by 2039 was announced in February 2021.

Jaguar traditionalists might find it hard to take in all of this, perhaps even harder to adapt to it from behind the wheel. But the marque is set to transition to a new automotive era that is transforming the whole car industry rather than being consigned to its own glorious history. And for that Jaguar fanatics should feel only happiness.

ACKNOWLEDGMENTS

My grateful thanks to the many people and sources that have helped me write this book and also to Zack Miller and Dennis Pernu at Motorbooks for asking me to do it. At Jaguar I have been hugely helped by UK PR manager Tracey Tompsett, Jaguar Heritage Trust archivist Karam Ram, and Tony O'Keeffe who for over forty years has been championing the company's heritage from within. Over the years it has been my privilege to interview Sir John Egan, Ian Callum CBE, Michael Quinn, Richard Bellamy, and Syd Creamer, whose comments, perspectives, and recollections have enlivened this story once again on these pages. It is marvelous to have the 125-year-old archives of *Autocar* magazines to draw on (and many other publications besides), and to be able to quote from the writing of my erudite friend Steve Cropley. Another former editor of *Autocar*, Matthew Carter, very kindly agreed to read through my first draft, and, as ever with wise friends, was able to alert me to details where I might otherwise have slipped up.

PHOTO CREDITS

ALAMY:
pages 14, 35, 38, 53 (top).

BRIGHTWELLS AUCTIONS:
page 31 (top).

RICHARD BELLAMY:
page 109 (top).

AUTHOR'S COLLECTION—
GILES CHAPMAN LIBRARY:
pages 12 (top), 13 (both), 15, 20–21 (all three), 30, 31 (bottom), 47 (top), 50, 53 (bottom), 55 (bottom), 58, 59 (both), 62 (both), 63 (both), 64 (bottom, right), 68 (top), 69 (top), 70 (top), 71 (bottom), 72, 73 (both), 78, 79 (top and bottom), 80, 81, 82 (both), 83 (top, left and bottom), 84 (both), 85 (all three), 96, 97 (top, left), 98 (both), 99 (top and bottom right), 103 (both), 104 (left and bottom, right), 106, 108, 109 (bottom), 112 (both), 113 (both), 114 (top left), 115 (all three), 116 (both), 117 (top and bottom), 118 (all three), 119 (all three), 122–123, 124, 125 (both), 127 (both), 131, 132 (all three), 133 (both), 134 (both), 135 (both), 136–137 (both), 138, 139 (both), 143 (both), 144 (all three), 145, 146 (all three), 147 (all three), 148 (both), 149 (top, left and bottom, right), 150–151 (all three), 152, 153 (bottom), 156, 157 (top), 158 (top), 163 (center and bottom, left).

GETTY IMAGES;
pages 17, 34, 75 (top, right), 97.

JAGUAR CARS/JAGUAR LAND ROVER:
pages 2, 6–7, 9, 12 (bottom), 22 (top), 28–29, 32 (both), 44–45, 46 (top), 47 (bottom), 48–49, 51 (all three), 52 (both), 54, 55 (top), 56–57, 64 (left), 65 (both), 66–67, 68 (bottom), 69 (bottom), 70 (bottom), 71 (top), 74, 76–77, 79 (center), 86 (top), 88–89, 90, 91, 92 (both), 93 (both), 94 (both), 95 (bottom), 97 (top, right), 99 (bottom, left), 110–111, 117 (center),, 120, 121, 128–129, 149 (top, right), 153 (top), 154–155, 157 (bottom), 158 (bottom), 159, 160–161 (all four), 162 , 163 (top and bottom, left), 164–165 (all four), 166–167 (all four), 169–169 (all four), 170–171, 172–173 (all four), 174–175 (all four), 176–177 (all four), 178–179 (all three), 180–181 (all three), 182–183 (all three), 184–185, 186–187 (all six), 188–189 (all six), 190–191, 192–193 (all four), 194–195 (all four), 196–197 (all five), 198–199, 200–201 (all four), 202–203 (all four), 204–205 (all four), 206–207 (all three), 208–209 (all three), 210–211, 213 (both), 214–215 (all five), 216–217 (all five), 218–219 (all four).

JAGUAR HERITAGE TRUST:
pages 10–11, 14, 16, 39 (all three), 40–41 (all four), 42.

JAMES MANN:
pages 18–19, 23 (both), 24–25, 36–37, 43 (both), 60–61 (both), 114 (top right, bottom).

MAGIC CAR PICS:
Front cover (Robert George), 4-5 (Robert George).

MOTORSPORT IMAGES:
86 (bottom).

NEWSPRESS:
pages 27, 33, 83 (top, right), 95 (center), 100–101, 104 (top, right), 140–141, 149 (bottom, left).

RM SOTHEBY'S/DARIN SCHNABEL:
page 142 (top).

SOCIETÀ EDITRICE IL CAMMELLO:
page 142–143 (center).

BIBLIOGRAPHY

Balfour, Christopher, *Roads to Oblivion: Triumphs & Tragedies of British Car Makers 1946–56* (Bay View, 1996).

Berry, Robert, *Jaguar: Motor Racing and the Manufacturer* (Dutton, 1978).

Chapman, Giles, *The Jaguar Story* (History Press, 2019).

Clarke, R. M, *Le Mans: The Jaguar Years 1949–1957* (Brooklands Books, 2005).

Dugdale, John, *Jaguar in America* (Britbooks, 1993).

Georgano, Wood et al, *Britain's Motor Industry: The First Hundred Years* (Foulis, 1995).

Grimsdale, Peter, *High Performance: When Britain Ruled the Roads* (Simon & Schuster, 2020).

Hutton, Ray, *Jewels in the Crown: How Tata of India Transformed Britain's Jaguar Land Rover* (Elliott & Thompson, 2013).

James, Brian and Starkey, John, *Jaguar from the Shopfloor: Foleshill and Browns Lane 1949–1978* (Veloce, 2018).

Montagu of Beaulieu, Lord, *Jaguar: A Biography* (Cassell, 1962).

— — —, *Jaguar* (Quiller Press, 1990).

Porter, Philip, *Jaguar E-type: The Definitive History* (Automobile Quarterly, 1989).

— — —, *Jaguar Sports-Racing Cars* (Bay View, 1995).

Robson, Graham, *Jaguar XJ Series: The Complete Story* (Crowood, 1992)

Skilleter, Paul, *The Jaguar E-type: A Collector's Guide* (Motor Racing Publications, 1986).

— — —, *Jaguar: The Sporting Heritage* (Virgin, 2000).

Thorley, Nigel, *Jaguar XJ: The Complete Companion* (Bay View, 1991).

— — —, *Jaguar: The Complete Works* (Bay View Books, 1996).

— — —, *The Complete Book of Jaguar* (Motorbooks, 2019).

Turner, Graham, *The Leyland Papers* (Eyre & Spottiswood, 1971).

Whyte, Andrew, *Jaguar XJ40: Evolution of the Species* (Patrick Stephens, 1987).

— — —, *Jaguar: The History of a Great British Car* (Patrick Stephens, 1980).

— — —, *Jaguar Sports Racing and Works Competition Cars to 1953* (Foulis, 1982).

INDEX A-L

INDEX L–Z

Brimming with creative inspiration, how-to projects, and useful information to enrich your everyday life, Quarto Knows is a favorite destination for those pursuing their interests and passions. Visit our site and dig deeper with our books into your area of interest: Quarto Creates, Quarto Cooks, Quarto Homes, Quarto Lives, Quarto Drives, Quarto Explores, Quarto Gifts, or Quarto Kids.

First Published in 2021 by Motorbooks, an imprint of The Quarto Group,

100 Cummings Center, Suite 265-D, Beverly, MA 01915, USA.
T (978) 282-9590 F (978) 283-2742 QuartoKnows.com

Motorbooks titles are also available at discount for retail, wholesale, promotional, and bulk purchase. For details, contact the Special Sales Manager by email at specialsales@quarto.com or by mail at The Quarto Group, Attn: Special Sales Manager, 100 Cummings Center, Suite 265-D, Beverly, MA 01915, USA.

25 24 23 22 21   1 2 3 4 5

ISBN: 978-0-7603-6866-4

Digital edition published in 2021

eISBN: 978-0-7603-6867-1

Library of Congress Cataloging-in-Publication Data
Names: Chapman, Giles, author.
Title: Jaguar century : 100 years of automotive excellence / Giles Chapman.
Description: Beverly, MA, USA : Motorbooks, 2021. | Includes bibliographical references and index.
Identifiers: LCCN 2021015838 (print) | LCCN 2021015839 (ebook) | ISBN 9780760368664 (hardcover) | ISBN 9780760368671 (ebook)
Subjects: LCSH: Jaguar automobile--History. | Automobiles--Great Britain--History.
Classification: LCC TL215.J3 C43 2021 (print) | LCC TL215.J3 (ebook) | DDC 338.7/6292220941--dc23
LC record available at https://lccn.loc.gov/2021015838
LC ebook record available at https://lccn.loc.gov/2021015839Acquiring Editor: Dennis Pernu

Page Layout: www.traffic-design.co.uk

Printed in China

Front endpapers:
Mike Salmon pilots a D Type at Silverstone in 1961. *National Motor Museum/Heritage Images/Getty Images*

Rear endpapers:
Steve McQueen drives his XK-SS on Sunset Boulevard in Hollywood, California, May 1963. *John Dominis/The LIFE Picture Collection via Getty Images*